SO-AHS-760

was clearly dominant in a circle noted for rugged personalities.

"All in all the experiences of Mary Blackford and her family, as here related, constitute a most interesting and revealing account of ante-bellum Southern life. *Mine Eyes Have Seen the Glory* points up the fact that Southern society had many nuances, and that the traditional picture is inaccurate in many of its details. The book contains important new material on Southern opposition to slavery, the experience of Negroes sent to Liberia, the Nat Turner insurrection, and the reaction of the colored folk to thralldom. This material is the more significant in that much of it comes from the Negroes themselves. I know of no slave writings comparable in fullness and charm to the missives sent from Liberia by James Cephas and Abram; and Betsy's story of the selling of her children is the most eloquent commentary that I have seen on the stark inhumanity of the South's peculiar institution.

"Dr. L. Minor Blackford, grandson of Mary and son of Launcelot Minor Blackford, is, of course, with such a heritage a veteran of both World Wars. He is obviously and rightfully proud of the Blackfords and their achievements, but he shows no disposition to gloss over weaknesses or to exaggerate virtues."

IINIVERSITY

MINE EYES HAVE SEEN THE GLORY

Mary Berkeley Minor Blackford
at 76

MINE EYES HAVE SEEN THE GLORY

The Story of a Virginia Lady
Mary Berkeley Minor Blackford
1802–1896
Who taught her sons to hate Slavery
and to love the Union

L. MINOR BLACKFORD

REMBERT E. STOKES/LIBRARY
WILBERFORCE UNIVERSITY
WILBERFORCE, OHIO 45384

HARVARD UNIVERSITY PRESS
Cambridge, Massachusetts
1954

F 230 .B65 B6
Blackford, L. Minor
Mine eyes have seen the
glory

Distributed in Great Britain by
GEOFFREY CUMBERLEGE
Oxford University Press
London

Copyright 1954 by the President and Fellows of Harvard College

Printed in the United States of America

Library of Congress Catalog Card Number 54-5018

To her Grandson
COLONEL STAIGE DAVIS BLACKFORD
Medical Corps, Army of the United States
Croix de Guerre, 1918, Legion of Merit, 1945
Professor of the Practice of Medicine, University of Virginia
1898–1949

CONTENTS

ILLUSTRATIONS

Introduction

Several years ago I had the pleasure of reading *War Years with Jeb Stuart* by Lieutenant Colonel William Willis Blackford. I found it to be one of the best of Confederate memoirs. Not long afterward I experienced a similar treat in *Letters from Lee's Army*, the correspondence of William's brother, Captain Charles Minor Blackford. These source works revealed that William and Charles were members of a family that sent five sons to the Confederate Army; they also suggested that the family was a remarkable one.

Recently my attention was called to the fact that a son of one of these five Confederate brothers was practicing medicine in Atlanta and that he had compiled a documentary history of his father's family. A reading of his manuscript revealed that Mary Berkeley Minor Blackford, mother of the five Confederate soldiers, was the central character of his story. In Mary Blackford I discovered not only an explanation of the remarkableness of the family, but a portrait of a most unusual and dynamic woman.

Mary Blackford and her immediate family were remarkable for their intense and undeviating hatred of slavery. "Think of . . . all the nameless horrors that are concentrated in that one word *Slavery*," wrote Mary on one occasion, and on another she solemnly predicted "that the time will come when we shall look back and wonder how Christians could sanction slavery." She was a loyal member of the American Colonization Society and *Uncle Tom's Cabin* was one of her most treasured possessions.

The Blackfords were also remarkable in their devotion to the Union. Aristocratic in their associations and Whig in their politics, they deplored the reckless excesses of the fire-eaters and applauded the refusal of Virginia to rush headlong with the Cotton States into secession. But when Lincoln's call for troops made necessary a choice between fighting for or against Virginia, they lined up quickly with the South and supported the Confederacy loyally to the end.

Another distinguishing characteristic of the Blackfords was their consistent devotion to God. Mary was intensely religious and her letters are replete with spiritual exhortations. Her husband was an active and devout churchman and in an era when drinking and carousing were an accepted part of being a young Virginia blue blood, her sons ran the gamut of both university and army without partaking of the evils that encompassed them. At the University of Virginia the sons were pillars in the temperance organization, and as soldiers they were active in religious affairs. But they were not prudes; and they had the respect and warm affection of their associates.

One of the most remarkable things about Mary and her flock was their relation to the slaves. Mary's mother, when left a widow in debt, sold the family home rather than put her servants on the auction block. Mary's undying ambition was to free the slaves and send them to Liberia. She sought by personal interposition to alleviate the harshness of the local traffic in Negroes. More than that, she defied the slave code and the hostility of neighbors to teach colored children to read the Scriptures. One of the choicest items in this account of the Blackford family is the deed of manumission given by Mary's brother, Charles, to his servant Ralph. To all the Blackfords, slaves were persons, made in the image of God, possessed of reason and dignity, and hence to be treated as humans and not chattels.

The emancipation enforced by war, without preparation for the responsibilities of freedom, produced serious misgivings in Mary and in many other benevolent Southerners. But the realization that Negro children could no longer be denied education or be sold away from their parents caused Mary to exclaim, "Praised be the Lord."

The forcefulness displayed by Mary Blackford in her relentless fight against slavery and sin prove her a striking exception to the stereotyped views of Southern womankind. No clinging vine or pliable ornament was she. Undoubtedly she was pretty and feminine, and most of her mature life she was a semi-invalid. But she was strong-willed, persistent, and a scrapper through and through;

and she was clearly dominant in a circle noted for rugged personalities.

All in all the experiences of Mary Blackford and her family, as here related, constitute a most interesting and revealing account of ante-bellum Southern life. *Mine Eyes Have Seen the Glory* points up the fact that Southern society had many nuances, and that the traditional picture is inaccurate in many of its details. The book contains important new material on Southern opposition to slavery, the experience of Negroes sent to Liberia, the Nat Turner insurrection, and the reaction of the colored folk to thralldom. This material is the more significant in that much of it comes from the Negroes themselves. I know of no slave writings comparable in fullness and charm to the missives sent from Liberia by James Cephas and Abram; and Betsy's story of the selling of her children is the most eloquent commentary that I have seen on the stark inhumanity of the South's peculiar institution.

Dr. L. Minor Blackford, grandson of Mary and son of Launcelot Minor Blackford, is, of course, with such a heritage a veteran of both World Wars. He is obviously and rightfully proud of the Blackfords and their achievements, but he shows no disposition to gloss over weaknesses or to exaggerate virtues.

BELL IRVIN WILEY

Emory University
January 5, 1953

Preface

In the spring of 1945, the 43rd General Hospital, "the Emory Unit," was established in Southern France, near Aix-en-Provence. Across the hall from me lived a young line officer, disabled by an honorable wound for further combat and therefore assigned to less arduous duties in the hospital. Before World War I, his parents had left a miserable hamlet in the Balkans — he had been shocked in 1938 to see the squalor in which his relatives were living — and Ed had been born and bred in the United States. At college he had specialized in American history and at the time of our association he was reading *Lee's Lieutenants*. One day he asked me if I had ever heard of Lieutenant Colonel William W. Blackford. "Why, certainly: he was my father's oldest brother." And of Captain Charles M. Blackford? "He was the second brother." I could feel my elevation in my friend's esteem, though he knew more about American history then than I did.

Baylor Blackford, Uncle William's grandson, had placed Colonel Blackford's memoirs at the disposal of Douglas Southall Freeman in the preparation of his second great work, and he rescued the book from oblivion. Ed introduced me to *Lee's Lieutenants* and the frequent quotations from Uncle William brought back happy hours I had spent as a child poring over my father's copy of the manuscript, of which we were all very proud. The day of my return to Atlanta I learned it was to be published as *War Years with Jeb Stuart*.

Fifty years earlier Uncle Charles had asked his wife to prepare a history of the family in the War between the States. Thirty-five copies were printed, but the book was not published. My copy, inherited from my father, is beyond price to me. Their grandson edited and abridged this two-volume work, which was published in 1947 as *Letters from Lee's Army*.

The interest aroused by these two books caused me to think that my father's war letters might well be prepared for publication too. Long considered lost, they and many other family documents were found in a heavy green chest made in Bogotá about 1844 — it turned out to be mahogany an inch thick when the green paint was scraped off — that had stood for many years in the semi-open corridor connecting the parlor at the Episcopal High School with the north "office." In that little house for twenty-five years my grandmother had lived with Mam' Peggy, and there Mam' Peggy lived fifteen years longer. My father was devoted to his four brothers: he would have been pleased with a book including them all, though, since William and Charles each already has a book devoted to his military career, he would have expected them to be touched on only lightly during the War. He would have been especially pleased to see published an account of the gallant career of Eugene, the youngest, for whom he always felt "more sympathy and intimacy" — as well as admiration and love — than any of the rest.

The more I studied the subject, however, the more apparent it became that the most noteworthy member of the family was the mother of these five young Confederate soldiers. Born in 1802 in the heart of old Virginia, brought up at a time when women were supposed to be seen and not heard but to bear plenty of children, she was an independent thinker and a fearless fighter herself. She hated slavery with a holy passion and she loved the Union with a passion no less intense. She was "shocked and overwhelmed" when Virginia seceded, but she managed to give each of her five boys her blessing when he entered the Confederate Army. She did her best to be a loyal Virginian, but she did keep a copy of *Uncle Tom's Cabin* hidden under her bed throughout the War.

Mary was paradoxical in other respects. Hating slavery with all her heart, she bought a slave in 1846 and kept her in bondage for fifty years — not that there is any evidence that Mam' Peggy ever wished to be released. Professing great humility and glorying in her poverty, she was proud of her blood and demanded that no son of hers should marry beneath him. She gave her own children dry bread for supper to speed the redemption of a mortgage on a slave in order to send him quicker to Liberia. She loved atten-

tion; for the last seventy years of her life she complained of ill
health and talked constantly of her approaching death. It is impossible to say how much of this prolonged semi-invalidism was
based on organic disease; some of it, I think, was. Her husband,
who must have been a very charming gentleman, may have hu-
mored her a bit too much, but he never wavered in his devotion
to her, nor did any of her children. My mother stood in awe of
her and felt for her only a dutiful affection.

Beautiful, Mary must also have had charm, though it has been
hard to find traces of it from interviews and correspondence with
those who knew her. But this work was begun fifty years after her
death, and those consulted were young when she was very old.
Her writings reveal a forceful personality. She was a domineering
woman who never hesitated to exact in full the prerogatives she
thought her due.

She was too, deeply and sincerely religious. A devout Episco-
palian, she was broad enough in her outlook to attend the services
of other Protestant denominations when she could not attend her
own church. Her great fault was that she was totally devoid of
a sense of humor.

In 1833, after recording some examples of generous conduct
on the part of the slaves, she wrote: "Such instances of faithfulness 'twere pity should be lost. I here record them hoping that some
day they may appear in better garb for the honor of the poor negro,
and to prove how much of goodness and kindness there is in his
nature." In fulfilling that hope I believe I am earning pardon for
any apparent lack of sympathetic respect.

Another reason led me to work on this book: I was brought up
to believe that my father and his four brothers did *not* fight to
preserve slavery. In my adult years, I blush to confess, I sometimes wondered if their recollection of the reasons which impelled
them to fight might not have been incorrect after the passage of
years. Their contemporary letters prove them to have been consistent.

The major part of the source material comes from that old
mahogany chest. The present whereabouts of the individual items

is listed in the notes. Many of the most important manuscripts have been consulted in the original. I have not thought it necessary to indicate every inconsequential omission and in the interest of readability I have freely altered punctuation and paragraphing, but the original spelling I have scrupulously observed.

I expect to hear from some of my kin that I have been guilty of various inaccuracies; for example, there is a family tradition that General John Minor choked on a chicken bone at a banquet in honor of Lafayette. Lafayette left this country twenty-three years before the General's death and did not return till eight years afterwards. Many other legends have been exploded by examination of contemporary records, which are apt to be more reliable than recollections written fifty years after the event. I have striven earnestly for historical accuracy.

My brother Staige was very much interested in the preparation of this book. He made many just criticisms and offered encouragement at times when it was needed. He suggested the title. My brother Randolph not only has loaned me his large collection, but has also read with unflagging interest and generous advice each version of the book. Charles Minor Blackford III has given me permission to use any hitherto unpublished parts of his grandparents' book and lent me his copy of his great grandfather's *Address* in 1828. Great-uncle Lucius' grandson, Berkeley's son, James F. Minor, has loaned me his father's invaluable Recollections with copies of so many letters; and he has rechecked the dates. Great-uncle Lewis' grandson, the late Dr. Landon White, showed me many old letters now in the University of Virginia Library, and Anne Minor Klingman, granddaughter of Cousin John B. Minor, pointed out to me the letters he received from my grandparents and also (probably) the only extant war letters Eugene wrote. Many others have helped too.

It is difficult to list all those not related by blood who have aided me. Perhaps topping the list should be Harriet Beecher Stowe's great-niece, Nancy Hale, who learned from this manuscript much about the South she had not learned in some twenty years in Virginia. Her interest has been inspiring.

Francis L. Berkeley, Jr. and John Cook Wyllie, of the division of rare books and manuscripts, Alderman Library, University of Virginia, have extended every courtesy and encouragement and checked a number of references for me.

J. de Roulhac Hamilton, recently Curator of the Southern Historical Collection, University of North Carolina, has also been most helpful. Mrs. Lucille T. Dickerson of the Jones Memorial Library, Lynchburg, has placed her facilities at my disposal, has sent me books, checked references, and brought items to my attention. The Atlanta Public Library, and the Libraries of Emory and Atlanta Universities have also been utilized. Carrol H. Quenzel, Librarian of Mary Washington College in Fredericksburg, gave me several valuable references.

Robert D. England gave me editorial assistance. W. G. Suhling, Jr. told me of the Confederate ruse that saved Lynchburg and supplied the references. Margaretta Douglas, M.A., searched the files of the American Colonization Society in the Library of Congress and provided me with copies of a number of documents, especially letters from ex-slaves in Liberia. The Reverend Churchill J. Gibson has checked various items and offered some suggestions.

Mr. and Mrs. Walter Chinn showed me the sights of Fredericksburg and Edward A. Hummel of the National Park Service the battlefield.

Olive Howard and the late Sarah Tryanham were tireless in copying old letters and typing successive drafts of the book.

To my colleague on the Faculty of Emory University, the well-known student of Confederate history and the author of various books about it, Bell Irvin Wiley, whose critical study and editorial suggestions have made possible the publication of this book, my thanks are most justly due.

Finally and most recently, I would be remiss not to acknowledge my appreciation of the interest of the staff of the Harvard University Press, especially Miss Ann Louise Coffin.

L. MINOR BLACKFORD

Atlanta
January 7, 1954

MINE EYES HAVE SEEN THE GLORY

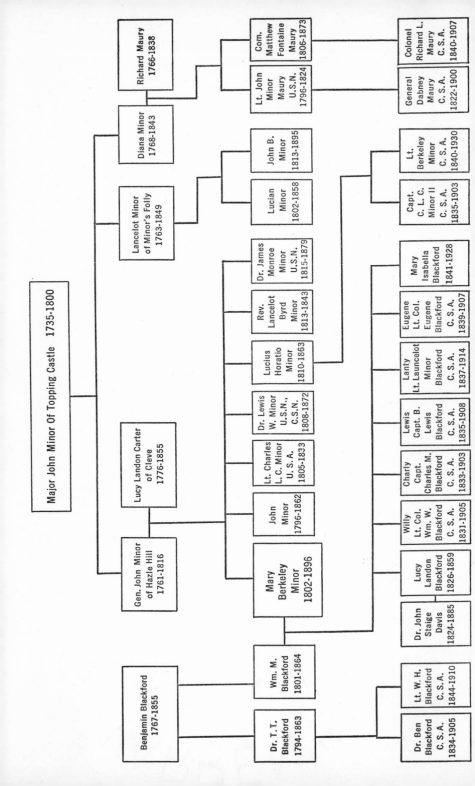

Major John Minor Of Topping Castle   1735-1800

Richard Maury 1766-1838

Diana Minor 1768-1843

Com. Matthew Fontaine Maury 1806-1873

Lt. John Minor Maury U.S.N. 1796-1824

Colonel Richard L. Maury C. S. A. 1840-1907

General Dabney Maury C. S. A. 1822-1900

Lancelot Minor of Minor's Folly 1763-1849

John B. Minor 1813-1895

Lucian Minor 1802-1858

Lt. Berkeley Minor C. S. A. 1840-1930

Capt. C. L. C. Minor II C. S. A. 1835-1903

Gen. John Minor of Hazle Hill 1761-1816

Lucy Landon Carter of Cleve 1776-1855

Dr. James Monroe Minor U.S.N. 1815-1879

Rev. Lancelot Byrd Minor 1813-1843

Lucius Horatio Minor 1810-1863

Dr. Lewis W. Minor U.S.N., C.S.N. 1808-1872

Lt. Charles L. C. Minor U. S. A. 1805-1833

John Minor 1796-1862

Mary Berkeley Minor 1802-1896

Mary Isabella Blackford 1841-1928

Eugene Lt. Col. Eugene Blackford C. S. A. 1839-1907

Lanty Lt. Launcelot Minor Blackford C. S. A. 1837-1914

Lewis Capt. B. Lewis Blackford C. S. A. 1835-1908

Charly Capt. Charles M. Blackford C. S. A. 1833-1903

Willy Lt. Col. Wm. W. Blackford C. S. A. 1831-1905

Lucy Landon Blackford 1826-1859

Dr. John Staige Davis 1824-1885

Benjamin Blackford 1767-1855

Wm. M. Blackford 1801-1864

Dr. T. T. Blackford 1794-1863

Lt. W. H. Blackford C. S. A. 1844-1910

Dr. Ben Blackford C. S. A. 1834-1905

CHAPTER I

In Old Virginia

On September 4, 1832, William Matthews Blackford of Fredericksburg, Virginia, wrote the Reverend R. R. Gurley, Secretary of the American Colonization Society:

"We have had reason to curse slavery within the last day or two from a painful exemplification of its evils occurring right under our own eyes. A year ago I bought a negro woman from a trader to prevent her separation from her husband. She was truly gratified and has made us a faithful servant ever since. Her husband belonged to an estate. In dividing it, a sale was necessary and, without letting me know of it, he was sold to a trader. He was seized on the streets and handcuffed, and then was permitted to take leave of his wife, who had not the slightest idea of such an event. I leave you to imagine the feelings of the wife, — and of Mrs. B. It has preyed upon the latter's mind very much and will, I fear, make her sick. The man was addicted to drink, but was civil and industrious and made her an affectionate husband. But I needn't pain you by reflections on this subject." [1]

Blackford's ideas as to the effect of the Negro's sale upon his wife, Mary, were quite correct. The incident burned so deep into her heart that she began a journal entitled, "Notes Illustrative of the Wrongs of Slavery." [2] In her "Notes" she inscribed this version of the tragedy:

"We were at dinner when I heard that my cook's husband had been sold, and he had come to take leave of his wife. I went out immediately to see about it. When I got into the yard he was standing there heavily handcuffed and leaning against the kitchen, his tears dropping upon the irons.

"Jane was engaged, as well as the agony of her feelings would permit, in collecting at a moment's notice, his little wardrobe; some of his clothes she was wringing out of the tub. He had left her early in the morning to go to his work, which was driving a dray on the Street. The first notice he had that he had been sold was the Trader coming up to put handcuffs on. This was occurring almost every day. They feared to let them know beforehand that they were sold lest they should make their escape.

"I shall never forget the silent agony of his looks as he cast his eyes on the irons on his wrists: they seemed (to use Sterne's expressive words) 'to have entered into his soul.'

"When all was ready and he had shaken hands affectionately with us all and had taken one more parting look at his wife, he turned and said in a steady voice to the white man, 'Now, Sir, I am ready.'

"The poor wife is almost heartbroken for, as he is sold to a Negro trader, there is no probability of their meeting again in this world. She says, 'if he was prepared, I would rather have seen him die than going off with those handcuffs on.'

"I offered to let Jane be sold to go with him that they might not be seperated,[3] but the young man who acted as agent for the Trader told me candidly that that would not secure the end I desired, for they would be sold wherever they got the highest price for them.

"The frequency of these sales and the high prices offered by the Traders and above all the deadening effects of Slavery upon the feelings have steeled the hearts of the people to its enormity.

"In the same drove of human beings that poor Henry goes with, there is a young woman whom the trader kept in the capacity of his Mistress until, either from weariness of her or in the hope of gain, most probably from both, he sent her along with the rest to be carried South and sold, probably in the New Orleans market, where a branch of this inhuman traffic is to sell pretty girls for Mistresses for white men: These command a *very high* price."

2

This version was not a sudden emotional outburst, but rather a crystallization of sentiments that Mary had absorbed from her father and, especially, her mother. Such sentiments were not uncommon in Virginia early in the nineteenth century.

Mary had been brought up to look upon slaves as human beings whose hard lot deserved not contempt but sympathy, to look upon them as persons capable of selfless devotion and worthy of deep affection. This was the attitude of her mother, the great influence in her life. This lady had been born Lucy Landon Carter, the daughter of Colonel Landon Carter [4] of Cleve and Mildred Washington Willis [5] (and she never let Mary forget her blood). She never tired of telling her daughter of the love lavished upon her by Mammy Betty when she was a child in the Revolution.

Colonel Carter lost his wife when Lucy was only six. She and her sister, two years older, "were left very much in the care of Mammy Betty . . . Mammy's rule was kind but firm: she knew how young ladies ought to behave and she kept them rigidly up to her own and her Master's requirements. Dressed in silks, with their hair powdered, they were carried around by her in state to pay visits of ceremony to the neighboring gentry. Mammy always threw linen mantles around them as soon as they got in the coach to keep the powder from falling on their dresses, and just before the coach reached the house where they were to pay a visit, she would give an extra touch of powder to their heads and take off their mantles." [6]

Colonel Carter did not remain a widower long. The very day he brought home his new bride she began to discipline her little stepdaughters, whipping Lucy "soundly to cure her of her extravagance," and she demanded ever after rigorous economy.

"But the burden of little Lucy's life was her anxiety about her beloved Mammy. The old woman could not reconcile herself so easily as the little girls to the new régime. The new mistress announced that Mammy should not idle away her time in the nursery and gave her as task work a certain amount of sewing to be done each day, and threatened to have her punished if she did not obey her orders.

"The idea of Mammy's being punished was agony unspeakable to the children, yet they saw plainly that the old woman had made up her mind she would not do the daily task. Mammy sat by the fire with the sewing in her lap and nodded over it, but not a stitch was done. The little girls dragged chairs around the room and still Mammy nodded. Then they threw down the shovel and the tongs and made a tremendous clatter but all to no purpose, for Mammy only roused up long enough to say, ' 'Tain't no use, honey: I ain't gwine to do it.' " Regardless of her sins of omission, however, "Mammy never was punished."

At sixteen Lucy left the dominion of her parsimonious step-mother to marry John Minor, a personable young widower. The old house servants at Cleve did not approve of this match: for all their sterling qualities they were snobs and they considered John Minor a self-made man. But they were willing to grant, "He sho' knew the quality: Miss Mary Berkeley and Miss Lucy Carter was the mostes' quality thar was." [7]

On his discharge from Virginia's army in 1784 — he had been a trooper in Nelson's Light Horse — young John Minor had come to Fredericksburg to practice law.

The citizens of the town, like many other Virginians, saw nothing paradoxical in considering themselves aristocrats in the Republic they had done so much to establish. George Washington had been brought up in the neighborhood; his only sister (Betty,[8] the widow of Colonel Fielding Lewis), many kinsmen, and old friends lived there. Mount Vernon was only a day's ride to the north, and General Washington was a frequent visitor to the town. "Many entertainments were arranged in his honor and he was always an appreciative guest. . . In that cultured society conviviality reigned. Dinner parties flourished and the safe return of the guests had to be carefully considered." [9]

Fredericksburg was wealthy enough to support such a society. It had been strategically located at the head of navigation of the Rappahannock by Colonel Henry Willis. A bustling port before the Revolution, its prosperity became greater as a shipping point and trading center for the rapidly filling up back country. It was on the main highway from Richmond to Washington, indeed from South to North, a highway that was traveled not only by public stages but also by "gigs, chaises, phaetons and, not least often, splendid silver mounted coaches, with driver and postilion, guiding the four, sometimes six, horses." [10]

Into this society John Minor was quickly accepted: he was always good at making friends. Among his intimates those early days in Fredericksburg was another young lawyer, James Monroe, also a veteran of the Revolution. Both were promptly elected to the legislature. At the age of twenty-two, two years after the surrender of Cornwallis, Minor introduced a bill for the emancipation of the slaves. His uncle, Peter Minor, wrote concerning the defeat of this bill: "I think it met with a very good fate for we might as well let loose a parcel of Indians or lions as to let our slaves free without they could be sent from the country." [11] Many of the wealthy people of Fredericksburg looked down their aristocratic noses at the young legislator with even more vehement disapproval.

But John Minor had come by his advanced views honestly. His immigrant-ancestor had stipulated as to his slaves in his will (1677): — "them and there Increase, Male and Female, are not to be sould nor Mortgadge & further my will is that the two ould Negroes Degoe and Sallis his wife shall serve but ten yeares after my deseace & then to be free & none of my other Negroes to serve any longer than forety yeares a pece, them nor ther Increase." [12]

Prospering, the young lawyer bought land on the Rappahannock just south of Fredericksburg. There, on a knoll partly encircled by Hazle Run, he built for his second bride, Lucy Landon Carter, a large, rambling frame house. He was very proud of his home: he loved to sign himself, "John Minor of Hazle Hill." [13] Hospitality there was unbounded. Soon he was made a Brigadier General of the Virginia Militia.

Neither his activities in public affairs nor the practice of law dulled Minor's devotion to his ever-growing family. John Minor, fourth of the name, was born in 1796. The father's great heart was filled to overflowing on December 2, 1802 when a little girl was born at Topping Castle.[14] Lucy Landon, whose heart was equally great, consented to name their daughter for his first wife, Mary Berkeley of Airwell.

Mrs. Minor never forgot the lessons in thrift so painfully administered to her by her stingy stepmother. When Mary was six, she wrote the General, "This is our Mary's birthday. If you make her a present, let it be a plain straw bonnet of the kind called leghorn, because it lasts the longest." [15]

The principles the General strove to inculcate into his children are set forth in his letters to his fifteen-year-old son attending college in Baltimore:

"Delectus sumus Epistola Fili meus quae praebit Industriam tuam ac etiam votum delectore Parentis — My dear boy, I intended to write you a Lattin letter in answer to yours, but I find myself pressed for time, and am not sure that I am writing good grammar. I will therefore postpone it for the present and write you in English. I write in so much haste that you will be saved the trouble of reading my advice in this letter — except one line —

"Be polite and respectful to every Body." [16]

He expected his namesake to be careful with his money: "I would send you some Pocket money but that I think it improper. You should feel the effects of yr own imprudence to make you act prudently. I gave you Pocket money in abundance when I parted from you. It is all gone. How? You loaned it. This seems generous but it is not so: a hundred to one it was applied to gratify some vice or extravagance of the Borrower, or at least induced him to violate the Rule of Oeconomy which shd have induced him to use only so much as was allowed him. This is an important subject; think well upon it and act accordingly." [17]

Two years later the father echoed the same theme: "I have lost about 6000 dollars by this kind of easiness. I once called it benevolence, — but I have lost both money and friends. Not one of those to whom I loaned but dislikes me." [18]

Despite his counsels of prudence, the General suffered from worry over his own debts. "His mind was so disturbed that he would walk the room at night when all others were sleeping at Hazle Hill." [19]

Mrs. Minor wrote many letters to her oldest son too. She tells him of the baptizing of the successive babies and gives him many stories of the children; she describes their various ailments. In 1812 she wrote, "our little Mary goes to school to a Mr. Strebeck. She is at the head of 3 classes, & has got a medal." [20] And the following year, "I suppose you will expect to hear something of the bright star that is to gild our hemisphere, — but I can only tell you what I heard Miss Smith say, which is that she reads to greater advantage than any person she has ever seen, progresses rapidly in her history, & understands every paragraph most perfectly. I fear her historical knowledge will put some of our young gentlemen to the blush, but besides this her other accomplishments are progressing in the same proportion." She added, modestly, "This is the opinion of others." [21]

She had her troubles too at Hazle Hill. On January 3, 1813, when Mary was ten years old, her mother wrote John: "In the midst of the greatest confusion imaginable I have undertaken to write you a letter. So great is the noise and confusion that I cannot be heard to speak, but as this is the first leisure moment I have had for a long time I must take advantage of it. *Thank God*, I have almost gotten thro' Christmas. What a slave a holiday makes of a mistress! Indeed she is always a slave, but doubly and trebly so at such times."

Mrs. Minor had lived through one war with the British. On March 27, 1812, she told her son: "They talk much of War in this town . . . I hope we shall have it in our power to give a check to British insolence." Soon the war came closer home. She wrote the General in 1814:

"Our little Molly" — it was only to her father that she used this pet name — "fasted yesterday till a late dinner, and is certainly, tho' not without fault, the best child I ever saw. . .

"Since it has pleased God that John should be called into service,

I submit; knowing that what he permits will ultimately be for the best, and I hope that I shall be so blessed as to be enabled to continue in this way of thinking for the balance of my life: but we are frail mortals, when we think we are strong it often happens that we are most weak. Will you, my dear General, ask our boy a question I often asked before he left College: 'Are you prepared to die?' It is an awful question, and should not be answer'd lightly. Endeavour to fix his attention and obtain if you can an answer more the result of reflection than from the impulse of the moment. Religious principles inculcated by a father have much more weight than any exertions of the Mother, let them be ever so great. Our boy will soon be placed in a situation where we know not how soon he may be number'd with the dead." [22]

To the boy himself she wrote, "The hope that my dear John is what I wish him to be enables me to bear with something like resignation the thought of his present situation." [23] Although things were not going well with the American forces at this time — the British burned Washington five days after these letters were written, — John saw no action in the War of 1812.

In June 1816, there were five younger brothers, Charles Landon Carter, Lewis Willis, Lucius Horatio, Lancelot Byrd and James Monroe. Mary, though but thirteen, was a singularly mature little lady. She left no account of the events of the evening of June 8 that year, but a hundred years later her daughter Mary Isabella recorded what she had heard from her uncles:

"My mother never did tell me this ghost story at all. I never heard it till after I was grown . . . My grandmother had kept it a dead secret forty years. The servants had strict orders not to mention it in Fredericksburg or anywhere. In those days servants had to mind. As far as I know, they never did tell it.

"General Minor was at that time a member of the General Assembly that was meeting in Richmond. My grandmother was not expecting him at all. She was sitting in her dining room at Hazle Hill about 6 o'clock that evening . . . with her sons, their tutor and my mother, when suddenly the door opened and the butler, an elderly colored man, came in and said, 'Mistress, did you know Master had come?' She rose from the table quite excited and said, 'No, Ben, I was not expecting General Minor. Where is he?'

"Then they all followed Ben out in the hall and saw [the General] at the lower end and just about to go upstairs. He turned a moment and looked at them and then went on up. He was in full evening dress. They could see his hand on the banister as he went up, and the ruffles at his wrist. Some went upstairs and searched every room but he was no where to be found. The family were all excited and distressed, not knowing what to think.

"At that very moment General Minor was at the Governor's Mansion attending a state dinner. Several hours later a man on horseback, his horse covered with foam, dashed into the yard with a letter to Grandma telling the sad news of the General's sudden death at the dinner party." [24]

3

When that heart attack so dramatically cut short the career of General John Minor of Hazle Hill, his oldest son was twenty, and there were six children under fourteen. It was then a delicate tribute to Lucy Landon that the General left her his whole estate provided she did not marry again.

In spite of his prudent counsels to his namesake, however, the General had endorsed notes for too many of his friends and, like many other Virginia gentlemen of that day, he left his estate considerably encumbered. The accepted way at that time to raise money quickly to pay off the deceased's debts was to sell the necessary number of slaves: slaves could always be converted into ready cash.[25] But to sell off human creatures, perhaps to break up families, was something that Mrs. Minor was not willing to do. She remembered too well the love lavished on her as a child by Mammy Betty. She could remember too the division of the estate of her father-in-law, Major John Minor of Topping Castle. She made that scene so vivid to her daughter that Mary could recall the details in her old age:

"There was [a] Sale of the property, slaves and all, as was customary on such occasions," she wrote in her journal. "Joe Tyree, a free man of color, one of the most humble and sincere christians [she] ever knew, was there. Joe worked at the wheel wright trade & had by his honest industry put by enough (as he thought) to purchase his family, whom he knew would be sold. . .

"On the day of the Sale a crowd of persons attended. When the wife and children were put up to be sold he stepped forward to bid. . . A rich man bid against him and ran the price up higher than the sum poor Joe possessed. [Mrs. Minor] whose heart was ever open to the claims of justice and pity . . . had never witnessed anything so truly touching as the expression of his face as he looked up and could only say, 'More, more,' from deep emotion, knowing the sum was beyond his means.

"[She] could not stand this, so insinuating herself through the crowd she laid her hand upon the arm of the gentleman who was bidding against Joe and begged him not to bid any more, with which request he complied."

The incident must have made a striking picture under those "large and beautiful trees in a grassy yard of a country home, [Mrs. Minor] a woman of remarkable beauty," as yet unmarred by age or care, the slave "wife and Mother surrounded by her children, Joe bidding for them and the man bidding against him; [Joe's] face fine in its expression of goodness and piety, upturned towards the [auctioneer] and quite absorbed with the one great desire of his heart and the fear of losing for want of means those precious ones who were standing before him." [26]

John Minor of Hazle Hill assisted Joe to pay what he had bid over and beyond his means.

In 1816, though it was not necessary to divide the estate, the General's obligations had to be met; his widow was not willing to sell even one slave, so she sold Hazle Hill, the home that had been built for her, and retired to Topping Castle.

The responsibility for her slaves weighed heavily on her heart. She could not legally free them until all of the General's debts had been paid, nor could she be sure that emancipation would better their lot. She could talk with Mary about them; she could interest herself in the health of those dependent upon her and she could correspond with her oldest son, who had started to practice law in Fredericksburg. From Topping Castle in 1821, she wrote him:

"Dick informs me of the illness of one of Charlotte's children. I am sorry that I did not know of it sooner. I fear that he has suffer'd. Pray attend to it. I will send some things by Ben. I do not think doctors know so well as ladies what to do for babies." [27]

In another letter to her first-born, Mrs. Minor revealed an obsession for the proper upbringing of her family: "The night after I wrote you my last letter," she said, "when I awoke in the night I recollected that I had spell'd *neighborhood* wrong. But is it to be wondered at that a member of that despised class of beings called women, especially one educated in the last century, sh'd deviate in this particular? I think not. I have no doubt that this often happens. However, there is this advantage from my ignorance. I have felt the pain & mortification arising from it & have endeavoured to spare my children such mortification by giving them every advantage in my power." [28]

Most of Mary's education after her father's death was acquired at home. Her brother John may have instructed her in some branches, though not in Latin, and the younger ones added to her knowledge of the world. Undoubtedly all six united in making much ado over her: early in life she became accustomed to being treated like a queen. The most important factor in the development of her mind and character, though, was her constant association with her mother. Notwithstanding her humility, Mrs. Minor was a cultured woman who not only knew much of the Bible by heart but who could also quote from Horace or Lord Chesterfield with equal facility, or gossip about historical personages. She was "a woman of lofty mould . . . and resistless will and yet a lady of infinite tenderness, distinguished for her great beauty, for the benevolence of her character and for the sweetness and grace of her manner." [29]

Mrs. Minor was sensible enough to realize how hard it is for a lone woman to make men of her young sons. Therefore, though she could not bring herself to part with her baby boy, in accordance with a request in her husband's will, she entrusted Charles, Lewis, Lucius, and Lancelot to the General's brother, Lancelot Minor of Minor's Folly. He instilled into his nephews, as well as his own sons, the old-fashioned virtues of truth and honor and hard work by precept and example, while teaching them the fundamentals, farming, and discipline by the liberal use of his cane. His foster sons loved him like a father.

For six years Mrs. Minor and Mary rusticated at Topping Castle. In the spring they particularly enjoyed the lilacs and laurel along their favorite walk down to the river. But the widow's mind was never idle: she was an astute business woman and she managed her affairs so well that by 1822 she felt entitled again to own a residence in Fredericksburg. Accordingly, she purchased on Main Street a house [30] dating back eighty years. It had been solidly built of brick against raiding Indians; openings in the heavy shutters had been provided to let men within shoot at the savages. Into this house she moved to provide a home for Mary and her brother John, for little James and any of the other boys when they had a chance to come.

Mary and her mother did not stay home all the time. They made long visits to their relatives in Virginia, especially those at Minor's Folly; once they spent several days at the home of another old friend of the General's, Thomas Jefferson.[31] Business occasionally took Mrs. Minor to Baltimore and in 1824 the ladies made the arduous journey by stagecoach and boat to see Third Classman Charles Minor at West Point: they agreed that he was the best looking man in the Corps.

In the summer they would spend weeks at Bath.[32] There Mary attracted many admirers. Her six years in the country and the long walks through the woods had given her slim figure grace and symmetry which the fashions of the day did not conceal. Her complexion was flawless and the lavish use of cold water, unusual in that era, had intensified her naturally high color. Her eyes were hazel-brown, set wide apart. Her black hair with overtones of red,

innocent of any tendency to curl but gleaming from much brushing, was parted in the middle and caught in a knot at the back.
Though she never sang, her rich contralto with the old Virginia
broad "a" was pleasing to the young men.

While at Bath the summer of 1824, her cousin, Lieutenant John
Minor Maury, U.S.N., introduced to Mary his friend, William
Matthews Blackford. William "fell in love at sight" [33] and Mary
smiled on him. The following January, young Blackford felt justified in moving to Fredericksburg. Though he had qualified as a
lawyer, at that time he was "more noted for his sartorial elegance
than for his skill in winning cases." [34] His father, however, was
more than glad to give him all the money he wanted.

That winter at Topping Castle, another of Mary's suitors was
George Washington Nelson. "When asked why he ceased to go
any longer, he said he knew from the way Mr. Blackford stirred
the fire that it was useless for him to continue in the race." [35]

Only one letter from William to his fiancée has survived. It
was from West Point in August 1825:

"I arrived here night before last. On Yesterday morning I saun-
tered over the plain to 'Camp Adams.' Whilst standing without
the lines I saw a cadet in deshabille pass by. I knew him — it was
Sergeant [Charles] Minor. Having heard of my arrival he immediately recognized me and met me with cordial attraction. He had
been on Guard all night. The relief however in a short time left
him at liberty — and having a permit as long as I stay, we have
been constantly together and have just returned from visiting the
ruins of old Fort Putnam and the beautiful monument up the
river. Last night we walked for three hours on the plain in delightful concourse and the subject, as you may well suppose, was you,
being the one nearest the hearts of both. The praise of the lover
fell on the ear of the brother in grateful strains and met with
cordial response, — all was confidence and mutual regard — and
I can safely say that since in the shades of Topping Castle, your
arm supported by mine and your gentle eyes beaming affection
upon me, I have not passed so happy an evening.

"I spent six days in Baltimore and received much kindness and attention . . . I was frequently asked most innocently whether the —— Miss Minor (supply the blank as you think proper) was yet unmarried. Well might I have said,

> " 'Many a shaft at random sent
> Finds mark the archer little meant.'

I generally kept my countenance — although my heart would throb with pride when I heard every tongue loud in praise of my beloved Mary. . .

"It would not sound nice every where, but to you I will say that to me West Point is more interesting than any place I have yet seen on my travels. My attention is distracted in a city and I soon weary of Brick walls; I prefer romantic and beautiful scenery. The delightful corps of young and gallant warriors — the future leaders of armies and the pride and hope of their country — and then the crowd of revolutionary associations — you know I am enthusiastic on that subject. And yet another association — I still recollect that my dearest Mary's eyes beamed with delight on all around and from her lips I have heard a glowing description of what my eyes are now witnessing. So on the whole I am fascinated with the spot and 'twill be with regret that I shall leave here tomorrow. . .

"I can not say when I shall see you, but I hope I need not assure you that the period will not be postponed a moment longer than my business — or rather your mother's — will make necessary. I shall have a thousand things to tell you — and look forward with powerful impatience to the time of our meeting." [36]

They were married at Topping Castle on October 12, 1825. Mrs. Minor, faced with the prospect of loneliness in her new home — John at twenty-nine was not yet a confirmed bachelor and ten-year-old James would soon be leaving for college — invited the Blackfords to come and fill up her house. William was always glad to concur in whatever his wife desired, so they moved in to live with Mrs. Minor. The next June, Mary had to give up her plan to travel again to West Point to attend Charles' graduation: a few weeks later she became the mother of a little girl. For this child she never considered any name but Lucy Landon.

Lucy Landon Blackford her life long was to be the darling and delight of her father, but from the day of her birth her mother complained of miserable health.

CHAPTER II

Dragon's Teeth

In Revolutionary days some of the most vehement enemies of slavery were Virginians. In 1788, Colonel George Mason of Gunston Hall (twenty-five miles north of Fredericksburg), who had already secured the passage of a bill prohibiting further importation of slaves into Virginia, fought the adoption of the proposed Federal Constitution largely because of the clause permitting the slave trade for twenty years longer. He thundered:

"This infernal traffic originated in the avarice of British merchants. The British Government constantly checked the attempts of Virginia to stop it; but the interest of the African merchants prevented its prohibition. It was one of the great causes of our separation from Great Britain. Its exclusion has been a great object of this State and of most of the States of the Union. The augmentation of slaves weakened the States; and such a trade is diabolical and disgraceful to mankind. Yet by this Constitution it is continued for twenty years. As much as I value an union of all the States, I would not admit the Southern States into the union unless they agreed to the discontinuance of this disgraceful trade, because it would bring weakness and not strength to the union." [1]

Virginia had already made it possible for her citizens to free their slaves, but, in spite of the urgings of Mary's father, the State was not yet ready to require them to do so. Most Virginians, like Peter Minor, opposed the emancipation of the slaves "without they could be sent from the country." Mason faced the difficulties of sending such large numbers back to Africa; a consistent advocate of emancipation (like Thomas Jefferson, with compensation to the slaveholders), he stressed the "necessity of educating them before taking such a step, teaching them to make good use of their freedom."[2]

However much the Virginia slaveholder might hate the institution, however sincerely he might wish to free his slaves, what could he do in the 1820's? "The free negro in the Free States was an 'alien, an outcast, a pariah,' wrote an Englishman intimately familiar with the United States. The increasing prejudice against negroes which impressed Lafayette so powerfully on his tour of the United States more than forty years after the Revolution was exclusively in the Free States. There was, in fact, an unquestionable hatred of them in the North."[3] Indeed, many Northern states would not even permit free Negroes to live within their boundaries.[4]

The plight of the free Negro in the South was hardly better. His condition in Virginia was depicted by Mary's husband:

"In your daily walks you meet with him whose looks proclaim more eloquently than I could the degradation of his lot. With the prefix 'free' to a word which with us is a synonyme of slavery, he enjoys of freedom only the name and the necessity — no blessing to him — of self support. It is in vain his muniments declare him a freeman — his color is an effectual bar to any claim which he urges to participation of privileges. Feelings, prejudices, call them what you will, consign him, despite it may be of personal merit, to abject and hopeless inferiority. Philanthropists may mourn over the fact, but the feeling is instinctive, or susceptible of explanation on the principles of association; it has ever existed and will ever exist. . .

"Here we do not ameliorate the condition of the slave by emancipation. Freedom to him is not a gift fraught with every blessing. He is still a negro, and as such is under the ban of color. . . The free black, too lazy to wish it or unable to obtain work, depends for his subsistence upon the nightly success of his predatory excursion or, it may be, on the profit accruing to him as the medium of an illegal traffic between the slaves and a portion of the whites more depraved than either. . . . .

"Do you wonder that the free negro feels not the impulse of generous emulation? How can he when every incitement to exertion is wanting, every avenue of distinction closed? His very virtues become objects of suspicion, and the instinct of self-preservation would nip in the bud the first development of superior intellect; or, supposing him not to be in a slave-holding community, to be endorsed with talents of the first order, and that accident led to their cultivation, to what calling or profession could he devote himself with the hope of obtaining any honour or emolument which the hand of the white man bestows?" [5]

The free Negro might be ordered out of the State on short notice or, worst of all, he might be kidnaped and sold again into slavery. He had no security.

The white people in the South were not able to enjoy security either: always in the background of their consciousness lay the fear of insurrection of the slaves. During the Gabriel insurrection of September 1800, John Minor had written from Richmond to his wife:

"By my brother's servant I have an opportunity of informing my dear Lucy that I arrived in good health last evening. I found the road lined with Guards and the town filled with soldiers. The delusion of the poor blacks has been much more extensive than it was at first apprehended. Ten have been executed and four more are under sentence of death. And the prisons are crowded with those yet to be tried.

"My heart bleeds for them, and yet this severity is necessary. How dreadful the situation! to be obliged to be cruel and unjust as the only means of self defence. I am sick of such thoughts!! Be sure to give my servant a Pass." [6]

As early as 1801 the Legislature of Virginia began to investigate whether territory "could be procured without the limits of the United States to which our free colored population could be transported. Mr. Jefferson suggested the coast of Africa as the most eligible situation." The Napoleonic Wars caused the project to be for a time abandoned. "But no sooner did peace again 'heal the wounds of humanity,' to use the words of the resolution, than the

Legislature again took up the subject of African colonization,"
passing unanimously a resolution again asking the aid of the President "in procuring a situation on the coast of Africa for colonizing
the free blacks and such as might afterwards be emancipated, and
requesting our senators and representatives in Congress to lend
their exertions to effect the same." [7]

On December 21, 1818, through the zeal of the Reverend Robert Finley of New Jersey, a meeting was held in Washington, attended by many of the distinguished men of the country, to establish a national society to carry on the project. Thus was founded
the American Colonization Society. The following month a memorial was presented before Congress and in the course of the year
the legislatures of Georgia, Maryland, and Tennessee passed resolutions in support of it.

The fate of the Colonization Society was one of the tragedies of
American history. Founded for the primary purpose of repatriating
"free people of color," it sought to enable slave owners who wished
to emancipate their slaves to be sure that they would be better off
free. [8] Some of the founders hoped to see the day when all Negroes
would be freed and sent back to Africa. But, instead of being a
powerful organization supported by all who wished the Negro
well, the Society ran into immediate difficulties. As a proponent of
the Society said, "In the North, the ground of hostility is that we
wage not war against slavery — in the South we are called an
abolition society in disguise . . . We would in a spirit of conciliation ask our brethren if the incompatibility of the views which
they severally ascribe to the Society is not, in itself, a presumption
that each may be gratuitous and that we have hit upon the golden
mean between those conflicting opinions." [9]

In 1828 Professor Silliman of Yale declared: "Slavery is now
generally acknowledged in this country to be an enormous evil. . .
costly to the proprietor . . . a source of increasing domestic danger; an insult to the purity of our religion and an outrage on the
Majesty of Heaven. This language is not stronger than that which
lately resounded in the Capitol of Virginia. This is not the proper
occasion to discuss the subject of the *entire* and *immediate* abolition

of slavery; it is enough that it is, at present, impracticable; nor will
we take upon us to reprehend with severity the intemperate, un-
courteous and unchristian language with which the friends of Colonization are from certain quarters assailed through the pen. . .
Should their attempt fail through the unfair and unjust opposition
of its enemies, the latter will have much to answer for to Africa
itself, and to the African race in this country and to the world."[10]

That strong speech gained circulation in the pages of the *African
Repository and Colonial Journal*, the official organ of the Colonization Society. Here Mrs. Minor saw it and she approved of it thoroughly. While she was inundating Charles on the frontier with
religious tracts (not at all to that young officer's delight), she took
pains to see that he read the Silliman speech, and Lieutenant Minor
concurred in her approbation of it. But the Virginia lady had not
waited for inspiration from Yale: as early as September 1826, she
had set about sending two sisters and their six or seven children to
Liberia. The slave women were not willing to go until after the
death of their mother six months later. By that time Mrs. Minor
was planning to send with them several Negro men. She also emancipated her house servants, but they preferred to remain in Virginia. She was secretive about her activities for she did not believe
in letting her light shine before men, but she knew that her widow's mite would find favor in the eyes of the Lord. Even her own
son the Lieutenant wrote her a year after she had sent the first
group to Liberia:

"How is it that you never told me anything about the emancipation of our servants? What hopes are there of general emancipation
in our State? It will greatly increase the wealth and importance of
the State, but when wealth becomes the great object of attention,
that refinement of feeling, that precious suavity of manner I fear
will fade and vanish."[11]

While young Blackford's father had the reputation of being
generous and kind to his slaves, — he was called "Old Master" so
affectionately that many of his relatives and friends took it up —
the sentiments of William as to slavery before he was introduced to

Miss Minor are unknown.[12] Certainly before she married him she must have been sure that his views on this vital subject were in harmony with hers.

On February 23, 1828, William Blackford delivered a very long speech in behalf of colonization before the Fredericksburg Auxiliary Colonization Society. He tried to temper his wife's views enough to avoid antagonizing his audience of slaveholders, belaboring the extremists of both sides.

While it was necessary for a private society to begin the project and prove its feasibility, he argued, the founders had always expected the Federal Government to complete the work. The expense would not be prohibitive and it could be spread over fifteen years. "Shall it be said," he queried, "that the energies of a great nation are incompetent to the restoration of some 10 or 15,000 souls to a land from which the cupidity of individuals annually purloins ten times the number in defiance of all the legislative denunciations which British and American humanity has prompted? . . . The slave trade still flourishes to an extent and under circumstances sickening to humanity. The question has been raised whether all the efforts at suppression which have been made have lessened the number annually taken from the coast, and whether declaring it piracy has not increased the aggregate of human misery and suffering."

Blackford cited other grounds for federal interference. "A colony on the coast of Africa is indispensable to the execution of some of our most important laws," he said. "Without it the acts of 1818-19 for the suppression of the slave trade would be entirely inoperative" for there would be no haven to receive Africans taken from traders on the high seas.

"We have taken the lead in measures for its abolition, but our exertions have been more legislative than physical," he went on. "The vigilance of our cruisers avails but little on a coast indented by a thousand streams, each affording a lurking place for the trader. The combined fleets of England and America would be inadequate to maintain a blockade so strict as to suppress the traffic entirely.

The evil must be cut off at its source, colonies founded along the coast and markets opened at which the tribes of the interior may find a ready sale for everything but human merchandise."

After commenting unfavorably on Free Negroes, Blackford continued: "I do not wish to libel this unfortunate race, nor do I believe I have used expressions too harsh in speaking of it collectively. Exceptions there are, striking, heart-warming exceptions. But the instances of good conduct and success in life which we see among the free blacks . . . suffice to demonstrate their capability of improvement under circumstances propitious to the development of mental and moral energy." Benefits would flow from the Colony to much wronged Africa herself; and the United States, both North and South, would be better off purged of "a sable lazzaroni, vicious and degraded."

In his peroration he exclaimed: "The Society does indulge the hope that the colonization of the free blacks will open the door to gradual emancipation, emancipation not effected by the agency of federal or other extraneous power, but the result of individual, spontaneous benevolence."

After that address Blackford wrote to the Reverend R. R. Gurley, the Society's Secretary:

"My address was of considerable length. I was anxious to lay before the people all the facts concerning the origin of the Society, and especially to counteract the opinion which prevails that it is a project of northern benevolence. I aimed indeed to excite if possible a feeling against them for not cooperating more generally; as it is the only time, I trust, that I shall be guilty of encouraging sectional feeling, I hope to be forgiven. . .

"I can not omit to state, as evidence of the progress of our cause that the announcement of our intention to have a public address excited no other feeling than that of approbation, whereas had any one attempted 6, 8 or 10 years ago to make a speech on the subject, he would in all probability have been *mobbed*. . .

"I have reason to believe that a great change is about to take place in Virginia. She will, I have no doubt, become decidedly the advocate of Colonization. The coming year . . . is big with her fate. Should reform be decreed by the people, it will extend further our political institutions: the whole character of the people will be new modeled."[13]

On March 31, 1828, enclosing a reprint of his speech to Mr. Gurley, he remarked: "I am fearful that I obtrude too frequently upon your time; if I do, attribute it to zeal in behalf of a scheme which, as the Maryland report says with truth, 'is the last hope of the slave-holding states.'"

That October Mr. Blackford bought from Mary's brother John his paper, *The Fredericksburg Political Arena*. He commented to Secretary Gurley: "I think not the least pleasing circumstance of the change of my vocation is that I shall have it in my power to advance the interest of the great cause of Colonization."[14]

When John Minor had sold the *Arena*, he no longer needed the services of his slave James Cephas. Two months later Mary's mother was writing Mr. Gurley:

"My son John Minor has for some twelve months past been preparing a man servant of his, who is about twenty years of age, for the Colony. He has been that length of time at the printing business and can read and write and is approved to becoming a printer, in consequence of which we have concluded to send him immediately lest he might form some connections which would forbid his removal. He is a boy of some principles, perfectly honest, understands all family work, but is not remarkable for his industry; this last is all that can be laid to his charge. He has been raised partly with my children, and I think I can say that he is a very upright, honest man. We wish to send him by the ship which is now going."[15]

The first letters that James Cephas wrote after his arrival in Africa have been lost, but on May 6, 1830, Mr. Blackford proudly announced to Mr. Gurley:

"I was highly gratified at the receipt of the *Herald*; it places the colony 50 years in advance as regards civilization. Could they not publish it oftener? Our boy James is the printer. He seems from his letters highly delighted with his vocation, and says he gets $20 per month. His account of the incredulity of the people as to his being a printer is amusing; as soon as the paper was issued he says several men came to him wishing to be taught the trade, but 'in consequence of their unbelief' as he observes, this he refused to do."

In September 1829, Mary Blackford was busy with her needle ("we all know the sums that have been raised by this feeble instrument") with other members of "female societies," trying to raise money for Colonization. But "partly due to the great objection made by gentlemen to anything that can in the remotest degree draw the attention of the Negroes to a Society they can not understand" the sale of their handiwork in the United States was not going well. She asked if their products could not be sent to Liberia, "for, as I mentioned before, our object is not sufficiently popular to help us in our sales, and we are obliged to be exceedingly circumspect as we are rather looked upon as intruders into a subject we have no business to meddle with, always excepting the more liberal and benevolent of the other sex . . . The gentlemen are so prone to think that a plan devised by females must be visionary and not worth noticing as rational."[16]

2

By the spring of 1831, three years after Mr. Blackford's address, many churches in New England would not allow agents of the Colonization Society to enter their portals to appeal for funds. A little later Mary Blackford was telling its Secretary: "From childhood I have bewailed the unnumbered ills of slavery. Colonization is the only plan at all practicable of lessening or removing the evils of slavery and fervent are the love and gratitude I feel towards those who like you are doing so much for this great cause." She was pained to read in Garrisonian periodicals wholesale denunciations for she knew "many persons at the South who make the most noble sacrifice for the benefit of the negro."[17] These sentiments were echoed by a friend of hers who said: "The expense of slave estates keeps Virginians, at least many, unable to give freely unless a new spirit of stronger faith and love could actuate them to deny accustomed self-indulgence. . . If I ever get out of debt, all I want with money is to further [the Society's] plans."[18]

Gabriel's insurrection of 1800 had been all but forgotten. In

Virginia the slaves appeared docile: they seemed quite reconciled to their lot, indeed happy in their lack of responsibilities. The sentiment for emancipation had made such progress in the State that one house of the legislature that spring of 1831 failed to pass such a bill by a narrow margin: sixty members voted for it, but those who objected to emancipation per se and those who deemed it impracticable at the time totaled sixty-seven. The prospect that summer for the passage of an act of emancipation by the State Legislature at its next session appeared good.

And then, the night of August 21, Nat Turner, a demented young Negro preacher who had been taught to read by his master and who had acquired a following among the slaves in Southampton County, decided that the signs in the heavens were propitious for carrying out what he had long been plotting. He and seven of his men entered the home of his master and slaughtered the whole family. Continuing with the dawn, he and his ever increasing band "murdered 61 whites, nearly all of whom were women and children. Savage barbarities were committed. The Negroes went wild with ferocity and bathed their arms in blood." [19]

After this crime it required a bold spirit to stand up for the slaves. Such a spirit was Mary Blackford: she even attempted to extenuate the enormity of the massacre. She wrote in her journal:

"In travelling in the summer of 1832, about a year after the Insurrection in Southampton, I met with some members of the Whitehead family who suffered so much at that time. This was the son (& his wife) of the old lady of that name whose family and herself were nearly all butchered by Nat Turner and his gang of ruffians. This Gentleman and his wife did not live with his Mother, but at some distance, and so escaped. I was so much struck with some instances she gave me of the fidelity of many of the slaves to their owners at that time that I took down *from her words* the following incidents to show that justice had not been done them generally in the recital of the crimes committed by a comparatively small number." [20]

Mary went on to record young Mrs. Whitehead's "recital of what occurred at her Mother in law's house in Southampton":

"A few minutes after the negroes were seen riding up the lane leading to the house (in this lane they killed her son, a young Minister), they were in the house and had commenced their work of slaughter. The Mother of the family, who had always enjoyed the affection of her negroes, was among the first killed. Her own servants had nothing to do with the insurrection; on the contrary (as will be seen), did all they could to protect the family at the risk of their own lives.

"A little negro girl clung to her Mistress and begged for her life until her own was threatened. She then fled and hid under the bed. An old negro man named Wallace vainly entreated for the life of his Mistress. After murdering the good old lady, they threatened to kill him. He told them to do it as he cared not to live now she was dead.

"The youngest of the daughters happened to be a little way from the house in some very high corn, which concealed her, and might have escaped, but losing all presence of mind (on hearing what was going on) screamed loudly in spite of the entreaties of a young negro girl who was with her; drawn by her screams, the murderers rushed upon her. Aggy, the girl with her, endeavoured to shield her young mistress at the risk of her own life, but was torn from her with such force as to tear the strong Virginia cloth dress she had on from her shoulders and thrown to the ground where she expected to be killed herself, but they contented themselves with the murder of her young mistress.

"A young Negro named Tom was in the yard watering the horses preparatory to their going to work (for it was very early in the morning). As soon as he saw what the gang were after, he set off full speed to give the neighbors notice of their danger, flying from one plantation to another. At one place the Master gave him a hatchet to defend himself should the insurgents attack him. Feeling however they might get hold of it and use it against the whites, he hid it. He afterwards met companies of white men assembled for the purpose of putting down the insurrection and it was thought that, had they seen him with a hatchet, they would have killed him on the spot, for at that time the innocent were often confounded with the guilty. The poor things would frequently fasten white rags on the end of a stick in token of their peaceable intention, but the innocent sometimes suffered. Tom ran until noon of that day when he arrived at the Guard house. He was altogether spent, it was a year before he recovered; it was thought for some time he would not survive the effort so much beyond his strength. Many lives were saved by it. Much praise and a certificate testifying to his exertions in saving the lives of so many whites at such an expense was all his reward in the world.

"Old Mrs. Whitehead and her four grown daughters, a son and a grandson were all murdered by these deluded fanatics. The only one of Mrs. Whitehead's family (who was at home) whose life was saved was her daughter Harriet, who hid between the bed and the mattress; her Sister was killed at the foot of the bed she was concealed in. After the company of banditti had left the house some of their number who were well acquainted with the family, remembering that there was one more to destroy, sent two of their number back to find and kill her. In the meantime, her own slaves had contrived to disguise and were actually carrying her out of the house to a place of concealment when they saw these men coming on foot to the back of the house for the purpose of surprise. Some of the slaves went immediately to meet them & contrived by some means to turn their course. The young lady was then carried and concealed in a swamp near the house until the pursuit was over.

"Out of forty negroes on this plantation, only three joined in the Insurrection, and they not until they were intoxicated. It afterwards happened that one of the negroes, Hubbard, an old man who had assisted in saving Miss Harriet, was brought out as one of the murderers to be shot. His young mistress, who had been conveyed to the place for safety, heard accidentally of it and ran out and saved him by relating the circumstances of his conduct in aiding to save her life.

"In the same neighborhood with Mrs. Whitehead lived an extremely amiable lady and gentleman of the name of Porter. A negro woman ran from a distance to warn them just in time for them to escape to the woods in sight of the house. By a point of the finger of any of the slaves there, the family might all have been murdered, but so far were they from betraying them they contrived to direct the steps of the murderers in another direction. Strange to say, that three of those who went along to divert their course joined the murderous crew after having saved the lives of their Master and Mistress.

"Another lady of the neighborhood (Mrs. Nicholson) who was too weak to move, having just recovered from a bilious fever, was taken up in the arms of her slaves and hidden in the woods."

After recording these bloody stories, Mary went on to say:

"Such instances of faithfulness 'twere pity should be lost. I here record them hoping that some day they may appear in a better garb for the honour of the poor negro, and to prove how much of goodness and kindness there is in his nature, notwithstanding that *as a people* they have so many wrongs, though many slave owners I know are among the most excellent of the earth, and this turns aside the wrath of Heaven when such things are committed as are recorded in the preceding notes. Bishop Meade [21] said truly, 'They are the most amiable people on the earth.' For though I have recorded fearful wickedness in this insurrection, we must remember how few those have been, and how ignorant and deluded the Negroes who joined it were. I only know of one insurrection before this of Nat Turner's, and of none since. And I am sure that with an hundredth part of the wrongs they suffer we white people would have risen in arms fifty times. . .

"O thou Almighty King! Look down in pity on those forsaken ones, forsaken of almost all but Thee, and open a way for their deliverance. Thou governest the hearts of men. Grant that the approaching meeting of the legislature may be productive of good to them and fix some date to their misery. Shew the people their sin and let them not go on until Thy judgments over take them."

Mary Blackford however failed to realize the impression left on the minds of her fellow-Virginians. While at first it was believed that Turner was merely insane and that the Southampton uprising was due solely to his crazed influence over his credulous and superstitious followers, a view had developed before the legislature met again that Northern Abolitionists had been at the bottom of the horror: all hope was thus destroyed of Virginia making herself a Free State.

3

"When [my brother] Charles was about three or four years old," Mary recalled years later, "Dr. Sprat of Urbana left him in his will a Slave boy named Ralph. When he came to our house my Mother soon found out that he was an uncommonly good child and (although extremely careful about the character of the boys she allowed hers to associate with) he became the nurse and playmate of my brother, being a little older than he was.

"On one occasion my Father and Mother were looking on while the children were at play. The little one, who was always the pet with my Father, took something away from Ralph that belonged to him and he was taking it back when Papa said, 'Don't take it away from him Ralph.'

"My mother who was sitting by him said (at the same time putting her hand on his arm gently), 'No, General, teach him to respect the rights of others.'

"Nothing could exceed his pleasure at hearing this sentiment from my Mother: it was the feeling and principle on which he had always acted, only this time betrayed by his desire to indulge his youngest pet." [22]

Mary and Charles were always devoted to each other. They were congenial souls and in no respect were they in closer accord than on the subject of slavery. When they were staying at Minor's Folly in 1808, Mary was already turning to Charles for sympathy and help. Her mother reported to the General one day that summer:

"A little Negro girl here had behaved amiss and was lock'd up in the Meat House. Mary found it out and came with tears in her eyes to get Charles to prevail upon his aunt Minor to let the child out. . . She stated the case to him in a whisper. I overheard her with great emotion tell him that the poor little thing was lock'd up and could not get out, that she was crying and had said, 'please, Miss Mary, ask your aunt Minor to let me out.' Charles enter'd immediately into her feelings and went to try his influence. I wish you could have heard him plead the cause of the distress'd and seen little Mary a little on one side waiting the decision. At first sister Minor attempted to prove that it was right and proper she should be lock'd up, but Charles overruled all her objections and the key was obtained, which poor little Molly was so much rejoiced at. . ."[23] There the old manuscript is torn.

As their years increased, the bonds that united them became stronger. Charles felt as deeply as she did "about the inconsistency of his Country's making such loud boasts of liberty while we kept many of our fellow creatures in abject slavery, denying them some of the dearest rights of human beings."[24]

In January 1832, the Lieutenant liberated Ralph, the only slave he owned; he had learned a trade while his master was at West Point and had been hired out for several years. Charles gave him his back hire and when Mary said to him that she thought "giving him his liberty was enough, he answered gently, 'I did not want Ralph's money.' That was indeed 'respecting the rights of others.'"

Lieutenant Minor labored hard on a letter of manumission for his slave. He was so proud of the finished product he sent several copies home. It read:

> "Dear Ralph:
>
> "I am no longer your master, but I am still your friend, and as perhaps we shall never meet again, I have determined to give you this assurance of my esteem.
>
> "You have ever maintained a character for honesty and gentlemanly deportment, and I trust that now you are free you will never give me cause to blush for having emancipated one who was unworthy of it.
>
> "You were my playmate and nurse and the good will which you won of me in my boyish days is still warmly cherished, and if I ever hear of your being otherwise than a *Virginia gentleman*, I shall be grievously disappointed.
>
> "I have once said it, and here repeat it:
>
> "I pronounce you *free* in the name of Almighty God.

"I strongly advise you to go to Liberia and if you will do so I will add fifty dollars to your earnings.

"If you go to Tennessee you will very probably be taken up and sold to the highest bidder, perhaps some wretched Negro trader, who will take you off to Louisiana, or some distant part of the country, and you will never see your wife afterwards. At Liberia you may become one of the first gentlemen of the country, your trade affording you a competent support. You must write to me as often as you can. You shall have your money whether you go to Liberia or not. At all events you can go over and try the place and if you do not like it, can return.

"No more your master but always your friend,
               "Charles L. C. Minor, U. S. Army.

"P.S. Write to me as soon as you make up your mind whether you will go to Liberia or not.

"If any suspicious-looking fellow should take you up, do not show him your papers or he will take them away from you, but wait until he brings you into the presence of some one whom you can depend upon as a witness. Take good care whom you trust."

Lieutenant Minor's requests that Ralph write him were to no avail but he kept in touch with him through his brother Jim who was still in Fredericksburg. On June 10, 1832 he wrote Jim: "You must tell me in your next all you can of Ralph's affairs. It was my wish for him to go to Liberia, but as his own is different I am satisfied. I hope he will lead a happy life wherever he goes." [25]

When the Virginia Legislature so narrowly defeated the emancipation bill shortly before the Turner Insurrection, it did so with misgivings. The preamble of the committee report recommending rejection admitted that emancipation was in just accordance with the feelings of the community on the subject; rejection however was necessary for the cost, including the expatriation of the free Negroes, "would absorb all our present means." Commenting on that Charles wrote his mother:

"I rejoice to see that the question of Abolition is put to a rest for the present. Enough has been done to make the people reflect &

prepare for carrying the measure into execution at some future time. The skulking sophistry with which they have hitherto tried to excuse their injustice has been dragged into the light, & all its hidden deformities exposed. The removal of the free blacks will occupy all their means for some time to come & I feel certain that voluntary emancipation will far outstrip the utmost efforts of colonization. The plea for holding slaves with many conscientious persons is that there is no way to get rid of them. This excuse will soon be destroyed." [26]

Though Mrs. Minor had freed her house servants in 1827, she had not been able to persuade them to go to Africa; accordingly she employed Maria West and her sister Lucinda at their old duties. Those of her remaining slaves who, in her opinion, would make good citizens of Liberia she planned to free as rapidly as the Colonization Society could provide funds to transport them to Africa; this expense she could not meet if only because she still had to support her old and sickly Negroes.

The first beneficiary of her plan after 1828 was young Burwell. Mary Blackford wrote to Mr. Gurley on October 12, 1832:

"Mother has in possession a young man whom she has kept in slavery only because he had a wife who was a slave. He is now seperated from her, and Mother wishes him immediately to go to Liberia; he is also willing. She has given him to our Society, hoping by that means to do it good, for many complain that the money raised does not seem to carry any of *our immediate* coloured population. We will, therefore, send him as far as Norfolk, and then consign him to the American Col. Soc. He has always borne an excellent character, and I hope Burwell will prove a useful member of society where he is going. He has not received any education, nor has he been taught any trade. But he is a steady, honest, industrious labourer. It may be that the delightful consciousness of freedom and equal rights may draw forth, like the sculptor's tools, hitherto hidden qualities. . .

"I wish I could say that the cause of Colonization was flourishing here, but here and elsewhere in the State people seem to me to have sunk into the same supreme indifference to it they felt before the Southampton affair. They keep muskets in the houses and train military companies for their defense against their domestic enemies. But to do justice, 'to let the oppressed be free' and to 'break every yoke' enters not into the arrangement. Though it appears to me the plagues sent upon the Egyptians that 'they might let the people go' were slightly more marked than those visited upon the slave-holding states."

Her mother's worries over colonization were paralleled by worries over the education of her younger sons. When John and Charles became of age she had given them shares of their father's estate. She had sent the other boys to Kenyon College in the Free State of Ohio, an institution recently founded by the Episcopal Church but not yet famous.

Lewis had left Kenyon to enter the medical school of the University of Pennsylvania. Former President Monroe, who had appointed Charles to West Point eight years earlier, still recalled their father as "one of [his] oldest, warmest and most estimable friends,"[27] and he arranged for Lewis to enter the Navy as a surgeon upon graduation.

Lucius had married Catherine Frances Berkeley, heiress of Edgewood, and had transferred to Yale where he was to win his bachelor's degree with honors.

Lancelot Byrd, winding up his work at Kenyon, was planning to enter the Virginia Theological Seminary. James, also still at Kenyon, aspired to follow Lewis through the medical school of the University of Pennsylvania into the Navy.

Such educations were expensive so, not be denied her ambition to give her sons "every advantage," including formative years in a Free State, Mrs. Minor sold Topping Castle,[28] the home of her children's ancestors for more than a century.

The year 1832 was an important landmark in the history of the United States: omens of civil war were already on the horizon. South Carolina objected to the new tariff law and was arming to prevent its enforcement. On November 24 her legislature proclaimed the law void and "not binding upon this State or its citizens after February 1, 1833."[29] Jackson warned on December 10,

1832, that nullification was the equivalent of "Dis-union" and that he would enforce the law: he prepared to do so with the army and navy. A gradual lowering of the tariff had already been promised and Henry Clay was able to persuade Calhoun to accept this as a face-saving measure and the South Carolina law was repealed.

When the excitement was at its height, Lieutenant Charles Minor wrote his brother John: "You allude to the subject of nullification in your last and I am pleased to see that we agree on that subject. South Carolina does not appear to meet with such cordial cooperation from the other Southern States as she probably anticipated."[30] A few weeks later that gallant young officer died, probably from tuberculous meningitis, far from those he loved.

4

Burwell's arrival in Liberia was announced to John Minor in a letter from James Cephas, dated Monrovia, February 11, 1833:

"I have received your letter . . . by the arrival of the ship *Lafayette*, with an hundred and fifty-four emigrants, all in good health. Among them was Mr. Burwell Minor, in whose care came your letter. . . When he first approached my presence I had no knowledge of him; but the name he bore, after a little discourse, caused me to recognize him. He is now comfortably settled at Caldwell, the Middle Settlement. . . He is working for 75 cents a day. He came down here on yesterday. He intends working by the day until he can purchase some farmer's tools to commence farming for himself. . . When he first arrived, he acted like a young horse just out of the stable, — he tested his freedom. I gave him the best instruction I could. . . We express great joy and thankfulness to your Mother and her offspring for permitting of his liberation.

"On the 16th of January the bark *Hercules* arrived in our port, with an hundred and seventy emigrants from Charleston, South Carolina. . . We have been favoured with the above mentioned numbers to come over on this side of the great waters to join this federal head so to speak. We are looking every hour for the arrival of the ship *Jupiter*. We hope many months will not pass away before we shall see our harbor glittering with ropes that have been the bonds of the people destined to return to the land of their forefathers.

"Affairs of the colony appear quite smooth at present. The war Horn is not heard here. The Natives are more friendly with us. Our recaptured Africans seem somewhat presumptuous at times.

"I thank you for the papers, and the book which my worthy friend, Mrs. Minor, sent me, called *Pilgrim's Progress*. All these were received and are much valued by me. I hope months will not elapse before I shall receive more presents of the same kinds from you all and that I am trying to live a Christian's life in this dark and benighted land.

"There is, as you will see, inserted in the 10th No. of the *Liberia Herald*, three extensive buildings lately erected solely for the accommodation of new comers. Ho! all ye that are by the pale faces laws oppressed, come over to the above mentioned destiny. The Charleston people (the most of them) are very intelligent. The major part of them are living in Monrovia keeping shops.

"You are desirous to know the exact number of the colonists. I will give it as near as I can (counting the last arrivals), 1829 in all.

"Nothing do I hear of the coloured inhabitants of Fredericksburg migrating to Liberia. The laws of Virginia must be more favourable to the men of color than the laws of South Carolina. Surely they do not shrink back for the fabrications of its enemies. Will they still lay down in Turkish apathy? Africa is a land of freedom, where else could the men of color enjoy temporal freedom but in Africa? They may flee to Hayti or Canada, but it will not do. They must fulfil the saying of Thomas Jefferson: 'Let an ocean divide the man of color!' Seeking refuge in other parts of the world has been tried; it is useless. We own that this is the land of our forefathers, destined to be the home of their descendants.

"Our infant commerce is stretching out her hands, and inviting the weary wanderer of the ocean to call. If your readers will peruse the *Liberia Herald*, they will see for themselves the number of vessels that arrive and depart in the course of a month.

"I have given you my brightest ideas on things at present that I am capable of doing. Pardon my errors and overlook my inferior discoveries. Remember my best regards to the family and particularly my friend, Mrs. Minor." [31]

The official records of the Colonization Society credit Mrs. Minor after Burwell, with only four slaves sent back by the *Rudolph Gröning* in 1841. But, if one assumes that "A Lady in Fredericksburg" was Mrs. Minor, there is verification of what her first grandson, William W. Blackford, wrote in his old age:

"Parties of a dozen or more young Negroes would be sent up from Cleve at a time, to be clothed and prepared for their journy to Africa. At night they would be ushered into Grandmother's room to be prayed for, and the writer can remember the intense amusement with which we youngsters watched the proceedings through the shutters. They were only perhaps the second or third generation of their race in America and, upon a large plantation, had changed little from the first imported savages. As soon as Grandma knelt down to pray they collected around the candle to gouge out the grease, with which they rubbed their faces until they shone like a polished boot." [32]

In after years Mary recorded another illustration of her mother's interest in the repatriation of the Africans:

"My dear Mother . . . owned a negro woman named Sarah with several children, — I do not remember how many. My Mother was principled against Slavery . . . but this woman's husband was owned by a Gentleman who was about moving to Tennesee, and as she would not be the means of seperating man and wife, she wished the gentleman to liberate his man that he might accompany his wife to Liberia, where Sarah wished to go. But [the Gentleman], not being willing to do so, offered to buy Sarah and her children that she might accompany her husband. This he did. And my Mother, after giving Sarah quite a large sum (I do not remember how much), gave one thousand dollars to the Colonization Society that it might help bear the expense of others who wished to go." [33]

After Mrs. Minor had freed slaves that might have been sold for thousands of dollars and spent hundreds on transporting some of them to Liberia, she felt understandably that she had done her part. When therefore her own son Lancelot decided at the Virginia Theological Seminary to follow them to Africa, she objected. He however was a determined young man; he did fast and pray one Sunday that she might be reconciled to his decision.

Lancelot Minor "was fully aware of the dangers to be encountered from the unfriendly climate of Africa. To the objections of his friends, his reply was decided and conclusive: 'If every foot print were on the grave of a missionary, still the command must be obeyed: Go ye into all the world and preach the Gospel to every creature.' A relative said to him, 'You will not live ten years in Africa.' 'True,' he replied, 'true, my dear cousin, but may I not do more in ten years for the Kingdom of Christ in Africa than I could in seventy here? Let me crowd the actions of a century in ten years, — 'twere sweeter than to rust out a lifetime.' " [34]

On May 19, 1837, he bade his mother and sister goodbye in Baltimore and sailed with his classmate, the Reverend John Payne, for Liberia. The Reverend Thomas S. Savage, M.D., who had arrived in Monrovia the preceding Christmas to study health conditions there, was on hand to welcome them.

Minor's first charge was a church for repatriated Colonists at Mt. Vaughan, but this meant that he was living in a community more or less civilized. He may have felt that on the coast there were preachers enough among the Negroes who had lived in America; at any rate he soon became more interested in the natives. Scorning danger, he decided that "in order to do them good I must throw myself among them; I must become as one of them; they must feel, as they would say, I am their 'God man.' "

Soon he was making missionary journeys alone into the interior. He took nothing to buy food, but trusted entirely to the hospitality of the natives for sustenance and shelter. In one letter he said, "In that beautiful valley dwelt the Krebbo, and all the tales which I had heard of their cruelty and cannibalism rushed on my mind and awakened impressions far from pleasant, but there was no retreat." He consoled himself with the thought that the most savage tribes would have no reason for detaining him, "for, to an African, brown linen jackets and trousers are of small value, and even a cannibal would turn with despair from a carcase so attenuated as mine."

His mother "spent money like water in keeping him supplied with everything on earth that could possibly contribute to his health and comfort, and these things he considered it his duty to scatter broadcast among others. He came home once after an absence of three years [to be elevated to the priesthood] . . . He was a handsome man, tall and powerfully built, with a sweet expression of face, but with an air of abstraction as if all that was passing around him had little interest and that his thoughts were directed towards something else far, far away. Saving souls he regarded as the only vocation for him on earth." [35]

Mrs. Minor and Mary Blackford had felt sincere interest in Liberia from the founding of the Colony; letters from slaves they had repatriated increased this interest, but Lancelot's presence there made Liberia as real to them as their own backyard and vastly more fascinating. With him there to welcome them, they tried harder than ever to persuade Negroes to venture back.

Young Minor did not surrender to tropical disease until 1843. That spring he sent home his shortest letter:

"The time is approaching when this flesh will return to the dust; but I know that my Redeemer liveth. I am too weak to write you, dearest mother, but I shall welcome you at the right hand of God." [36]

In his last illness Lancelot talked often of those at home, especially of his aged, blind mother and of his beloved sister. Peaceful and resigned, this hero died in Cavallo, Cape Palmas, on May 29, 1843, aged twenty-nine years. The stone which marks his grave bears his last words, "Let the mission go forward; let it go forward more than ever."

5

"The following notes," wrote Mary Blackford at the beginning of her journal in 1832, "are not isolated instances of wrong and oppression, but daily occurrences, so common as scarcely to excite a remark. And yet we had many good and Christian people among us, those who would have shuddered at such a thing done to white people. And yet they pass daily by the Slave Market and Slave jail, or gangs of chained human beings going South, with indifference. Why? Because property in human beings hardens the heart, dims, ay blinds, us to human rights and human suffering." [37]

She added to her Notes only as the spirit moved her, and she often neglected to specify the date. In one of her first entries, she recorded the following:

"Diagonally across the street from our house in Fredericksburg lives a Negro trader of the name of Finnall. Last summer a young negro was sold to him who was strongly suspected of the crime of wishing to make his escape to one of the Free States. So his Mistress sold him to this Trader, who confined him in his cellar, not having a jail at hand then. The Mother of this young man was an old woman whom I know, an excellent and pious woman. This was her only son, her greatest earthly comfort. She would often come to visit him in his cellar. She had sometimes been admitted as far as the iron grated door, but that favour was only granted by the special interposition of the gentleman with whom she lived; after a while this was denied. Her son remained several weeks in this confinement; about twilight those confined used to be brought out and walked about the garden for exercise.

"When the time drew near for them all to be driven South," she continued, "the Mother came to the house and very earnestly solicited the young man who had charge of them (the Trader being away), to permit her to see him once more. This was refused!!! She came over the street to our house. When I discovered the cause of her silent grief, for she made no complaint, I asked her if she thought my intercession would do any good. She answered perhaps it might. So I put on my bonnet and went over with her, she waiting at the gate while I went to the door. The young man I addressed, pleading for permission for the Mother to take leave of the Son face to face, but in vain. Though he was quite a youth, his heart seemed quite hardened toward these poor people. I asked him how he would feel were he in the place of the young man now in confinement and his mother waiting to take a last farewell of him. Wearied with my importunities he said he would step in and ask Mrs. Finnall, that she had the liberty to permit it if she chose. I then begged to see her, hoping from one of my own sex to find that mercy I looked for in vain from a man. I was still standing at the door. She would not come down stairs, but sent me word that she had nothing to do with it. The only reason the young man gave me for this unnecessary cruelty was that when he saw his Mother it caused him to give himself airs for some time after.

"When I found all hope of prevailing with him was over, I fixed my eyes steadily upon the hardhearted being before me and asked him if he did not fear the judgments of an offended God. I warned him that such cruelty could not long go unpunished, and reminded him of the affair at Southampton which had just occurred. He seemed to quail under my rebuke. After it was over I wondered at my own courage but I was entirely carried away by the enthusiasm of my feelings. He had then many human beings who had committed no crime, in close confinement in a damp cellar, I believe, handcuffed and chained.

"I saw them some weeks after set out, the men chained two & two; the women and little children in large Carryalls, an indulgence not always allowed. The mother I interceded for was down there. She clasped her son to her bosom, but he was quickly pulled away by the inhuman driver. Large droves continually pass here, the men often chained, the women limping after, and their stern Drivers bringing up the rear. Not long since a slave about to be carried off in one of Smith and Finnall's droves cut the sinews of his wrist so as to render his right hand useless."

Early in 1833 she entered this lengthy story as to the local slave traffic:

"There is within a few yards of our house in Fredericksburg a tolerably large brick house owned by Judge Green. By Deceiving the son (who managed his father's business) as to their object, the Negro traders, Smith and Finnall, bought the property to turn into a jail to put the slaves they purchased for the Southern Market in. They have now nearly completed a brick wall 16 feet high so as to form a small yard behind the house in which these innocent prisoners can come out to take the air, the front and side of the building are on the street. The windows are grated with iron.

"They have been using the town jail for their purpose, though it is expressly contrary to law, there being no one possessed of moral courage enough to go forward to have this abuse corrected. The town jail faces the Presbyterian Church and I have sat there during the preaching and looked at the innocent prisoners peeping through the iron bars, and have thought that they were kept there for the crime of desiring to be free and to return to those whom God commanded them to protect and care for. The words would occur to me as I looked around on the worshippers in the Church: 'Is not this the fast that I have chosen, to loose the bonds of wickedness, to undo the heavy burdens, and to let the oppressed go free, and that ye break every yoke.'

"At a time when my heart was weighed down by watching each day the progress made in building the brick wall that was around the negro jail spoken of above where guiltless prisoners were to be immured, and I looked around in vain for a remedy. (My dear husband did all he could to stop it.) I was called to the door to see a plain looking country gentleman who wished to see Mr. Blackford on business. I told him Mr. B. would soon be at home and asked him to be seated. On entering into conversation with him, I discovered he had been directed by that good and holy man Father Kobler (a Methodist preacher) to get advice from my husband as to the steps necessary to be taken to procure a passage to Liberia for a young woman, the only Slave he possessed. He told me he was about to remove with his family to Illinois, and he wished to give her her freedom and every advantage. He could have gotten, he told me, four hundred dollars for her in the neighbourhood.

"This act of disinterestedness cheered me; it was the green spot in the moral desert I had been wandering through. I thanked God for showing me just then that there were some who felt for the oppressed; it cheered and refreshed my spirits, and I can better bear to witness the progress of the jail, though I trust I shall never be hardened to such sights.

"The young woman who was liberated by the old gentleman . . . was sent to town to the care of the Female Colonization Society, and was sent to Liberia by them under the protection of some missionaries who were going to that place. Along with her we sent another freed girl manumitted by Mr. Morton. . .

"My distress was great about the jail, or rather the Bastille, to immure innocent persons. Every time I passed the wall and saw the poor Negroes working on it (not knowing but that they themselves might be the first to be confined there), my heart seemed bursting with indignation at the great wrong to be committed. Yet what was to be done? No one in the neighbourhood could afford to buy the property for the high price the traders asked.

Finally, "Mr. Wm. K. Smith, a generous, rich, kind-hearted Yankee, finding out how much all the neighbourhood dreaded the Bastille being erected in their midst, purchased the lot from the Traders at an exhorbitant price. I have now, thank God, the infinite pleasure of seeing the high brick wall pulling down and the iron grating taken out of the windows. Mr. Smith is preparing to make it a handsome dwelling house.

"But alas! the poor Negroes are not benefitted as the same men have erected another jail in a part of the town less respectable, near the river. 'Disguise it as thou wilt, Slavery, thou art a bitter draught.'

"How the practice of injustice hardens the feelings is perfectly wonderful; what is done under our own eyes would shock us to the last degree were it not for this hardening process. I am convinced that the time will come when we shall look back and wonder how Christians could sanction slavery. . . Professors of religion think themselves justified when a slave attempts to make his escape to a Free State from a most natural and laudable desire of freedom, to have him immediately sold to a Negro buyer, seeming to consider he had committed a great crime."

On February 20, 1833, she entered this note: "This morning in taking a walk up the street I met one of the Negro traders with a few negroes; he sat in a Carriold by the side of a young negro woman. Three negro men walked before his horse, two of them chained, the chain extending from the arm of one to the arm of the other. I heard the Trader call to them to 'walk like Devil.' I thought to myself, 'How would those persons who contend that Slavery is no evil like to change places with these chained men, driven through the streets like cattle to market, perhaps leaving behind them a beloved wife & children whom they were never to see again? indeed the circumstances of their being chained shows their extreme unwillingness to leave home and kindred.' God have mercy upon these poor people!! for mercy is not in man when interest and power unite in drawing him from it."

When Fredericksburg celebrated Washington's birthday that year, the effect upon Mary was quite different from that made upon her fellow citizens. She wrote of the day:

"I always feel strongly affected when I see the mob of poor slaves that follow our troops of Volunteers who come marching in the streets on our great anniversaries. I think how little reason they have to rejoice in an independence that has left them in such abject slavery, and yet so profoundly ignorant as not to understand why they have no interest in the rejoicing. These companies have been gotten up since the alarm of the Southampton insurrection. It grieves my heart that my brave countrymen should be preparing for a servile and dishonorable warfare when the way is opened to gradually abolish Slavery, the cause of so much wrong."

In a long entry dated five days later she reverted to the slave trade: "To day Finnall, the Negro trader, set off with a large gang of Slaves for the Southern Market. There were many women, girls and boys who set off from this place, the *men* coming afterwards. *They* were generally chained and handcuffed. Capt. Henry Philips, who lives very near us, has sold to this gang a little girl, twelve or thirteen years old, named Melinda, tempted by the high price, though he is rich. She was a favorite with those who knew her. My good neighbour, Mrs. Stevenson, told me that when she came to take leave of her 'every limb of her delicate frame trembled.' The sale had been very sudden. The only reason given for selling her was that Mrs. Philips said she could do her own work. I saw companies of females weeping as they walked before the Drivers, stopping occasionally as they proceeded to take leave of their relatives and friends as they met them.

"A call was made not long ago upon the charity of some ladies of my acquaintance in behalf of a negro woman who had been left by a Trader to be confined. The child it appears was his own, though he had left the wretched Mother destitute, depending upon her supporting herself. This she could not do during her confinement, she had not even clothes to put on the poor naked infant but for the charity of these ladies, who felt it more than the hard hearted father. It is one of the most dreadful circumstances of this traffic that the women frequently become the prey of the brutal lust of their oppressors, even those who perhaps have torn them from the arms of a beloved husband and children.

"The light manner in which female virtue is regarded among colored persons is truly appalling, and it is owing entirely to their being treated as property, their marriages not being recognized by the law of the land. The conjugal tie can be broken at the will of the Master at any time, though God has said 'that what He hath joined man must not put asunder.' This evil of our own creating recoils often on ourselves, our enemies are sometimes 'those of our own household,' producing a degree of profligacy among the male part of our Society truly alarming, and threatening to break down all sense of virtue among them.

"Our laws require that the Slaves be kept in profound ignorance, the penalty being fifty dollars fine or three months imprisonment for any one who should teach one of them to read unless it were his or her Slave. I have myself been twice threatened by the Grand Jury for teaching on Sunday a few colored children to read their

Bibles. I know they can not get any white witnesses to witness against me, and the colored people would not be received as witnesses in the eyes of the law, even if they were willing. But I am forced to refuse frequent applications to receive colored children, for if I were to enlarge my Sunday School at all, the threat so often given of breaking it up might be put into execution. These poor creatures being denied Sabbath School instruction which they so much covet! Even oral instruction (which the law allows) being forbidden by public opinion! Is it not a wonder they possess as much virtue and religion as they practice?"

In a later entry Mary related another incident: "Between Fredericksburg and Mountain, about half way, there is a pleasant little way side inn, white washed, with a pretty green yard before it, where I like to stop to eat my lunch and to enjoy the intelligent conversation of its Mistress, who is so deeply interested in the best welfare of our negroes. She is in the habit of circulating pamphlets in favor of the Colonization Society that I leave with her. She told me of her giving one of these to a Negro trader that stopped there with a gang of Slaves he was taking South. Twenty of the men were handcuffed, two and two, a chain passing between them. There were, beside, women who were not chained. A gentleman there asked one of these women, 'Are you willing to go?' She answered, 'No, I am not willing.' She then said, 'Master, do you know why God has sent this cholera among the people? (It was then raging in this country.) He asked her why. She answered by pointing to the twenty men chained together. It is remarkable that the opinion was universal (when cholera was approaching Virginia) among the negroes that they should be exempt, because it was a judgment from the Allmighty for our sins in holding them in Slavery."

Once (probably after 1840) she had something pleasant to record. "I have been this morning," she wrote, "to witness the departure in the Steam boat from this place to Norfolk on their way to Liberia of one hundred and eight liberated slaves (liberated by the will of Dr. Hawes of Rappahannock county). They are to form the nucleus of a new colony at Grand Bapa. This ship was

chartered and provided with every convenience by the Colonization Societies of Philadelphia and New York. Mr. Eliot Cresson of
the former place was a most active and eficient worker in this,
and came to Fred'g to attend to the embarkation of their people
in whom he took the liveliest interest.

"I went down to the wharf to see them off. It was indeed a
sight of the deepest interest to me. They were very neatly and
comfortably clad, and the generous men who had undertaken to
send them had furnished them I knew with everything they might
need in founding a new colony. Thus opening a way, I humbly
trust, for great good to Africa and to this country. Though the
Colonization Society does not claim to do more than send *free*
people of color *by their own consent* to Liberia, it is opening an
asylum I trust, and gradually preparing a country for the whole
unfortunate race when Slavery shall be abolished, and for Chris-
tianizing and civilizing that great, dark continent in the only way
it could be done, and gradually putting a stop to the iniquitous
Slave trade, all this beside the infinite good to our own Country.
But shall I ever live to see that dark stain of Slavery wiped away
from my beloved Country? Now too when they are becoming so
valuable on account of the high price of cotton. Yes!

> " 'God moves in a mysterious way
> His wonders to perform.
> He plants His footsteps in the sea
> And rides upon the storm.'

"And does He not cause 'the wrath of man to praise Him' and is
not the time coming 'When every man shall sit under his own
vine and fig tree with none to molest him or make him afraid'?"

Then followed one of her most eloquent outbursts against the
institution she so thoroughly abhorred:

"Thank God! that I am permitted to breathe the pure air of
Heaven! that no one can deprive me of this privilege unless I have
broken through such laws as are essential to the order and well
being of Society.

"Forever praised be His name! that I live in a land where no white man at least can be unjustly thrown into confinement until just cause can be shown why. Thank God!!! that I live in the land where the 'Writ of Habeas Corpus' exists for the white man and woman. And may I live to see the time when the poor down trodden negro too shall enjoy this great privilege!

"These feelings have been called forth by the delightful sensations I experienced just now (a clear October evening), on walking out and breathing the fresh air of Heaven. In the midst of these feelings of pleasure, I remembered with shame there are at this moment in the negro jail very near here three men whom I can see (when I look that way) through the iron grating of the windows. They belong to Smith and Finnall, traders in human beings, who keep this jail to confine men whose only crime is that they wish to return to their families.

"Think what it is to be a Slave!!! To be treated not as a man but as a personal chattel, a thing that may be *bought* and *sold,* to have *no right* to the fruits of your own labour, *no right* to your own wife and children, liable at any moment to be seperated at the arbitrary will of another from all that is dearest to you on earth, & whom it is your duty to love & cherish. Deprived by the law of learning to read the Bible, compelled to know that the purity of your wife and daughters is exposed without protection of law to the assault of a brutal white man! Think of this, and all the nameless horrors that are concentrated in that one word *Slavery.*"

CHAPTER III

Mission To Bogotá

Mrs. Blackford's miserable health did not prevent a rapid augmentation of her family between 1831 and 1840. William Willis was followed by Charles Minor, Benjamin Lewis, Lancelot Minor, Eugene, and Mary Isabella. Before the second of these arrived Mary realized that she needed help in taking care of the children. Therefore, in spite of her abhorrence of slavery, William Blackford hired from her owner a slave girl named Peggy at $30 a year. Peggy "growed after [she] got thar." [1] Even more than in stature did she grow in favor with Mrs. Blackford and all the family. Mistress and servant began an affectionate friendship that was to last more than sixty years.

However much Mary Blackford may have repressed her little boys at home, they had a good time. They roamed through the countryside, hunting, fishing, swimming, riding, skating, often under the tutelage of their young uncles, especially Uncle Jim. They learned every bypath and stream for miles around Fredericksburg. But their greatest thrill was in seeing long trains of bell-wagons, each with six horses, come from their grandfather Benjamin Blackford's foundries in Luray across the Blue Ridge to seek shipping at Fredericksburg, the nearest port. "The circus was the only thing of the kind that created half the entertainment, and in the circus [they] had no proprietary interest. There would be trains of thirty or forty wagons, all with magnificent horses with bells on each, and every wagon covered with white sheets and in perfect order. He had hundreds of such horses and took great pride in them." [2]

But the Blackford boys did not have long to enjoy the sight of their grandfather's wagon trains. The panic of 1837 entailed heavy losses to old Mr. Blackford and in January 1841, when he was called on to pay a note for $150,000 that he had endorsed for a friend, he could not do it. Their grandfather's failure had other and more momentous consequences for the little boys than the disappearance of his wagon trains. Their father who, since abandoning the law in 1828, had been editing the *Fredericksburg Arena*, writing reviews for the *Southern Literary Messenger* and enjoying "other cultural pursuits which his refined tastes suggested" [3] but which did not increase his income, could no longer look to his father for money. Already in debt, with a large family to take care of, he sought a government job. On March 12, 1841, his old friend, Vice President John Tyler, wrote to the Secretary of the Navy recommending William "in the event of a vacancy for the position of Navy Agent at the Washington Navy Yard, [for] Mr. Blackford has long been favorably known to the public as the Editor of the *Fredericksburg Arena*, a paper which has been devoted to the advocacy of sound principles and enlightened views." [4] Nothing came of this request.

Though President Harrison died a month later, President Tyler did not get around to doing anything for Blackford until the following February when he appointed him, by and with the consent of the Senate, chargé d'affaires to the Republic of New Granada. This position carried with it "power and authority . . . to conclude and sign treaties . . . between the United States and the Republic of New Granada." [5] It also carried with it a salary of $4,000, a large salary for the day. He sold the *Arena* and accepted the diplomatic post with alacrity.

Mr. Blackford took Willy, his oldest son, with him, but he felt it necessary to look over the lay of the land before he could have his ailing wife and the other children join him. "The excitement in the family at the prospect of his going, the pain of parting . . . and the general family upsetting" [6] made a lasting impression on the young folks. Mrs. Blackford continued to live with her mother, helped by her faithful Peggy in the care of the children. There were too many of them however, so Charly was sent to Mt. Airy, "a prim, old-fashioned Virginia plantation with thirty or forty negroes and much thrift and comfort." [7] Here Mrs. Blackford's lifelong friend, "Cousin Betty" Hill, maintained a home school for small fry.

2

During his absence from home Mr. Blackford wrote voluminously to his wife. His first letter was from Norfolk, June 10, 1842. "How did you bear up under the parting?" he inquired. "I hope you have been supported under the trial. I fear for your health. The excitement made you insensible of the fatigue. Now that it is over, I dread the effect of reaction. I hope you will continue the use of port wine and bathe whenever the weather will allow." [8]

Mr. Blackford thoroughly enjoyed his formal reception on the sloop of war *Falmouth*. "Now you may tell mother I preserved my composure throughout, and was not in the least elated at their unwonted honors which I received with great soundness as a tribute to my official status and not to personal merit," he wrote. "Willy behaved very well and the officers seem disposed to make a pet of him. He will be in danger of being spoiled and made vain by the foolish flattery which his hereditary beauty elicits." [9] William, who was not by any stretch of the imagination handsome, could never pass up a chance to pay his Mary a subtle compliment.

At sea he mused: "I dreamed of home last night & had you all very vividly before me. I don't like to trust myself to dwell much upon you, I should get melancholy. Indeed sometimes, when I think of the difficulties I have left as a legacy to you in your feeble health, I am inclined to doubt whether I am in the path of duty in thus expatriating myself for so long a period. As to the hardships or privations which are personal to myself, I value them not at a farthing. But when I think of you on your valetudinarian bed, perplexed by all the cares of a large household with no one to rely upon for support, I am almost tempted to regret that I ever accepted an appointment which thus severs us." [10]

On Sunday, June 26, he repeated the nostalgic strain: "I fancy the children & *Gramma* just about this time returning from church. You, I presume, are not able to go, but have spent the time on the bed reading or listening to Lanty who I presume still bores you with his inveterate propensity to read aloud to you" (Lanty was five.)

Captain McIntosh of the *Falmouth* lauded to him the virtues of homeopathic physicians, and he passed it on to his wife. "I am willing to try anything," he assured her, "as most assuredly you have suffered many things of many physicians and all in vain. I hope you continue to use the port wine, the cold bath, and to wash yourself carefully. You can in no way please me better than by taking care of your health and presenting yourself on my return restored to health and vigor." [11]

After a stop at St. Thomas, William reported on a subject always high in his wife's interest: "I saw hundreds of blacks and mulattoes on the street. I could not tell who were bond or free. They were better dressed and had a gayer and happier air than the colored population of our Town. They seemed the happiest beings: I never saw a class less calculated to excite pity. We all remarked that we had not seen a single person at work, white or black." [12]

After resting up at La Guaira he told her of his excursion to Caracas: "In crossing the mountain I frequently wished for Lucy L. I did *not* wish for you, believing your enjoyment of the scenery would be more than counterbalanced by your sympathy for the sufferings of the multitudes of cargo mules and Donkeys which we were continually meeting or passing. The loads they carry on their backs are incredible. I saw donkeys with a barrel of flour on their backs. Frequently we would find a strapping negro or native sitting upon the little animal behind a considerable load. One could not but think that the man should have carried the donkey to town. Mr. Hall says he delights in the belief of the transmigration of souls, and that their burden mules & donkeys now encase the souls of the Spaniards of the olden time who oppressed the natives.

"There is, at least as far as the law can make it, an entire equality of political & social privileges in Venezuela," he commented. "Slavery was abolished immediately after independence was achieved." [13]

A few days at Curaçao brought another reference to Negroes: "I went to see the institution of the Sisters of Charity. They have now about 150 girls, from the highest to the lowest classes, under their care. We saw a large class which were taught gratuitously, and there are slaves also in the school; a large number of them will be taken in when a reinforcement of nuns, now shortly expected, arrives. The little prejudice as to color which exists is really astounding when we know that slavery is still here. But slavery is on its last legs in the Island. A grown man will not bring $150, and the owners are very willing to let their slaves support themselves. They are considered of no value. The Dutch will not abolish slavery in their colonies because in the East Indies it is very profitable, but in Curaçao it is abolishing itself. By treaty with England they are not allowed to export them to any other islands than their own for sale." [14]

Periodically William was constrained to warn his wife against depression. On one occasion he enjoined her: "Don't above all things get melancholy, nor write in low spirits, — if you do I shall be seriously offended. I want your letters to cheer me and nourish me, and not to unman and distress me — so, mind, no blue devils if you love me." [15]

3

After a 500-mile ride across the mountains, attended with dangers and hardships, Mr. Blackford and Willy were happy to reach Bogotá three months after they first set foot aboard the *Falmouth*. The diplomat felt it incumbent upon him to uphold the dignity of his country, so he rented "one of the largest and most elegant houses in town" for $60 a month. "It is completely furnished in the most superb manner," he boasted. "Now that I am in a house of my own and have a semi-domestic establishment, I feel the void created by your absence more than I had expected. It is such a dull business to sit down to breakfast & dinner with nobody but Willy. . . I want to bring you and a portion of the brats here if possible." He gave many arguments in favor of her coming. "What will you do for a servant?" he inquired. "I hope you can bring Peggy, or Maria West or her sister Lucinda. Indeed, if Jane could be induced to come, I would not care if you brought two servants."[16]

On October 12 he celebrated his wedding anniversary with a tender love letter, but one not intended "for profane eyes." He went on to exult: "For the first time I hoisted my flag to day and feel quite proud of the display it makes against the mountains. I have also over the door the arms of the U.S., — so I am well protected, you see, by the moral force of the republic — and there is something sublime in the consideration of the protection this piece of striped bunting and painted board would be to me in case of civil commotion here, which occurs every eight or ten years."

From his pride in representing America he turned to the less happy subject of the persecution of the Negroes. "I got three Philadelphia papers, bringing news as late as the 6th August," he wrote. "I read with great pain the account of the riots in Philadelphia on 1st August in which the negroes were so unjustly treated: The lower class of whites, in all respects inferior to the objects of their rage," (he is echoing her thoughts) "were the aggressors, and there seems to have been a great supineness in the authorities in repressing the tumult. The incident is another exemplification, however, of the impracticability of the negro co-existing with the white on a footing of even nominal equality. As the means of subsistence become of more difficult attainment in the northern states, or rather cities, there will be greater competition between the blacks and the lower class of laboring whites, which will engender jealousy and hatred, and end in a repetition of the Phila. scenes, greatly aggravated indeed, til at last the blacks, as the weaker race always does in such a contact, will succumb and, if not removed, will perish. This catastrophe, so far from being prevented by the foolish attempts of the abolitionists to place them upon the basis of social equality, will be precipitated by those very ridiculous measures. If these fanatical efforts are persevered in (and when did fanaticism ever listen to reason or experience?) I look forward to something like a St. Bartholomew Massacre in some of the large towns of the North. The low Irish & Germans who compose so large a portion of the *caniella* of N.Y. & Phila. would join with pleasure in exterminating a race which they hate and despise."

After reading over his gloomy forebodings, Blackford felt inclined to destroy the page as he feared it would give his wife pain. But he refrained, advising her, "I wish you to accustom yourself to have your most cherished notions controverted. On all that relates to this subject I am aware that you are not very accessible to reason, — but you ought to show your confidence in the opinions you hold by tolerating dissent from them; above all you ought not to shut your eyes to facts. This is unjust to yourself and injurious to the cause you have so much at heart."

William was aware of a possessiveness in his wife: "I send herewith a poetical Epistle to dear Lucy on her birthday — you need not be jealous — as you will see that all the flattery and soft things are said *at* you *through* her. Indeed it may be considered as addressed to both."[17]

In a later letter he discussed again the advantages of her joining him in Bogotá: "You will have no benevolent societies here to occupy your thoughts. This, by the way, I shall not regret. One of the advantages I propose in your coming is the weaning you from your fierce philanthropy. . . You will have no measure here of wearing out soul and body in Negro-philism or other philanthropic schemes. This forced state of quietude will do more to restore your health than all the drugs in the world administered by the ablest of the faculty."[18]

4

Though all but one of Mrs. Blackford's letters to her husband on his diplomatic mission have been lost, her correspondence with her son has fortunately been preserved. Her letters reveal much about herself. Two weeks after they sailed for South America,

Mary admonished eleven-year-old Willy: "*Always* remember that you are continually inclined to *evil* rather than good, that we are born with corrupt nature which we inherit from the race of Adam. Fix this *truth* continually in your mind; at the same time know that God stands ready for the Savior's sake to give us the *constant aid of his Spirit*, so that it is only when we trust to ourselves that we need be corrupt."[19]

Anxious that her boy not forget "the Wrongs of Slavery," nor lessons in charity, she gave him this story: "A feeble, poor-looking black woman called here with a paper signed by Colonel Clarke, the Mayor, stating that she with her two youngest children must, according to an act of the court, leave the state before the next July court, or they would be sold as slaves. She was trying to collect something to enable her to go to Ohio. You must understand she was a liberated slave and this is the law. She intends walking. One of her sons has had an abscess on his hip which has lately broke. When she spoke of his inability to undertake the journey she wept. I thought my children would all approve of their dollar being given to this forlorn being, and I did it."

She appended a long description of a Temperance Parade in which Lewis, Lanty, and other little boys in Fredericksburg took part, and anecdotes of Eugene, Mary Isabella, and Peggy.

She acknowledged Willy's first letter from St. Thomas with a scolding: "I hope you will practice writing a great deal that you may do yourself more credit than you did in that letter." After further moralizing, she continued: "Lewis Herndon got home yesterday looking remarkably well and with a most ferocious set of whiskers. . . I have not heard whether the *glorious* war in which he was engaged is concluded; certainly the warriors who have succeeded in driving these poor Florida Indians from their country should be crowned with laurel. I wonder if your Uncle Charles would have fought in such an unrighteous cause."[20]

In December she wrote the boy: "I keep only two servants now. Lewis & Lanty saw wood without being told. . . I want to turn out a noble set of Spartan boys, inured to hardship and fatigue, afraid of nothing but God, despising luxury. And *unlike* the Spartans, never satisfied unless usefully employed, always bearing in mind that they are soldiers of Christ who 'choose rather to suffer affliction with the people of God than to enjoy the pleasures of sin for a season.'" [21]

She added a morbid little conversation: "I said to Eugene this morning,

"'Won't you take care of Mary Isabel if I die?'

"'Yes,' [he replied] 'but Peggy must not die; if Aunt Jane and Peggy die, I shall have no one to get my breakfast.'"

She concluded that letter with, "Tell your Papa I cling fondly to his promise of giving Abram his freedom in July when his bank debt will be paid. It will almost break my heart if he does not — God knows I have earned it."

On Christmas Day 1842 she began a letter to Willy on a more cheerful note: "Well, Christmas has come at last and I have been thinking what Willy and Papa are doing now. What sort of a Christmas have you had? Did you hang your stocking up? and did St. Nick put anything in? St. Nick has felt the pressure of these hard times and actually left nothing in the stockings but eatables. Pity 'twere this 'jolly old soul' should ever feel the pressure. However, Lu got a gold ring her Grandma had put away. . . Oh, I had like to have forgot to tell you of a famous big baby made of rags (the rag bag has been nearly emptied to stuff it) with cap, frock, shoes and staring eyes and red cheeks, painted by Sister for May Bell. She is taking her nap with it in her arms now; it is half as big as she is."

But as she turned to the subject of her health the tone of her letter changed. "They have all gone to Church but poor me," she bewailed, "and I am as usual propped up. I am afraid that I am no better than I was before I went to Philadelphia.

"We live much plainer than we did when you were here," she continued, "and though every one has plenty of wholesome food, beef steak, oysters and turkey are unknown delicacies. I made a resolution I would pay all the old debts *and do without* what I had not the money to pay directly for. . . My dear boy, make the same resolution, *never go in debt*. If you could see all the distress it causes, you would not mind denying yourself. Your Papa for the sake of clearing us of debt has submitted to the sacrifice of banishing himself from his family and Country. When I have paid these debts economy will enable me to have something to give away. We must deny ourselves before we can be truly generous. Every act of self-denial and economy I practice counts for something *now* I have a regular allowance and I know exactly the state of affairs; this stimulates and encourages me and I find ways I never thought of before to avoid going into debt."

Mary Blackford enjoyed her self-imposed poverty like a martyrdom. On January 20, 1843 she told Willy: "I expect to be poor all my life. I do not even wish to be wealthy and to cut a figure in the world, but I do desire above all things to pay all my debts, to give all my children the very best education, to be independent; and I know there must be money to do this. Never, my dear Willy, buy anything that you do not pay for immediately; do without what you can not pay for directly."

She discussed her possible death again with Eugene. This time the four-year-old answered, "I don't want my Mother to be died. You won't try to die, will you?"

The next month Mrs. Blackford scolded poor little Willy again: "I hope you do not eat as much as you used to do. One reason you were so *excessively* fond of eating was that you felt a vacuity of mind and action which must be filled in some way. Interesting employment will allay this craving. I remember some few times in your life I have known you so much interested in reading as not to hear the dinner bell. Lewis and Lanty are *not* remarkably fond of eating because they have so many interesting employments, reading, drawing and other things."[22]

Mary Blackford had been taught by her mother that overeating was one of the cardinal sins. By a strange coincidence, a few days before she admonished Willy on the subject, her brother, Dr. James M. Minor was writing from the *U. S. S. Independence* to Lucius:

"Let me tell you one thing, & I beg that you will not pass it by for what I say I *know*; it is this: I think that your chief stumbling block is your appetite. Now do not say that this is my hobby & ask what possible connection it can have with your affairs; as I said before, I speak knowingly & from actual experience; how often have I had my mind clouded & irritable from immoderate eating & been called on to exert it & found that not only did I do so with reluctance, but performed it most indifferently. It produces lassitude & obscurity & enjoins irritability. But this is not all: the body suffers in the end & brings on a train of diseases which will make life miserable. Had I time, dear brother, I could write a volume on the ill effects of indulgence & the exceeding benefit of abstemiousness." [23]

Sometimes Mrs. Blackford was able to sugarcoat her moralizings, as on February 22, 1843. "The soldiers are just passing by and the drum is sounding in my ears," she wrote. "I never heard it with more pleasure for they are to have a total abstinence supper to night at the town hall. They are gone down and are standing before Col. Mercer's."

5

The letters from Bogotá were more cheerful than those from Fredericksburg. Mindful of his wife's absorbing interest in the emancipation of slaves, he wrote her of what Colombia was doing about it: "By a law of the year 1821, every slave born after that period attained his freedom on reaching the age of 21. But in addition to this prospective measure for the emancipation," an inheritance tax is levied "to be employed by a commission appointed in every province in purchasing the freedom of such slaves as are distinguished by good conduct. There were six women and one man brought forward on the stage to be emancipated. They were neatly dressed but only one seemed to manifest any sensibility: one of the women cried during the whole time. A paper proclaiming their names and freedom was read aloud. A gentleman then made an address to the crowd and to the freed people; afterwards a deed of emancipation was given to each and they walked off & thus ended the ceremony." [24]

"A gentleman who has a sugar estate about 50 miles hence," he continued, "sent me a few weeks ago a cargo (250 lbs.) of the best white sugar I have ever seen here. When I went to pay him, he said he would receive nothing as it was a present. . . You would enjoy the sugar the more in as much as it is the product of free labor."

"I see Mr. McDowell has been elected Governor of Virginia," he remarked in February, "a good & able man. I observe the abolitionists are crowing over the election of a man who so ably advocated the abolition of slavery in the 1831–32 Va. legislature." [25]

On March 24, 1843, Mr. Blackford received a batch of letters from his wife. It took him an hour and a half to read them to Willy. "And first," said he in acknowledgment, "let me express the pleasure I feel that you should have gone to Philadelphia. What years of suffering might not such a trip have prevented if undertaken sooner."

The usual tenor of Mary's letters to her husband may be gathered from those she wrote Willy and from Mr. Blackford's letters to her. On leaving for South America he had provided her for the family expenses with an annual sum larger than he was to earn for another ten years; he wearied of hearing of her miserliness induced by her haste to liquidate all his debts. He also thought he was in a position to be the best judge of what was required of a diplomat in a foreign capital. It was not without justification therefore that he wrote her in 1843:

"I see with great pain that your self-tormenting spirit has led you to find sources of trouble in my supposed extravagances. Now economy and saving and getting out of debt are all very well and I can appreciate and applaud the sentiment which induces you to do all in your power to accomplish them. But like all other good things they can be carried too far and, as I know how terribly hard you ride a hobby when once fairly mounted, I expect nothing else than to hear you have put the whole family on an allowance of bread and water.[26] I know too that you take a sort of pride in talking about your poverty and tell every one how saving you are." [27]

"With respect to Abram," Mr. Blackford wrote that spring, "I promised you to emancipate him as soon as I could, and I will be as good as my word, but I am at a loss to know how to do it. Indeed I suppose it can not be done in advance. On the 1st July, however, he may consider himself free. I do this, I beg you to understand, from deference to your feelings and in fulfillment of the promise I made, and at the same time from a conviction that I am making no pecuniary sacrifice, but also I beg you to bear in mind that I believe I am doing the worst thing for him I could do & that I believe he would be far better and happier as our slave than as a free man. I protest against any undue influence being used to induce him to go to Africa, and I shall be sorry if he does go. I hope, as I have yielded my convictions of duty to him, you will yield your notions about the colony. If you could get him a situation in New York, he had better go there at once. If I record a deed of emancipation he will have to leave the state and can not return. Say as little about this as possible, I do not want any notoriety given to the act for many reasons." [28]

When the long-awaited day arrived, Mr. Blackford surrendered: "With respect to Abram all the responsibility rests upon you and, of course, you are entitled to the management of him. I have to repeat that no éclat may attend whatever you do in the matter, and that no coercive means may be used to induce him to go to the Colony, nor the truth concealed from him as as to the real state of things there." [29]

But Mary Blackford carried her point "with respect to Abram." She hastened to pass the good news on to Mr. Gurley: "Giving him his freedom and outfit is as much as I can do, being limited in my funds. My brother writes me he is very apt in learning any trade he is put to and suggests his being put to learn the carpenter's trade before he goes, but I fear if I kept him here for the purpose something might occur to prevent him having his freedom. He is about nineteen or twenty, very well grown, *honest* and well disposed. You can safely recommend him. I think he will make a useful colonist. My heart is greatly set on this plan. Pray ask that he may be cared for during the fever: if he were to die I should feel a heavy responsibility on me." [30]

The Colonization Society was, as usual, short on funds, so Mrs.

Blackford had to make other arrangements for him while she saved money for his passage. On May 13, 1844, she wrote to the Reverend William McLain, Treasurer of the Society: "The young man, Abram Blackford, whom we have liberated, I am anxious to send in the next ship that is to sail the first week in June. Will you tell me what tools would be most useful for him to take with him? I placed him nearly the whole of last year with my brother [Lucius], who is a farmer, and who took much pains in instructing him in agriculture and other country employments. . . Could you give him letters recommending him to the kindness of the Governor or some other individual in whom you place confidence?"

Abram finally sailed on June 18, 1844, on the *Virginia*. Soon afterward Mrs. Blackford corrected Mr. McLain: "You are mistaken in thinking Abram educated; he would not learn when he was a boy, though I tried hard to teach him; now he is anxious to learn and hopes to do so in the colony."

That winter Mary Blackford felt richly repaid for all her agonizings over Abram by the following letter from Monrovia, dated September 9, 1844:

"Dear Madam:

"I am well at present hoping these few lines may find you enjoying good health. I embrace the opportunity of telling you of my travels when I left Fredericksburg for Richmond. I put up to the Exchange Hotell ther is the place I lodge at night. In going the next morning to settle my bill, expressing myself to the landlord where I was agoing, he charge me nothing. I set oft to Norfolk next morning and arrived ther that evening. I was very politely ask up to Mr. Bell's house where I was accomodated until friday Evening, which I had directions from Mr. McClain to see all of the passioners on bord by three oClock, which I did, so after I saw all on bord, me and Mr. McClain came ashore again, which he advise me when I got to Monrovia to set me out some coffee trees, which I had not done as yet, being as I has not had the opportunity.

"When we arrived to the Jolucal Mountain we did not meat the Govner, he was in the States, but I will make it my business to do so as soon as he coms. I has not been up the River as yet, but I has been inform that the land up thir is very good, but I am in hopes when I goes that I will make a living which it is my desires, for I believe an industrious person can live here.

"I wish you would rite to Mr. McClain, as he requested me to rite him how these passioners was. Thy is some smart a people as I would wish to be with and some had enough to pay for it. Since some of them has been ashore, thy has been some stealing, but I am in hopes that I shall never be guilty of that. Thy is some of them sily enough to say they wish themselves back, but ther is a great many going to school. I am included in that number, but I has regret very much that I refuse when I was there.

"Mr. McClain give me a letter to the assistant govner which I has visit. I find him to be a fine man. I amuse myself after I has said my lesson to Mr. James C. Minor and Dr. J. B. Luvenhal, a white gentleman which Mr. McClain gave me a letter to. I sate down at his office with surprise which I must say I never enjoy such life as freedom. My conversation to him when I call him is Dr. Luvenhal and his to me in a Ripli Mr. Blackford. It is much Better than to be in a State for them to call you Boy.

"Mr. James C. Minor has Received your letter and has giving me free access to his house. Mr. Minor sends respect to you and family, especially to your mother. He is not in town that is the Reason he has not riting you all, but says he will by the next opportunity. Please give my respects to the family, particularly to Mr. Blackford. I am afraid I can not return thanks enought to him for his kindness and also to you. Please give my respects to all enquiring friends.

"Mr. Freeman, the gentleman that will give you this letter, I has advise him to stop and see you and give a free estimation of Africa. He is so much please with the place, he is going back after his family. He is a very fine man. I am in hopes you will give him an invitation to Unkle James Wess house so that he can give him an estimation of it. Please give my respects to Mr. Luscious H. Minor and family when you return to him.

"When I left Norford I was in low spirit about eight days, but after the Captain put me as steward over the black and white, which I received from the Captain $20.00 after my arrival. He insisted me to go to Calcutta, being he was so please with me, but I felt loft to leave my old country and I did not go.

"I see they is a great deal of religious person heare. I has attended meeting very regular. Thy is a Presbyterian church and a Baptist and also a Methodist. I was a coming home one night from the Methodist Church and I heard a crying over the street and when I cam to find out, thy has been a woman died very sudden which was supposed to be well about a half hour ago. She was not prepared for death, I think, and I am studying about it every day.

"Nothing more to say at present, but remainds your acquaintance,

"Abram Blackford."

On February 2, 1845, Mrs. Blackford wrote to the Treasurer of the Colonization Society: "I thank you for your letter apprizing me of Abram's occasion of fortune. I remember the old man, Ben Lawson, but is it not strange that he should leave it to Abram when he had a family at home? I hope all this good fortune has not injured Abram. I have received a letter from him since his arrival in Africa," (and she gives him a carefully edited version of the letter) "and seen several letters he has written to others." She then quoted a choice and revealing paragraph (evidently also edited) that Abram had written to a colored woman in Fredericksburg:

"I am very pleased. My reason why is that I can use my own privilege in every respect. There are a very few white people here, though they are very polite. I meet them sometimes in the streets and they steps to one side of the pavement and touch their hats. I can call at their dwelling in the course of the day and sets down and talks a great deal about the States and religious subjects. The white men never calls me by any name unless they call me Mr. Blackford."

Ten days later Mrs. Blackford wrote Mr. McLain again, this time in behalf of a friend who desired to emancipate and send to the Colony her six slaves: "She will do her utmost in sending these people away, or rather in giving them their freedom, and I know it is entirely out of her power to furnish them the necessary funds. If some who judge slaveholders so hardly knew all that I do of the conscientiousness, generous self-denial, insurmountable obstacles which they would so gladly do away with, how differently would they regard them. In Virginia the owner is almost as much to be pitied as the slave." [31]

6

Mr. Blackford never tired of passing on to his wife his impressions of South America, his various experiences and his opinion on a wide range of subjects. On May 8, 1843, he commented to her on a political insurrection: "We who live in a country where life and property are secure, and where the very idea of civil war never enters the head of the worst citizen, can have but little notion of the paralyzing influence of a state of constant dread and apprehension of political disturbance."

In June he made the following good-natured reference to Mary's busybody tendencies: "You were always rather addicted to throwing pearls to ——— no, I must not write the word, — persons who don't know the value of them — and I was amused at your lecture to your neighbor about her encouraging the attentions of Mr. V. I have no doubt you said enough to make her determined to marry him. So much for your Quixotism." [32]

"A young gentleman from Popayan who was educated in England, took tea with me last evening," he wrote in July, to remind her of the dangers of too abrupt liberation of slaves. "He is exceedingly rich & is married to the only child of the richest man in this country. His father owned 900 slaves. He was a member of the Congress of Cucutá & voted for the prospective emancipation of slaves — but wished a fund provided for their education. He could not carry out his plans. The consequence is that the valley of the Cauca is filled with freedmen who are entirely uneducated, savage & filled with a bitter hatred of the whites. Hundreds have taken to the mountains as robbers and live by plunder. They won't work, and the whites are kept in a constant state of apprehension. The

Hacienda of this young gentleman was attacked by a party of negroes who once belonged to him. He was not there, but his Major Domo or manager was shot. There is in fact going on there a second Maroon War."[33]

"You are mistaken in supposing the Chagres to be near Maracaibo," he corrected her. "It is on the Atlantic side of the Isthmus, as Panama is on the Pacific. The River Chagres is navigable to within 25 miles of Panama. Here is the spot upon which they expect one day to connect the two oceans by a canal or Rail Road. There are no unsurmountable physical obstructions — but capitalists will not subscribe to a scheme which is to be executed in a country on the Government of which no confidence can be placed. If three or four of the great powers of the Earth were to guaranty the Independence of Panama & take it under their protection, declaring that no exclusive benefit should occur to any one nation from the work, it would soon be made."

To both William Blackford and his wife the Revolution was very real: both had heard stories of it from their parents. It was natural therefore that they wanted their children to understand the background and issues involved. While in Bogotá, Blackford specifically urged Mary in teaching their children, to "dilate upon the character of Washington."[34] This request was quite unnecessary for Washington had been closely identified with Fredericksburg, and Mary had known many friends of his.

William enjoyed copying from a letter to him from a citizen of Fredericksburg, "Lucy Landon will be quite as beautiful as I remember her mother to have been before she married."

Blackford revealed sentiments reflective of Revolutionary times when in August 1843, he referred to Irish activities in America. "England can not however complain," he argued, "as societies are openly formed there with the avowed design of interfering with the constitution of our country, the dissolution of the Union & the overthrow of the constitution being the avowed & only means of accomplishing their end in view, the abolition of slavery."[35]

Turning to home affairs, he wrote, "I regret to hear that Jane has been misbehaving. Now you are not in a state of health which will admit of being harassed by her or any other servant, and you must take prompt steps to repress her ill temper or get rid of her at once. I regret that I did not give John discretionary powers. Tell her for me that it will not be well for her if on my return I hear a bad report of her general conduct." [36]

"I was not surprised to hear of the abatement of the *fever* — for such it was — about Temperance," he added. "No community can long be kept at the pitch of excitement on any subject to which ours had attained on this. At the same time, you need not despond or think the cause abandoned or retrograding because of the difficulty of getting up a meeting for Lucian to address."

That summer Mrs. Blackford heeded her husband's request and spent some weeks at Old Point. William, convinced that emotional calm was no less essential to her recovery than a salubrious environment, counseled her:

"Your excitability on some two or three subjects — and indeed your general excessive sensibility — whether cause or effect of your physical sufferings — must greatly counteract the effect of any remedies. Thus the excitement into which you were thrown by the silly and false idea advanced by Lt. Davis [37] I dare say induced great lassitude next morning and undid the tonic effect of a week's bathing. What a pity there was not some way of giving a shower bath or steel pills to your feelings!

"Depend upon it, you will never be well until you cure yourself of this morbid excitability. Conversation on indifferent subjects even is too exciting and in all probability your being so little benefited by sea bathing was owing to the interest you naturally took in conversation with intelligent & well bred people. It is this first conviction that makes me deprecate so fervently your ever touching upon the subject of slavery. You know from sad experience the pernicious effect it has upon your health. You will hold up your hands in astonishment at the man who persists in draining the bottle, though he knows the destruction of his health and impairment of his faculties are necessary consequences. Now are you not nearly as infatuated when you persist in brooding over the wrongs, fancied & imaginary, of the blacks when experience has taught you that it does no good to them and is vitally injurious to your health?

"I am well persuaded that, could your mind be restored to something like equanimity it would do more for you than Dr. Meigs can. I conjure you by your love for me & your children to take this into serious consideration & strive to moderate the impetuosity of your feelings. This temperament may give interest to your discourse, make you eloquent (as I have often heard you) and excite admiration for your conversational talents —

> " 'But little they think who delight in her strains
> How the heart of the minstrel is breaking.'

"It has often been a matter of wonder to me," he assured her, assuming a more conciliatory vein, "that you could not or would not 'build to lofty rhyme.' In all seriousness, I assert that you have every element of poetry in the character of your mind and heart. There are many who have achieved a reputation for poetry who possess not a tithe of your imaginative sensibility, romance of feeling and exquisite enjoyment of the beauties of nature. You only lack the quickness of association and the affluence of poetic language, which go to make up the comparatively inferior and in great degree mechanical capacity for versification. Though guiltless of a couplet, you are rich in unwritten poetry." [38]

Before closing he came back again to her dominant interest: "Have you read an article in the June *Southern Literary Messenger* on the condition of the negro race in the free states as deducted from data furnished by the statistics of the last census? It is a most startling paper. I have seen nothing so strong against emancipation unconnected with colonization. I know that you are not apt to read with any patience what does not coincide with your views and on matters connected with *blackmanity* your opinions are excited into conviction of conscience. Still you must read this remarkable paper — though I can not say on the whole that the author advances any thing much at variance with your notions. He laments the existence of slavery and is a friend of colonization."

A letter Mrs. Blackford wrote Willy just before Christmas that year betrays that she did not heed her husband's injunction against emotional strain. She wrote:

"Lewis went down to the Depot on some business for Mother and he told her when he returned he saw a poor negro woman sitting by the road crying and wringing her hands, 'Oh my children, my Lucy, my babies, my heart's blood! Oh Lord hear me!'

"It was Rachel weeping for her children and would not be comforted because they were not. They were just going in the cars, they had been sold. As well as I could find out this was the Grandmother and there was a man who I suppose was the husband of the woman. Her Master (a man by the name of Toles) is a drinker and has to sell his property to support his dissipation. These are some of the dreadul effects of slavery.

"A white woman crying thus for her children torn forcibly from her arms for purposes of trade would enlist the sympathies of *all*, 'a thousand swords would have leaped from their scabbards to redress her wrongs' (as Burke said of the French as regards Marie Antoinette), nay the whole nation would have gone to war for a less cause. Do you remember how near England and America were to being involved in war about Macleod? And yet this woman was scarcely noticed because no one is countenanced in appearing to interfere between Master and Slave. The idea of *property* in our fellow creatures hardens and pollutes the heart otherwise open to every generous emotion. But no one as he values his good name must pry into or endeavour to redress the wrongs of a slave!" [39]

Strong meat that for a mother to offer her twelve-year-old son so many miles from home at Christmas!

The next summer however, she was able to write more in the spirit of the season: "How I wish my dearest Willy could have spent his 4th of July with his Mother at home. The boys had their favorite Willy Morris here and the little Cannon was in requisition, and was fired twenty-two times, besides a number of fire crackers. Your Uncle John had given each of the little boys a four pence to which Willy added his, and thus procured the crackers and powder."

7

The one letter that Mrs. Blackford wrote her husband in Bogotá that survives was dated May 23, 1844. In it she explained almost pathetically why she had not been a better correspondent and she assured him of her love. It read:

"Dearest husband:

"If you knew how often I am sick & stupid you would make great allowance for me when for days and weeks my memory and understanding seem impaired by this slow and stupefying pain, though, thank God, it is never violent. Then I can not arrange or remember what I have to say, even when I am deeply interested in remembering. Such a time I have had lately, & I could not write and indeed I had not pens to write with.

"When I forget something, do not blame me but my disease. To write you is 'my time's employment and my leisure's charm,' but all must give way to this 'thorn in the flesh.'"[40]

Though William admonished his wife freely, sometimes to the point of scolding, he had great respect for her opinions. This is nowhere better illustrated than in an entry in his diary on August 30, 1844 (winter at 8,500 feet above sea level!). "I began this morning to spunge my body in cold water all over," he wrote. "I hope I may have resolution to keep it up. I do it in hope of strengthening my constitution and to lessen my susceptibility of taking colds. Mrs. B. has been very earnest in her exhortations that I should follow this practice. It will give her pleasure to hear that I have followed her advice & example. I hope I may have courage to persevere."[41]

The one extant letter that he wrote Mary from Bogotá in 1844 is without interest. However, that fall he tried to teach one of the little boys a lesson of great importance while discussing the rival fire companies in Fredericksburg. "So you are a Union man," he said. "I do not know which is the more dependable company or which has the better engines and apparatus, but I like the name of your party, and hope that when you grow up to be a man you will be at all times for the Union of the States if then, as they are now doing, wicked men should aim to destroy it. There is no Hope without Union." [42]

That summer, with Abram on his way to Liberia, Mary Blackford had — for the time at least — surcease from her mania on the subject of economy. She and her mother saw Natural Bridge and again visited the Virginia springs. Mary was attended by Peggy. Mrs. Minor was still waited on by Maria West whom she had liberated seventeen years previously.

Mary Blackford, it may be emphasized, was not provincial in her outlook. She had traveled some in the north, and she was well informed as to what was going on there. Her first cousin, Lucian Minor [43] of Minor's Folly, had taken an extensive walking trip through New England a few years earlier and had published a long, thoughtful account of it in successive issues of the *Southern Literary Messenger*. [44] And in 1843 she had seen this letter from her brother James:

"Having been for some months in Yankee land I have had an opportunity of observing some of their thrifty habits, & have come to the conclusion that the great secret of their success is a most persevering industry and an economy which takes cognizance of the smallest things: there is indeed nothing which they throw away, not even the most insignificant. . . This spirit in the majority of them produces meanness, & I do not believe the two qualities of economy and generosity to be at all incompatible." [45] That last sentence echoed his mother's teachings and his sister's beliefs.

Mr. Blackford's last letter from New Granada, dated shortly before the election of 1844, was to Lucian Minor:

"I observe with great pain and indignation the symptoms of another agitation in South Carolina on the Tariff question," he lamented. "I believe that there exists in that state a small clique who are bent upon the destruction of the Union. I believe that they will receive less sympathy than they experienced in 1832 and have no fear of their attaining their end. But it excites my indignation to see them making a movement in that direction. South Carolina is declining, not because of the Tariff, but because her people are not industrious, her lands are wearing out, and her population and capital are finding their way to other states and, not least, because the incomes of a large portion of the wealthy are spent abroad."[46] He was sure Henry Clay would be elected.

Mrs. Blackford was unwilling to move with the children to Bogotá. It would have been a huge undertaking for a robust woman. Probably too she felt it would be an extravagance. The chargé could not stand the separation any longer so he secured a leave of absence in December 1844. He expected then to continue in the diplomatic service in Bogotá or perhaps in some European capital, provided he could take his family with him. But he was a poor prophet: when he arrived in Brooklyn on February 12, 1845, he found that the Whigs had been turned out. He hurried on to Washington, stopping in Philadelphia to call on his wife's doctor. On the 15th he presented his treaty to the Secretary of State and was told that he had been "the most efficient and successful diplomatic agent abroad."[47]

CHAPTER IV

Mary's Training
of Her Children

The news of Polk's election in 1844 came by boat to Aquia Creek and thence by train to Fredericksburg. As the train crossed the bridge leading into town a prearranged signal on the locomotive announced the news to the assembled crowd, which included four little Blackfords. Sixty years later one of them said, "Though but seven years of age I recall the enthusiasm Clay excited, and hearing it said on that memorable day that many an ardent Whig in Fredericksburg shed tears at his defeat. It amuses me now to remember the profound conviction I entertained at that tender age of the utter insignificance of Mr. Polk and of his conspicuous unfitness to be President." [1]

He remembered too the day of his father's return, February 16, 1845, — "how as he entered the wide passage in our dear old house in Fredericksburg . . . a great Newfoundland dog we had sprang to greet him with a paw on each shoulder, thus actually toppling him over." [2] After "the happiness of embracing [his] wife" [3] that Sunday morning, he hurried off to St. George's Church to offer thanksgiving for his safe return home.

Soon after the inauguration of the Democratic president, Mr. Blackford returned to Washington, hoping to find that, although a Whig, the success of his recent diplomatic mission might serve to keep him on the Government payroll. He "called on Gen. Scott, — found him as vain & egotistical as usual, — fully persuaded had he been the Whig candidate for the Presidency the result would have been different, & equally persuaded that he will be the Whig Candidate in 1848. With all his foibles, I like Scott & a worse candidate might be selected."[4]

William had many friends who tried to help him, but sometimes their enthusiasm embarrassed him. "I regret one thing," he noted in his diary on April 3. "I learn in letters to the President allusion was made to the largeness of my family. I can not see how the fecundity of one's wife qualifies him for office." But even such appeals were unavailing and by June he was again in the ranks of the unemployed. Mr. Blackford remained without a job until March 1846 when, after an unsuccessful attempt to buy a share in the *Richmond Whig,* he was engaged to edit the *Lynchburg Virginian* at "$750 per annum."[5] Lynchburg was already the home of his father and older brother, Dr. Thomas Thornburg Blackford.

It was hard for Mary Blackford to leave a community where her roots went so deep. It was hard for her at forty-three to cut the silver cord and leave her mother's roof, but it was more than she could stand to part with Peggy. She "is so necessary to Mrs. B.," William noted in his diary, "to whom she is devotedly attached, that I could not think of letting her be sold to any one else."[6] Accordingly he bought her for $318.25.[7] "The poor creature was overjoyed when told that I had purchased her."[8] Mr. Blackford then carried out his threat to deal severely with misbehaving Jane: he sold her!

It did not seem expedient to move all the children to Lynchburg immediately, but this plan had its disadvantages. The father was alarmed that summer to receive "a letter from Mrs. Atkinson informing me of Eugene's indisposition and that she had given him 60 gr. of calomel in 24 hours. This is horrible and ought to be prosecuted as an attempt to poison."[9]

In July, Mrs. Blackford, Willy, Eugene, Mabelle, and Peggy arrived in Lynchburg, "also Rover." Lucy Landon told her father in September that she was going to marry Dr. John Staige Davis, "an uncommonly intelligent and interesting"[10] young man of twenty-two. Dr. Davis was their house guest a few weeks later but he could not screw up his courage to ask her father at that time; he finally did so by letter. They were not married until the following summer. By that time the rest of the family had been assembled under one roof.

In 1847 the boys all had a wonderful Christmas. Their stockings were full of nuts, apples, and homemade candy. Lanty described the day to his grandmother: "We shot our little cannon several times until the Police Master, Mr. Brown, came after us about it and was going to make us pay a fine, but let us off: the fine is $2.00 a shoot. I think we ought to have been excused anyhow as it was Christmas and every body else was doing it."[11]

Perhaps they shot off their little cannon too often, perhaps their mother felt too sick to celebrate the holiday, or she may have felt that the day should be celebrated only in a religious way. Whatever the reason, after 1847, Christmas Day at Mary's home was drear. Mr. Blackford, it is true, sometimes would have one or two lonesome young bachelors, an engineer or an army officer perhaps, come in to a simple family dinner. As children and later as college students, however, the sons often spent Christmas away from home without regret.

The education of his five sons impelled Mr. Blackford to start a little school. To help meet the expenses, he invited several other gentlemen with adolescent sons to join him. Among these was Lucius Minor, Mary's brother, who sent Charly and Berkeley over from Hanover to board with his sister. Though he frequently and sometimes violently disagreed with her, Lucius always greatly loved and admired her; he particularly wanted his sons to have the benefit of Mary's training. The fifteen to twenty boys of Mr. Blackford's school were "taught by a young man carefully selected as to his attainments and character, whose influence and good work"[12] could be relied on. The chief drawback to this plan was that such an erudite and exemplary young man could not long be retained in so small a school. Naturally in that day emphasis was placed on the classics, and the amount of ground the boys covered in their ten-month school year was all but incredible. Before he was seventeen, Lanty had read Caesar (several times), the Aeneid, the Bucolics, Cicero, Livy, Tacitus, Demosthenes on the Crown, Herodotus, and even some of Euripides!

In addition to Latin and Greek, the young Blackfords were well instructed in the history of their country; not all they learned of this history was taught them in school. They were brought up on stories of the Revolution that their mother had from her father and mother. The boys heard more stories direct from a veteran of that war, their father's father, who came to live with them in 1848. Old Benjamin Blackford loved especially to talk about General Washington. His grandchildren remembered always his account of a review held by Washington just at the close of the Revolution. Ben, only fourteen, but well grown, standing close to the General, was lost in admiration of his splendid appearance, "elegantly mounted and dressed, and surrounded by a brilliant staff." Though he "always worshipped Washington and his memory," he told, with pride apparently, that as each stand of regimental colors would pass and salute, the General's horse would whirl and rear, causing him "below his breath to use strong language beginning with a big D, just like ordinary mortals."[13]

At home the boys certainly had instilled into them devotion to the Union, and its possible disruption even that early provided them with themes for public speaking at school. At eleven, Lanty memorized Henry Clay's "Influence of National Glory." Sometimes the orations were original. On February 18, 1849, "brother Charly spoke on the importance of preserving the Union," and later Lanty made a similar speech.[14]

Debating was also encouraged and on May 26, 1849 the topic was "Is slavery the cause of the Superiority of the North over the South?" In reporting this debate, Lanty wrote: "Each side had two things to contend, first that the North is Superior to the South, and that slavery has been the cause of it, or the opposite. I was very much interested in the debate and the fact that most of the members were Southerners, of course that (wrong) side carried the popular vote. . . I cast my vote among 3 or 4 for the North, or as Gray Latham said in his speech (although I did not like it), 'the land of wooden nutmegs and yankee notions.'"

Lanty also told of arguing other weighty questions:

"Ought women to be allowed to vote? I defended the affirmative.

"Is foreign immigration injurious to our country?" Lanty was on the negative.

"Do the signs of the times indicate the downfall of the Republic? Although our side, the negative, was well defended, we lost it."

Mary Blackford's views often determined the subjects discussed. Her influence also determined the side her sons chose in each debate. She would attend the exercises Friday afternoon and, if things went to suit her, invite all the boys to her home for light refreshments.

On February 23, 1848, the day he became eleven, Lanty began to keep a diary.[15] This interesting document affords many glimpses of life in the Blackford household during the next several years. The first entry quite naturally had to do with the Mexican War, then just concluded:

"Yesterday, the 22nd, was such a bad day that the soldiers could not turn out and except for the firing of the cannon at daybreak, I believe it passed like any other day. We heard last night that peace was declared, but on what terms and whether true I am not able to ascertain. I hope it is as that will stop the flow of so much blood."

Five days later the young diarist recorded that Captain Smith Bankhead had come to the Blackfords' for tea. "I found him very agreeable," he wrote. "He told me a very curious fact that the wolves will not devour the bodies of the Mexicans that fell in battle, but will scratch up the Americans and devour them; the cause of it is attributed to the use of garlic by the Mexicans. He said . . . that they can not bury their dead unless they pile great piles of stones over the graves or the wolves will scratch them up."

On March 11 the war was still the dominant interest: "Capt. Selden and Lieut. Johnstone who have been in all the battles nearly of the Mexican War had tea with us last night. . . Capt. Selden has a very bad wound about his eye which is put out. They were both very interesting although I did not hear much of the former's conversation as so much talking was going on in the room and I was not by him, but Mr. Johnstone was speaking of the arrangement of the men in battle by which I was much interested. It seems to me that if ever any one had little idea of battle I have, I therefore like to get as much information concerning them as I can. The company staid till half past ten."

Some days later, Lanty wrote of another officer's visit: "Major Gwinne spent the evening here tonight. . . I was particularly amused with one of the things he said, 'boys were the most uncouth vulgar animals alive.' I who was present comforted myself with the assurance that he had been a boy himself." [16]

On September 14, 1849, when Mary's brother John was staying with them, Lanty escorted him out to see the railroad cut. "One tent is occupied by the negroes," he recorded, "and as they had nothing to do at this time they were as merry and as happy as you please; they were dancing and singing to the music of the banjo, jawbone and bones, and in all seemed as happy as larks."

And on April 1, 1850 he noted: "The streets were crowded with negroes from the country as this is a holiday, being Easter Monday. On market street the town people were selling to the country old second hand clothes. It was quite funny to see the display of broadcloths, silks and satins half soiled which were bought up with great eagerness."

In view of Mary's ardent opposition to even the minor vices — her program called for prohibition of tobacco as well as strong drink — it is surprising to find among his 1848 entries:

"May 11: I made some ginger beer this evening the hops and ginger are boiled and the yeast and molasses added afterwards, it stands for a night in the jar and in the morning it is bottled and kept for 3 days before it is fit for use. . .

"May 12: I bottled it and a little while ago it was first rate. I tried it. It is very active and seemed to be very popular. . .

"May 15: I made 3 gallons more of the ginger beer this evening. It cost me only fourpence a gallon, very cheap I think. The last I made is nearly exhausted now and it seems to be popular and is beneficial to mama — it revives her these hot days."

2

The typical Virginia boy before the War, according to writers of fiction, lived in a handsome Georgian mansion with big white pillars; except when hunting or fishing, he spent most of his daylight hours on his favorite horse, and he was constantly attended by at least one adoring little slave. Mrs. Blackford, even if she could have afforded it, would not have been willing to bring up her children in any such fashion. They were born, it is true, in the comfortable Fredericksburg home of their grandmother, but after moving to Lynchburg the family lived in a succession of unpretentious little houses. The contrast at first was all too evident to the children "as the whole of this lot could get into one of the grass plats at home." [17]

The Blackfords owned no horse. They did have a cow ("This morning until nine we all worked, brother Lewis and Eugene in the garden and I in one of the Herculean labors, viz., cleaning out the cow house." [18]) The boys worked: they tended the vegetable garden and raised chickens, they split wood and salted pork, they made household appliances, they even cobbled their own shoes. With Lucy Landon off married and Mary Isabella so young, Lanty had to help with the housekeeping. Many a time he mentioned "my monotonous walk to the market place to get something for dinner."

But, as in Fredericksburg, Mary allowed her boys to have fun too. They loved to meet the packet coming up the canal from Richmond, and they often rode in on it from the locks. Every Fourth of July a Sunday School picnic was arranged with transportation by canal boat. They watched with interest construction of a tunnel and of a deep cut for the railroad. In May 1852, engines having been brought up by packet boat, they were thrilled to get in the cars and ride out to Liberty. [19] On May 31, "Peggy wished to take an excursion to Liberty this evening (50 cents for servants round trip). There was a very long train of 2d rate cars filled with negroes hundreds; they presented a very curious appearance." [20] In 1853 Lanty was even predicting, "in two or three years we will be connected with Charlottesville and Richmond by railroad." [21]

In the summer they visited their kin at the University where there was so much of interest to adolescents. Sometimes they would go by canal boat to Scottsville and thence by stage to Charlottesville (twenty-four hours), or direct by stage to Charlottesville in eighteen hours. Every summer they went to Hanover County, going by packet to Richmond, completing the trip by stage. The traveling expenses were for the most part met with money they had earned. By the time the younger sons were at the University, they could travel by rail, but the canal survived the War.

At Edgewood they often found their grandmother. Mrs. Minor's sight was gone; she required the children to read the Bible to her (and Maria West) a great deal, but the old lady did not need her eyes to hear their catechism. Edgewood, Mt. Airy, the Nelsons' Mont Air, the Berkeleys' Airwell, the Cookes' Dewberry, and the Pages' Oakland (scene of the *Two Little Confederates*) were for their sturdy legs all within walking distance of each other. Each home was full of young people and at each Virginia hospitality was true to tradition. On these farms the boys pitched in cheerfully with the chores. Other relatives were farming near Lynchburg, and with them they often spent a few days too.

When a circus came to town they admired the parade, especially the white horses, sometimes ten to a wagon. Often they managed to get in to see the one ring and the menagerie, "the Zebra, Kangaroo, Burmise cow, hyena, Lions, tigers, cougars, etc." They also took in various entertainments, such as "General Tom Thumb" (they were disappointed he was not the famous original), mesmerists and hypnotists, magicians and jugglers, and they saw the big paintings and panoramas exhibited in Lynchburg. They loved every bit of it.

Their mother believed that strong bodies were necessary for sound minds. Regardless of her motives in allowing this freedom, the boys enjoyed snowballing, Anthony over, "Hickeme dickeme," blindman's buff, prisoner's base, pull over the bat, kite flying, chinquapin hunting, quoits, archery, gymnastics, bull in the pen, wrestling, "washing" in the James in summer and skating on it in winter, stilt walking, cutting jackets, knock and catch out. So soon after the Mexican War, naturally the boys played soldier, but hunting and even fishing were considered by Mrs. Blackford cruel and were therefore forbidden. Chess was the favorite indoor game, but with their heavy academic schedules they did not have much time to play in the house.

That the children's education might be broad, in the evening Mrs. Blackford usually read aloud to them while they were at drawing class; Willy and Lewis developed considerable proficiency in this line. In addition to religious works, Mary read good literature to them. Our diarist mentioned Marmion, The Lay of the Last Minstrel, Hamlet, King Lear, Merchant of Venice,[22] King John, Midsummer Night's Dream, and Much Ado about Nothing. Her readings were delightful and they left indelible impressions on her hearers.

The training of her children she considered the main purpose of her life, and in her opinion it was never completed. One of her methods was to have them copy verses from the Bible. For this they were paid by their grandmother about two and one half cents a page, or five to seven cents an hour: it was their principal source of spending money, for performing the chores was only their duty. This exercise served to familiarize them with the Bible and it also served another purpose: "If you will take pains to copy Bible verses and spell out each word as you see it there, you will soon spell beautifully and write beautifully too." [23]

The family were regular attendants at St. Paul's Epsicopal Church. Mr. Blackford was long on its vestry and he was a great friend of the rector, the Reverend William H. Kinckle. When for any reason there was no service in their own church on Sunday, the Blackfords went to some other Protestant church. Of course, family prayers were conducted every day. Sometimes in their home a neighborhood prayer meeting was held, which might assemble more than sixty persons.

Mrs. Blackford did not allow the children to neglect the practical aspects of Christianity. In December 1848, Lanty noted, "I went out on the hill this evening to carry some things to a very poor but apparently worthy couple whom Mama knows. The old woman is very low and will probably not outlive the present year." [24]

Unlike the fashion of today, Mary taught her children to face the fact of death and had them attend funerals. Lanty, who duly recorded them all, wrote of one on November 19, 1848: "Mr. Kinkle preached the funeral sermon of that young Mr. McKinney that was killed Thursday night. It was very good but, as funeral sermons admit of very little variation from the old tune, it was not much different from most others. Still, it was very interesting."

On August 31, 1849, tragedy was again his topic: "As I was going down the street, I met Charley Leftwich going down after his father and mine. He said that Mr. Clayton had just died and he had witnessed the death-bed scene. He requested me to go down with him after papa. I consented immediately but had not gone twenty steps before I met him and turned back. On my return I found mama was not here, but had gone over to Mrs. Clayton's. She came home in the course of an hour and gave us a long description (as she had heard it) of the death-bed scene. One piece of *good* news was that mama had heard from his mother's lips that he died happily, ay very happily, and, she had every reason to believe, easily."

3

Home routine was pleasantly interspersed from time to time by letters from Africa. Mail service was unreliable and expensive so communications were sent when possible by persons traveling between Liberia and Virginia. In 1846 Mrs. Blackford received a letter from her first African correspondent:

"Much Esteemed Marm:

"By the reception of these few lines you will know that I am still surviving the wreck of time. There arrived here on the 8th of December last, the ship *Roanoke* with emigrants from Norfolk, 96 in number, among whom was George and James Marshall, two young men from Fredericksburg, whom I was glad to see; they, myself and Abram gets together and sits down and cherishes the recollection of home and remembrance of old acquaintances. . .

"You have doubtless heard of the arrival of the *Pons* of Philadelphia in our harbor with 756 slaves on board, captured by the *Yorktown*, Capt. C. H. Bell, to the leeward of us.

"Yours with abundance of respect,

"*James C. Minor.*" [25]

But she enjoyed even more an enthusiastic one that came by the same ship from Abram, who in two years had made great strides in his education and who had changed his name to Abraham:

"As an opportunity offers, I now embrace it and drop you a few lines by way of remembrance, hoping that they may find you enjoying good health, as they leave me and my family at present. I am doing tolerable well at present, and I like the place very well, in so much that I have married, trusting that I may do as well as those who has come to this country years before me and are doing as well as it can be expected.

"As regards sickness, or this being a sickly climate, it is not, so far I never has enjoyed better health in my life than I has since I have lived here. It is very true, most all of the people who immigrate from America have had to undergo a acclimating process. I mean by that, that they have got to get the fever, and in many instances it is very slight, only lasting not more than two or three days. And if I were to go entirely by my own feelings, I can assure you that I have not lost three days on account of sickness. Since here I have had none, properly speaking, since I had the fever.

"Tell all those who want to come, come, — a free country this is, fine malicious fruits grow here, enough to attract the noblest minds. People speaking about this country tell them to hush their mouths if they are speaking anything disrespectful of it. If any man be a lazy man, he will not prosper in any country, but if you will work, you will live like a gentleman, and Africa is the very country for the colored man. There are a great many colored persons there that have the liberty to come but will not come. It is to those to whom I speak.

"Mr. James and George Marshall arrived here in December last in the ship *Roanoke* from Fredericksburg, Virginia. And the immigrants that came out at that time has already planted their produce and eating of the same. And out of two hundred and more immigrants, there has been not more than three or four of them died, and they was old persons. I would write you more about fine Africa, but I have a gob of work on hand, and the person it belong to are in a hurry for it, and the vessel by which this letter is to go is expected to sail in a few hours.

"Please to give my best regards to Mr. Blackford, and tell him that I would have wrote to him, but not knowing where he is. You will please inform me in your next. You will give my respects to all the family and also Mr. Lucious Minor. Also give my regards to all my friends and acquaintances, and tell them I would have wrote to them but I do not know where they live. They must write to me so that I may know where they are, and I will certainly answer their letters. Will you please be so kind as to write my Mother and tell her that I am well. I would write to her, but I do not know where she lives. She must write to me so that I may know where to direct my letters to her.

"I very often see Dr. Pattin and Capt. Cunigun, they talk with me much about old home. I will be very glad for you to send me some cloth and tobacco, which articles demands at times a pretty good price, also flour and pork, such articles demands a pretty good price. As I am keeping a little shop and such things I want very much. The freight shall not cost you anything. If Mr. James Marshall returns on a visit, as he expects to do, I shall send the money." 26

On March 6, 1848, Lanty recorded the arrival of letters "from Cephas and Abram and Uncle Lewis." The charming ones that Lewis wrote from distant ports, full of color and adventure, did not interest Mary Blackford nearly so much as those from the former slaves in Africa: she was directly responsible for Abram's being there and she felt entitled to a share of the credit for James Cephas. The latter had left Virginia before any of the little boys were born, but they had heard a great deal about him. Of course they remembered Abram if only because they had supped so often on dry bread to speed him to the Colony; then too he had not been gone four years. By the time the next packet was ready to sail for Liberia the family had a number of letters, papers, and packages to despatch to their old friends.

Mary Blackford would not let her children forget the continuing importance of sending "free persons of color" to Africa, even if her and their contributions to the good cause were of necessity small. Her emphasis on the Liberian venture is reflected in the following entries in Lanty's diary:

February 3, 1849. "Axman came here yesterday evening who is going to Liberia and the funds of the Colonization Society being at this time too low to send him, his wife and children, he is trying to collect some money to help him along, $120 being the required sum to be raised in 30 days in which time the next Liberia packet will sail. He offers to take papers and letters to James and Abram. . . We could muster then only 75 cents, but I believe Mama gave him 50 cents more this morning when he came for the letters and bundles. I wrote a long letter to Abram."

January 20, 1850: "I spent the evening principally in reading aloud to mama in the *Liberian Herald*, a paper published in that infant republic in which she (as well as myself) is so much interested."

March 24: "This evening mama borrowed a book from a lady near here, *History of the African Missions*,[27] in which much was said of Uncle Lancelot Minor, and a very interesting sketch of his life given. Papa read aloud this evening in it, and we listened with much interest for several hours."

June 16: "This evening I read a great deal in the *African Repository and Colonial Journal* . . . It is exclusively devoted to the interests of the republic of Liberia and is published by the Colonization Society."

April 29, 1851: "Mama opened the charity box which she keeps on hand during the year, and solicited our aid in making the sum up to $9, as she expects to send Frederick to the Colonization Society soon, to which we all contributed 'according to our ability.' "

February 27, 1852: "Bishop Payne came over last summer from Africa and has been taking a tour of the Union. Papa . . . invited him to come and stay at our house. This he accordingly complied with. The Bishop is a middle aged gentleman with the most refined manners and deportment, the more remarkable for his having lived the last successive thirteen years among savages. He is, papa says, very little changed since he last saw him. Conversation about Africa was very entertaining."

February 29: "Bishop Payne preached to day to a large congregation, white and black, and took up collection, at Mr. Kinckle's suggestion, night and morning both. They took up between $120 and $130."

The bishop to whom Lanty referred was the same Reverend John Payne who had gone to Africa in 1837 with Mary's brother.

Shortly Mrs. Blackford heard from James Cephas again:

"I was glad to hear that health prevailed among the family, — but was very sorry to hear of the poor health of your dear mother — we hope that she is much better by now. It would have afforded me much pleasure to have been present at the assembling of your brothers, and sons and daughters, and grandchildren.

"Bishop Payne was at my office and gave me much interesting intelligence of the whole family. He spoke of the personal interview he had with you and some of your brothers. He spoke of the healthy appearance of your brother John now that he had lived to be a man of advanced age;" (he was 56) "his head was white and withal he had not married. He spoke of the improvement that was going on in Lynchburg and Fredericksburg. He called the names of many of the residents of Fredericksburg (the scene of my youthhood); many of them I recognized as old acquaintances, others I had no recollection of. Very often, by reflection, I can take a view of Fredericksburg, Toppen Castle, Edgewood and many other places over which I have walked in your beloved country in the days of my early Youthhood. . .

"From the time that our Independence [1847] was declared to the present moment we have moved on smoothly with as even a tenor of our course as could be expected from the encounters that our Government have had to contend with during the five years of our national career. . .

"We have now a Brazilian Charge de Affairs living among us at present; but really, madam, I am not able to tell you what is his business here farther than by report, and that is that he wishes to negotiate with our Government for a tract of land to colonize the worn out or unruly Brazilian slaves, — a people that we do not want among us at all. . .

"The religion, habits, manners, customs and dress of the un-attended to portions of the aborigines among us are so vague and insignificant that the children are imbibing some of the lowest principles." [28]

In 1853, James Cephas thanked Mary's brother John for two volumes of Blackstone which had been delivered to him by a missionary. "It shall be my earnest endeavor," he wrote, "to make the best proficiency in the act of the study of the law that I can. As our community is on the increase and there may arise cases for adjudication which comes within the [province] of some of us who tries to do just between man and man." [29]

Getting out the *Liberia Herald* had not proved to be a money-making proposition. In seeking means to increase his income James Cephas' thoughts turned to the mercantile business. On July 6, 1853, he wrote to a free person of color in Fredericksburg:

"By reception of this letter you may know that I am living, thank God, and hope that you are well. Should you ever take a notion to come to this Republic, I would advise you to bring with you the following articles in as large a quantity as you can conveniently do: pork, beef, flour, fish, assorted mackerel, herrings, smoked and pickled codfish, soap, tea, coffee, butter, lard, dry goods, assorted, bleached and unbleached cottons, shirting cotton, domestic plaids, shoes, stockings, table knives and forks, bonnet ribbons, muslins of various patterns for ladies wear, white muslins, spools of cotton, skins do., pins, needles, tooth brushes, and in fine any and everything that you can. And if you have not the means to purchase these articles, you can get some friend to give you credit for some four or five hundred dollars for a few months, and you can soon sell enough of them to pay for them. In your selection of ladies wear, do get some lady to assist you to make choices for the ladies here are very flashy and wear no mean dresses." [30]

On October 1 he wrote his former master: "I would propose to you propriety of entering into a sort of commercial business by way of shipping a small lot of assorted domestic goods, fancy, of various patterns and kinds, and of provisions for sale and returns, provided that such proposition is not contrary to the cause of your business as the amount of two or three hundred dollars worth of saleable domestic goods and a varied assortment of fanciables of female and gentlemen's ware and wholesale provisions would find a ready market here. Should such a course sute and you make the experiment or venture, you may rely on my prompt attention in every respect.

"Abraham & his family has gone up the country," he added, "to live near Cape Mount. He was well when I heard from him last. And beged to be kindly remembered to you all." [31]

The same day he wrote his last letter to Mrs. Blackford: "There is nothing strange about which to write you. We have not had any alarming sensation of trouble nor any fear foreboardings of approaching difficulties. Affairs seem to be moving gradually along. A state of quietude and peace seems to be our chief companion now. The general interests of the country seem to engage the attention of the principle men of the Government. Our revenue is, I believe, on the increase. The imports from foreign countries amounts to several hundred thousands of dollars per annum, and the exports of the products of the country lies not far behind that amount. Our harbour has been lately visited by several U. S. Naval Cruisers, the *Constitution*, of which Mr. John Rudd is Capt. and the U. S. Ship *Marion*." [32]

4

Dr. Lewis W. Minor should have been Mary's favorite brother; he was always sympathetic in her troubles. In 1846 he wrote from the *U.S.S. Mississippi*: "The tenor of your letter gives me pain as it showed that your health was more impaired than when I saw you last. I hope that Dr. Blackford may have it in his power to give you some relief but I fear this will not be the case as you do not submit to be quiescent." [33]

The physician he referred to was Dr. Thomas T. Blackford, Mary's brother-in-law. Like her two brothers, a graduate of the University of Pennsylvania, "he was a good physician . . . well equipped in his profession and [he] kept up by constant reading with its progress." [34] Soon he had to give up her case, though he was often a guest in her home.

Mary always knew that she could turn to Lewis with whatever idea possessed her at the moment and gain a deferential hearing even though he disagreed with her views heartily. She found in him too unostentatious generosity. On leave the winter of 1849, he wrote from Edgewood:

"If you had rather keep Mary Bell with you for the present it is well, but on the contrary if the condition of your finances is at all in the way of sending her to Miss Betty's and but for such a condition you would send her, let me know and the means shall be forthcoming either now or hereafter, Deo volente. . . Charly and Lanty are staying here and are well. . . What a remarkably handsome boy Lanty is. I know not when I have seen one so much so."

Unlike Mary's other brothers, Lewis never gave advice unless asked for. "Your boys are so well trained," he continued, "that the advice you ask is scarcely needed by them. I will suggest however that the habit of speaking of Lewis' genius in conjunction with his laziness is calculated to engender a kind of pride which I have observed in other young men of quick parts, viz., a pride in showing to their fellows how little of their time they need to devote to their studies." [35]

By this time Mary's youngest brother, Dr. James Monroe Minor, had resigned from the Navy to marry Miss Ellen Pierrepont. He had settled in Brooklyn, the home of his wife, where he practiced surgery. After his marriage, he was not often in Virginia. However, he never lost an opportunity to tell anyone who would listen that he was a Virginian, that his heart would always be in Virginia, and that Virginians were always in the right. He strove to bring up his children as Virginians, and was to prove not very popular in Brooklyn during the War.

William M. Blackford, though unable to provide his sons with luxuries, was a wonderful father. He accumulated a large library of good books [36] and encouraged his children to read. He was an excellent craftsman,[37] whose masterpiece was a steam engine [38] with a walking beam and a fly wheel two feet in diameter, constructed in 1830, always cherished by him, and frequently exhibited. He was constantly doing things around the house: he built a shower bath for the boys and made book cases, cabinets, and gadgets. He liked to repair clocks and he made electrical batteries. In 1850 he constructed a telegraph instrument, two years before commercial telegraphy was introduced in Lynchburg. He maintained a chemical laboratory where he had his sons conduct experiments, and a shop where he instructed them in bullet molding, wood turning, cabinet making, and such prosaic things as the manufacture of mop and broom handles, as well as bedsteads. Sometimes the former diplomat even went "washing" in the James with his boys.

Mr. Blackford early inculcated in his sons a lively interest in politics. Pages of Lanty's diary are devoted to the election of 1848. The torchlight parades were minutely described. "They fired the cannon a hundred times this evening in commemoration" [39] of General Taylor's election. The General's death was duly recorded and the accession of Millard Fillmore. On August 14, 1850, the thirteen-year-old wrote, "Mr. Kinckle's sermon was about the death of Gen. Taylor on the text 'know ye not that a prince and a great man has fallen in Israel this day.' Without touching on his life, character or achievements, he endeavored to point out the hand of God in this dispensation and treated it in several lights, speaking of the effect it ought to have in bringing together the North and South and silencing the cry of Disunion, showing the evils of it and speaking against all who are for it."

Sometimes, however, the Blackford boys actually behaved like boys. While their mother was spending a few weeks in Fredericksburg, February 1852, her oldest son wrote her:

"I cannot let this package go without a contribution from myself. This is a cold disagreeable Sunday though I cannot say a dull one. Indeed Sundays are never dull to any one who has worked hard during the week. I have been reading all day with the exception of time I was at Church. It is now just the time at which you close your reading party and we all collect around the fire for a sociable chat until Church. I miss it very much. Papa has just left the room, your chamber, to go down to the office.

"The boys are all down in the dining room, they are behaving very well considering. There has been only one appeal to Paternal legislation this evening; that was on the part of Messrs. Eugene and Lanty who had been forcibly ejected by the rest and were prevented from returning by the door being fastened inside. The plaintiffs returned to the charge armed with a bull to which the besieged surrendered. A skirmish by way of revenge ensued, after which everything has gone on quietly. Before I finished the last sentence a distant sound like thunder came to my ears: it proceeds from the dining room. But now I hear them pursuing someone in the yard, so the carpet is in no danger. Eugene's yells indicate that he was the pursued person and that he is now expiating his crimes. This is all just letting off a little steam that has been accumulating during the day. I will march them all off to Church presently." [40]

Three months after writing this letter, Willy, a very self-assured young man just turned twenty-one, set out on an extensive tour of the North looking for a job. His first stop was in Fredericksburg, where he had to pay many calls "on Mama's account." [41] He was entertained by his mother's cousin, Lieutenant Matthew Fontaine

Maury, at the Naval Observatory and he described enthusiastically the wonders of Washington. The guest of friends in Baltimore, he inspected many factories and the port facilities. His Uncle Jim showed him the sights of New York and he enjoyed every one of them. From New York City he crossed the state to Buffalo. His long letters are still fresh, vivid, and delightful.

"Struck up an acquaintance with an Irish party of three gentlemen who are making a tour through the States," he reported from Toronto, June 16, 1852. "Find them agreeable, well informed people, especially the youngest who is about my age & has traveled in Europe. He can not understand why the Southerners will not liberate all their slaves. . . This evening we were strolling along the streets and passed some very well dressed, respectable negroes.

" 'Ah,' said he, 'There are some of your runaway countrymen.'

"We had not gone more than a few yards when we passed some miserable-looking Irish immigrants.

" 'Ah,' I said, 'There are some of your runaway countrymen.' . . .

"There are great numbers of these fugitive slaves here and hundreds are coming every year.

"Was much amused at a conversation which I overheard in the bar room this evening," he continued. "A man who had recently returned from the South was telling a great burly Englishman about the slaves there, he said they seemed to be two to one of the whites. 'Why,' exclaimed the Englishman, 'don't they play hell sometimes though? I suppose they keep a big standing army.' How wonderfully little foreigners know of our institutions."

Willy spent a few days in Boston. Again at Dr. Minor's in Brooklyn, on June 29, he wrote "about the hornet's nest of Abolitionists" he got into. "Confound them," he exclaimed, "I never heard such a hardheaded puritanical set of people talk in all my life. I am very much troubled about the Union. I did not believe there was such violent feeling existing. It is true this young man I was talking to was named Greeley, a relative of the notorious Horace, but I won't get into politics now."

The young engineer returned from his grand tour more than

ever convinced that his best prospects were to be found in Virginia:
he went to work for the Virginia-Tennessee Rail Road Company,
making his headquarters in Abingdon. That was not what his
mother had planned for Willy!

5

From his father William M. Blackford had inherited lifelong
devotion to the Whig Party. This was rewarded again in April
1850, when he was appointed postmaster at Lynchburg with a
salary of $1200. He resigned the editorial chair of the *Virginian*
at once to accept the more lucrative if less congenial job. Mary
had managed to feed her children on the smaller income: she had
learned thoroughly the lessons in economy drilled into her mother
by Mrs. Minor's parsimonious stepmother.

Henry Clay died June 29, 1852. He was a leader greatly beloved and widely mourned. His death was above all a great loss
to the Whigs. The Blackfords must have felt the loss of their
political idol deeply but they left no record of their feelings. It is
safe to assume that another Whig expressed them suitably:

"Cast into life when slavery was already widespread and deeply
seated, he did not perceive, as I think no wise man has yet per-
ceived, how it could be at once eradicated without producing a
greater evil even to the cause of human liberty itself. His feelings
and judgements therefore, ever led him to oppose both extremes
of opinion on the subject. Those who would shiver into fragments
the Union of these states, tear to tatters its now venerated Constitution, and even burn the last copy of the Bible, rather than
slavery should continue a single hour, together with their more
halting sympathizers, have received, and are receiving, their just
execration, and the name and opinion and influence of Mr. Clay
are fully and, as I trust, effectually and enduringly arrayed against
them." [42]

The name of that eulogist of Mr. Clay was Abraham Lincoln.

After the election of 1852, Lanty recorded, "By way of sorrow
for [General Winfield] Scott's defeat, Eugene as soon as the news

reached us went up and put our Scott's flag at half mast, tying something black around it and attaching a black streamer to the top." [43]

This Democratic victory [44] was a matter of grave concern to the Blackford family. On November 19, Mary wrote to her mother: "I think you and brother had better not send the boys money, it has a bad effect, particularly on Lewis, who hates all exertion. If it is given as a reward for labor of some kind or in some useful present, it would prevent this. I hope that the thought of their Father's being thrown out of employment will act as a useful stimulant; indeed I can see much good in our difficulties in this way. Eugene is quite an industrious boy, and Lanty too is so inclined. I hope Lewis and Lanty will be able to do something for themselves in about a year. I suppose there is no doubt but that Mr. B. will be turned out of his office, but we hope for good from it." [45]

One good Mrs. Blackford hoped for in her husband's being turned out of the post office was the opportunity of getting away from Lynchburg. She had not been happy in Fredericksburg because of the pain she so often experienced in seeing slaves jailed to be marched off in handcuffs, but, while she could be unhappy anywhere without the least effort, she was particularly unhappy in Lynchburg. Lynchburg at that time was really a wild frontier town. Shortly before that letter to her mother, Mr. Blackford's successor on the *Virginian* had been attacked on the street by a man who felt that his father had been insulted in the editorial column. Both men fired, mortally wounding each other. Murders with less extenuation were common, sometimes three in a week, and as a rule only whites were involved. [46]

Willy, understanding his mother's feelings, wrote her from Abingdon: "You have I think an unjust dislike for Lynchburg. . . Lynchburg is a very thriving place and where that is the state of the case education, talent and refinement will be the result; they are making great headway in Lynchburg. Your tastes were formed in a community where wealth had long been familiar with the people and where it was not so eagerly sought after. . . The worship of the golden calf, as you call it, is not a worship confined to Lynchburg. In the West it is a hundred per cent worse. There it makes not the *slightest* difference who a man is, what he is or where he comes from so he has money. You will not believe this until you go somewhere else and then it will be too late. Lynchburg will soon be in close communication with the eastern part of the state. You will then be able to visit there with comparative comfort." [47]

Charly, studying law at the University at his grandmother's expense, also felt the gravity of the situation keenly. "With all the advantages which I here derive, with the degree of energy which I know I possess (in spite of Mother's assertion to the contrary), with a tolerable facility for expressing myself, with sufficiency of brass, and above all with the many causes which incite me to exertion, I will not admit failure ever as a probability," he tried to reassure his parents. "I only wish it were a profession by which I might make money sooner, not on my account but on yours, for were William & myself both making money now, Pa need fear little the chance of being thrown out of employment. I hope as it is however, that he will commence looking out *immediately*, going on the supposition that the loss of the office is inevitable. . .

"The Whigs have been beaten most ingloriously," Charles continued. "I was not disappointed for I never expected anything else, & they deserved it for not sticking to Tilman. I can not say that I am particularly sorry except on your account, for it will bring about a change of parties which I am very anxious to see. I think from what I can observe in both, that there must be an affiliation and consequent amalgamation between the radicals of both, forming a new party under that name or some other equally odious, though equally qualified to catch the ragged muffin vote — which must consequently be opposed by a conservative party made up of conservatives of both. A party under whose banner all good lovers of their country can fight, though they will always have to struggle only as a respectable minority." [48]

And, even though Mrs. Blackford did not receive the letter till after matters had been straightened out, her devoted brother Lewis

wrote her from the *U.S.S. Levant,* anchored off Constantinople:
' "I have heard a few days since that Blackford has been removed
from his office, and it occurred to me that at such a crisis you
might be in need of pecuniary aid while waiting or preparing for
some new occupation. If such be the case, write to Lucius on the
subject who will supply you from funds of mine in his hands. I
have also desired him to purchase Peggy should she be sold. I
hope that you will remember that there is no necessity for speaking, out of the house, of pecuniary transactions between a brother
& sister.

"I am very anxious to hear what business Mr. B. expects to
enter upon, or has commenced. You have such a host of youngsters
that I fear B's loss of employment will seriously inconvenience you
all. I wish he could get some permanent business not subject to
the changes attendant upon all Government offices. The presidency of some extensive Rail Road would give him not only a
good income but full occupation with sufficient exercise. As that
office, however, is elective, he might at any time be replaced by
some one else; but with his skill in passing smoothly through the
world without jostling his neighbour, I think, if once seated in a
warm birth, he might keep it without difficulty." [49]

Mary's fears were justified: just one month after the inauguration of President Pierce, William M. Blackford was turned out
of office in favor of one whom Lanty designated as "the former
Editor of that most execrable and dirty Democratic journal in the
state, published in Lynchburg. This act of unprovoked and utterly
unjust proscription," he went on, "was, however sudden, not by
any means unlooked for. Suffice it to say that papa is without employment now and is anxiously looking for something to do. But
nous verrons." [50]

Fortunately Mr. Blackford was not long without employment.
The citizens of Lynchburg desired to establish in their city a branch
of the Exchange Bank of Norfolk and they sent him to see about
it. "The result of it all was that the Branch was granted (and papa
said mainly through his efforts), and such a President and Corps
of Directors appointed as would assure his election for the office

of Cashier, which place he was very desirous of obtaining. The election took place on the 4th of May, and the same evening we heard of it by Telegraph." [51] The new position carried with it a salary of $1500.

It is surprising that a man who had not managed his own finances very well should have been entrusted with responsibility for the money of others, but Mr. Blackford proved equal to his new duties. "His great industry and intelligence, his integrity and conscientious regard for duty, combined with his even temper, culture and charming manner, won to his bank the good will of all, and in five or six years it had outstripped all competitors and did a business more than double that of any other bank in the city, and nearly equal that of any bank in the State." [52]

CHAPTER V

Uncle Tom's Cabin

In the spring of 1852 a book appeared that was to influence the history of the United States and the opinion of the world. At first it created little stir in the South, but soon the Southerners reviled it. At least most of them did, but Mary Blackford always loved it. A contemporaneous opinion of one of her sons is found in his diary for 1853.

In early January of that year, Lanty, nearly sixteen, was at Edgewood. There he met "Miss Winner, a young lady from New Jersey, a teacher, very pretty and quite young. . . I found her very agreeable. . . I had a good deal of conversation with her on various subjects, among others *slavery*, to which we wandered from 'Uncle Tom's Cabin.' She has only been in Virginia a month and is a red hot *abolitionist*. I found her a very good arguer." [1]

On January 11 he continued: "Finding that Uncle Lucius had the book, I commenced reading that remarkable and ingeniously mendacious production of one Harriet Beecher Stowe, '*Uncle Tom's Cabin.*' I have long been anxious to read it because it has created so much disturbance in the United States. . . So far I have met with nothing to offend particularly a Southern reader. But scores of improbabilities and impossibilities in some places have come under my eye. As an example of the latter, a young female of delicate make and constitution is represented as crossing the Ohio River, where it could not be less than three quarters of a mile wide, on blocks of floating ice, by leaping from block to block in the quickest succession, and all this too after having walked some 25 or 30 miles with a child in her arms, which child she carries across the river. This is a sample of the book. This is sufficiently wild and improbable for the most highly wrought romance and yet it is represented merely as a representation of real life."

Two days later the boy added: "This evening by means of 'forced marches,' I finished 'Uncle Tom' and can now give my unbiassed opinion of it. Although it contains a great deal more truth than Southerners generally are pleased to allow, it is, to take it all together, one of the greatest collections of unvarnished and downright *lies* that I have ever met with. A total disregard of truth in many of her assertions, or rather in a majority of them, is the most remarkable feature of the work. From the time that Uncle Tom gets into St. Clare's hands the story becomes so entirely *ideal* as to excite more of disgust and ridicule than any other feeling in one's mind with regard to the authoress. But let me leave criticism of this remarkable work to better hands. Harriet! Harriet! what hast thou to answer for!! All *liars* shall have their part in the lake which burneth fire and brimstone."

While Lanty was fuming over *Uncle Tom's Cabin,* Charly at the University was in greater turmoil over a letter concerning his future that his mother had written him on January 5. Fervid excitement is apparent from the confusion in spelling and metaphors that marked his long, long letter of January 15:

"I will take up a sheet this morning in answer to that part referring to my future choice of a home. I have not yet determined on any place or even that I shall leave Virginia. But in regard to the question whether I shall remain in the South, I think I will examine it in a three-fold respect, viz.:

"1. Whether it is conscienciously my duty to remove to a free state and whether by doing so I can accomplish any good.

"2. Whether I should yield all my own convictions to my mother's wishes.

"3. Whether such a move would not be ruinous to my temporal interests.

"*First,* whether it is conscienciously my duty to remove to a free State and whether by doing so I can accomplish any good. In commencing this head let me give my present views on the question of slavery and give it as my conscience, not passion, dictates. Of course I agree with you as to its being an *evil,* but as we find it amongst us, and no means has yet been invented to eradicate it, though it must be confessed many steps yet remain to be taken to mitigate it. Any move toward the final emancipation and emigration of the Slaves or toward amelioration of their present condition can only be taken by those who own them and all interference by others only tends to perpetuate their fetters. These two facts none can deny who will examine the internal history of public sentiment in Virginia from 1833 until the present.

"Now when about to make a choice of my future field of labor I find myself by birth and education in the South where this slavery exists, — and if 'whatever is, is right,' I should presume that, at least to this extent, Providence had directed my course. All men have a mission to perform, and what that mission is they must judge from the circumstances by which they are surrounded and influences bearing on them, most certainly the duty of a person who takes the view of slavery which I do, is not to place himself by wilful removal beyond the power of affecting the slave for anything but harm, — and when I will be affiliating with a class who by their affected compassion but increase their suffering.

"*Here* I may alleviate their misery; *There I could not,* if I would. *Here,* seeing the evil before my eyes, I will ever be seeking to remedy it, and that with (at least to a moderate degree) the power of doing so. *There,* the evil being removed from my view would soon be forgotten, — and even if remembered, it would be but to mourn the loss of all power of remedy. What then would be my motive for leaving the South? Why, merely for the selfish wish to remove myself from scenes which shock my sensibility and which it is my duty to endeavour to prevent. A similar reasoning would have caused Wilberforce to fly from England instead of putting an end to the Slave trade; would have caused Howard to shun the dens of iniquity instead of alleviating the suffering he found there, — would in fact put an end to all philanthropy. The Good Samaritan stopped and healed the wounds, not passing over to the other side as did the Levite with a pitying glance. The Missionary does not leave his post because he may be disgusted with the idolatry of the heathen around him. Though I may not be either a Wilberforce or a Howard, nor yet a Missionary, I feel confident that with my education and views on the subject, I *may* do some good, — while I *know* it would be impossible for me to do ought but harm *there*.

"In view of these facts, should the dastardly fear of becoming habituated to the evils of Slavery make me throw aside the only means I have of abating them? Would such a course be philanthropic? Would it not be cowardly?

"I admit the full force of all you say of the evils of slavery: But would my going North cause these evils to recur less frequently? The same reasons which you apply to me should make *all* holding my opinions leave the South, — and suppose they did! Who would there then be to regulate public opinion? Who to prevent even more flagrant acts of injustice and cruelty? Who to lighten their yoke? You certainly would not have all to leave! When you would have *me* fly from a task which you must admit others in similar positions to perform. Thus to fly would not be to choose that path when I could 'loose the bonds of wickedness and let the oppressed go free!' *I should free* MYSELF *of the evils of slavery but not the slaves!*

"For these reasons, my dear Mother, I have conscienciously determined *not* to leave the South. Were I to do so, I firmly believe I should be recreant to my duty to my God, my country and my fellow men!

"*Second*: Whether I should yield all my own convictions to my Mother's wishes? In answer to this I can only put another: would I not, holding the views above expressed, be committing a *moral wrong* by going North? More especially when this determination was formed, not in a day or a month, but in earnest thought of years, — and I may add, not without consulting an Authority to which even my Mother's wishes must yield.

"*Third*: Whether it would not be ruinous to my temporal interests? (This of course I would not of touched had I believed the *affirmative* of the other two questions.) Undoubtedly it would. What confidence would the citizens of a Free State have in a young lawyer from the South? What amount of business would a New Hampshire lawyer get in Virginia? I *might* get along at some other business. But such a move would *certainly* involve my separating from a profession into which it is true I have not yet dived far, but to which I am closely wedded." [2]

But Mary Blackford was persistent. Five months later Charles was constrained to write her again, at even greater length. This time her son too had a great deal to say about the Harriet Beecher Stowe book:

"And first as regards 'Uncle Tom's Cabin' and my settling in the South. As to the former, I confess to its author the claim of genius, and to it the claim of more truth than most are willing to admit; in this point of view I only object to it because of its taking isolated facts and making a general impression with them.

"But it is not my intention to speak of its comparative merits or truth, I only ask what has been her object in writing it? What good has she done to the cause of *human liberty*? She has not advanced the interest of the Negro here in the South for if these things are so, we know them without having them told us.

"It is human nature to stick more closely to those faults with which we are tainted and to become obstinate in the vices of which we are too often reproved: the more this question is agitated by the North and by those who have nothing to do with it, the less it will excite interest in the mind of Southerners, the only class to whom the slave can look for aid. Already has this book elicited twenty 'Answers to Uncle Tom's Cabin,' 'Defences of Slavery,' etc., etc., and it has turned the public mind to looking rather for the contra-benefits of Slavery than to the wrongs which Mrs. Stowe points out; it causes thousands daily to join the ranks of those who hold the institution a Social and Political blessing. It is plainly obvious that here the fetters of the slave have only been riveted.

"But what has it done in the North? It has brought tears from many an eye that weeps for no suffering unless seen through the medium of fancy; it has aroused many a reposing or suppressed feeling of sectional hate or perchance it has elicited many a curse from more than one Syracuse Bloomer, but it has *not* brought a cent to the colonization Society; it has *not* relieved the miseries of a single one of the thousands of the same race who, not as slaves, compose the prostitutes and paupers of the Northern cities. It has not caused one of the States which have passed such, to repeal the law which prohibits on penalty of fine or imprisonment any colored person whether a run-a-way or not from entering its limits. It has *not* struck the yoke from a single slave!

"But worse than all this, it has greatly tended to open the widening breach between the two sections, to inflame one-half of the nation against the other, to produce *dis-union* and to stir up a civil war, a war in comparison with which all the bloody scenes of History would be but Child's play; can any *friend* of the human race, or any *friend* of the Negro desire such an issue? I pity, I despise, I hate the soul whose workings are so dark as to look forward to such scenes as an end, and when that soul pretends to beat in a woman's breast, I sicken to think that human nature can be so blood thirsty. Did Mrs. Stowe lay down any *plan* for us to follow by which the freedom of the slave might be accomplished? I should not blame her, but, knowing all the obstacles in our way and yet refusing even a suggestion, she uses all her great power to stir up the North, not the South the only source whence aid can be brought them.

"It seems to me that there are two kinds of phylanthropies, the *theoretical* and the real; the former invent great schemes for the amelioration of man which would be glorious if only *possible* but, not being so, they give up their ends because their means fail: they are as liberal with their tears over suffering humanity as they are sparce with their money. They are *idealists, sentimentalists,* they aim at perfection and because not obtained they give up all exertion in despair; they can picture woes but can not show how to relieve them, they weep and are satisfied: such are Mrs. Stowe and Horace Greely.

"The latter (the real phylanthropists) find out accurately where the evil lies and set about to correct it. If it can not be reformed all together they bring all the powers they have to bear upon it and do all *possible* good, they not only plan but they execute; they pay and they work: to this class belong such persons as Wilberforce, as Howard, and Mrs. Fry, and near at home as Cousin John [B. Minor]. Yes, though he occupies the most laborious chair in the University, every Sunday evening he is to be seen in the Church in Charlottesville, the guiding spirit in teaching some 50 or 60 of the race whom Mrs. Stowe has so *terribly* injured. Every Sunday morning in his office he reads, prays and sings with his own servants, and night and morning he summons them all to family prayers and explains such passages as they can not understand.

"Though he does this, his name is not known as that of a 'phylanthropist.' Over the civilized world he has not been presented with invitations from the Duchess of Sutherland and with £170 from the 'London Female Negroes Society,' he has not had his expenses to England paid, nor has he received from book-sellers the round sum of $70,000. (By the way, has Mrs. Stowe ever liberated any Negroes with this sum? None.) Who could not afford to be a 'phylanthropist' with such emoluments and so little expense! But though he has not been 'persecuted' with any of those things, who will not say that he does daily more for the good of the slaves than Mrs. Stowe ever has done, is doing, or will do, or ever can do?

"But, Mother, he does not think it his duty to *do so to the North*. When not serving the suffering he must soon forget it. No! he stays here where Providence placed him and attends to the temporal and spiritual wel-fare of the slaves around him, although as the Good Samaritan of old, he is not so over-come with his sympathy as to be deterred from examining the wound and doing all in his power to heal it. But no, you would have me to sympathize but to 'pass over on the other side' and then what good can be done? How can I then befriend the slave? Will that be acting the part of a friend of *Human Liberty*? No, Mother, No! Heaven placed me here in the South and this is my sphere of action." [3]

That book became a wide source of discussion on both sides of the Atlantic. William remarked: "I have been highly amused with the female international war now pending on the slavery question. I suppose the English countess thought that all she would have to do would be to descend to writing in such a common thing as the newspapers to carry conviction to the world. But what a scratching and hair-pulling there has been!" [4]

Mrs. Blackford was not easily discouraged. Charles proving recalcitrant, she tried again to get William to leave Virginia to seek his fortune in a Free State. But William loved the state of his ancestors; too, he had made a promising start in life. He answered her on May 8:

"At this time Virginia holds out inducements to an Engineer much greater than in any other state in the Union. Her engineers are rising in reputation in the West & Southwest. Her people are tired of Yankee Engineers and are now finding that they have among them those who are fully as well qualified & far more reliable. Virginia is at the dawn of a new state of existence. At the end of the next six years she will be a thoroughfare for the most fertile back country in the world. Hundreds of thousands of acres of fine land will be made accessible and the tide of emigration will set towards them. There is not a state in this Union where a brighter prospect opens than in this same old state of Virginia. The adage you quoted about Virginia's being a good place to hail from but a bad place to live originated & was true in times past."

2

While her sons were so vehemently denouncing Mrs. Stowe's account of slavery, Mary Blackford was with her own hand recording a story from real life no less in pathos than that of *Uncle Tom*. She prefaced the narrative:

"Betsy, whose simple narrative I wrote from her own words, was bought by Dr. Jno. S. Davis from a negro jail in Richmond. She bore an excellent character which induced him to purchase her. All her children had been sold away from her, the last, her youngest, a boy of five years old. Dr. D. would have liked to have gotten him to comfort his Mother, but she only knew that he had been carried away by the traders: she [knew not] where. The Dr. wanted her for a nurse to his little girl Lucy Landon. . . My little granddaughter Lucy L. became passionately attached to this woman and the attachment seemed mutual. I have seen her when any one hurt her feelings in any way, run crying to the kitchen and throw herself into Betsy's arms to sob upon her bosom. It was while my Lucy was on a visit to our home in Lynchburg . . . with this child that I took down from the words of this good simple creature the following narrative." [5]

Then followed Betsy's story:

"I lived in New Kent and belonged to Col. Christian. I was not quite grown when Mr. Burr George bought me, he lived in Richmond. He was a very rich man and owned somewhere about an hundred slaves. He had a farm in New Kent. I worked out when I lived [on his son's place]. I lived there about thirteen years and married his waggoner, Claiborne Holmer. He was a good husband to me & we have had each other ever since. We have had eight children, three died.

"My old Master died and my young Master, John George, took his share of us to Richmond and sold us all to the Traders. I was so old the Trader told me he could not sell me so well away, but to look out in Richmond for a home. Before this Martha, my oldest daughter, was sold by William George to a Trader. Then John, who owned the rest of us, had us put up. Jane and Patience & Edmund with me on a table to sell to the highest bidder. Patience was sold first, a widow lady bought her. Jane, about fifteen, was sold next. A trader bought her. She was carried to West Tennesee. She promised to write and let me know where she went, but I have never heard of her since. I can not write myself.

"A Trader bought Edmund and me, he was my youngest, only five years old. The jail I was in is divided into two parts, one is locked up closely and there is a high enclosure around the yard, but I was not in this part, but many men, women and children are there.

"Some little children stayed in the part that is not locked up and Mr. Grater (the Jailer who sells people for the Trader) lets them come to the fire and warm, — he had a tender heart for little children. They used to say to me that he said, 'They should go home and see their mammys,' but this was to please them for he was going to sell them, and did. I used to take care of them and wash them. Some of them are babies and have [no] one to nurse them, their Mothers being sold away, and others are sold to the traders very small.

"Each Trader has a jail of his own, sometimes there are two in partnership and have one between them. In the jail I was in they had a colored man who did the whipping. There are a great many jails in Richmond: There they keep a cob — a board with holes in it — to cob them. I heard the cries of a young girl not quite grown who was cobbed. She had run away from a bad Master who brought her there to be whipped. I sometimes think the world will not stand much longer, there is so much wickedness in it.

"[After a while I went] and stayed at the Trader's house with his wife. But there was a deep snow on the ground and [Edmund] was kept in the jail to keep him out of it. . . The colored people are not allowed to go to the jail to see their friends without a note from the Trader. I asked Mrs. Shaper (the Trader's wife) to give me one on Sunday to go to see Edmund. She told me to tell Mr. Grater the jailer to let me see him, and then she went away in a buggy. I suspected something was the matter, and so I went down directly with my husband.

"I saw Mr. Grater and he told us at the gate not to come any farther. My husband said, 'Law! Mr. Grater, don't you know me?' He answered, 'Who is that? Claiborne?' 'Yes Sir.' Then he said, 'Come in.' I felt doubtful whether he intended for me to come in, but he said to Claiborne, 'Tell your wife to come in.' Claiborne then said, 'Is our little son here?' He answered, 'No, your little son has been gone three or four days.'

"I cried and dropped the bundle I was bringing to him with his clothes and some cakes and apples, and turned to go back.

"Mr. Grater said, 'Claiborne, what makes you let your wife do so?' My husband answered, 'Law! Master, women you know can't bear these things like men.'

"I came out but Claiborne stayed, he told him that a good man from West Tennesee had bought Edmund. That Edmund wanted to see me before he went away and begged hard to go and get his clothes, but they would not let him. I thought if I had known when they took him away, I would have followed him unless they locked me up. For some time I could neither eat nor drink. I am always thinking of him and his young Sister who have gone where I can never hear from them.

"One of the women owned by the same man that sold me had *all* her children sold from her, four boys and two girls, some of them grown, the youngest about two or three years old. She and her husband were left together; two of the Traders wanted the one the husband the other the wife, and offered them five dollars a piece to part, but they would not agree to it. He was carried off handcuffed, as all the men were, but the women were not, but walked off to get in the cars. I have never heard from her since.

"Dr. Davis bought me and carried me to the University. He lets me sometimes go to Richmond to see my husband."

To Betsy's story Mary later appended this comment:

"Here ends her narrative, told me in a simple, unpretending manner and without bitterness; she seemed to feel none, though so heartbroken.

"Dr. Davis afterwards bought her husband, an old man, he found her so faithful a nurse to his little Lucy Landon. The child was devotedly attached to her, as I mentioned before, and seemed to come somewhat in the place of the little boy that was lost to her. A few weeks before the death of that sweet child of croup, my Lucy, the Mother overheard a conversation going on between Betsy and the nurseling whom she was washing preparatory to her going to bed. She asked her Mammy to tell her the story of her little boy being sold away. She was three years old and could not speak very plainly. Her feelings were much moved at the simple story of her Mammy's wrongs, and patting her cheek with her little hands, she said in a soothing, gentle way, 'Never mind, I'll be yo' child to you my own tef.'

"When I heard of the death of this lovely little one I hastened to the University to see and comfort my dear child. I was struck with the expression of Betsy's countenance, it was so sad & hopeless. The death of this child seemed to be the drop that made her cup of sorrow run over. I never thought she recovered from it, but gradually declined until she sunk into the grave, dying, I truly believe, of a broken heart."

3

Regardless of Mary Blackford's pronounced views on the subject, there were Southerners who honestly believed that slavery was good. One of these was her cousin, Captain V. Moreau Randolph, long the master of the schooner *Ontario* and later a planter in Greene County, Alabama. A long letter of October 2, 1858 from Captain Randolph to his brother Richard and carefully preserved by Mrs. Blackford set forth the writer's views:

"Had I read several passages in your last letter to me under the Editorial head in Garrison's *Liberator*, or Henry Ward Beecher's Religious (?) newspaper called the *Independent*, they would not have surprised me; but when I know that they were penned by one who was reared in a Southern State, and consequently who has had opportunities of knowing something of our peculiar institution and of the negro character, and to whom our Maker has given a reasonable share of understanding, I must express my astonishment.

"You modestly say that if I do not think as you with regard to the lamentable condition of the offspring of Aunt Easter and Doll, you pity and 'must also despise' my selfishness, and you also hope that it is not my purpose to hand them over to my sons to perpetuate their bondage. Your strong language and violent epithets do not anger me, we are both too old for that, but you will allow me in turn to speak plainly to you. . .

"I believe that bondage is the normal condition of the African race. I know that they (negroes) do not thrive when left to themselves, even under the most favourable circumstances. I have been much among them on the island of St. Domingo. Under French rule fifty years ago much of that beautiful island was cultivated like a garden, and the exports exceeded that of any island in the West Indies. *Now,* what is the condition of that island? The negroes on it are semi-savages. The beautiful sugar and coffee estates have *all* been abandoned, and are now of no value. The Emperor, whom I know, has absolute power, and he is a brute. His subjects would be infinitely happier even with French masters than they can ever be under the rule of Negrodom.

"I was much among the British West Indian islands for the years 1820, '21, '23 and '24, before the passage of the Emancipation act by the British Parliament. These islands were then comparatively prosperous, but I grant you would have been more prosperous but for Absenteeism. The proprietors of the large estates usually resided in the old country, leaving overseers and agents to manage them! *That* was an evil. In *that* and indeed in all respects our system in the Southern States is far better. Our negroes, in consequence of their masters, are better cared for. I have visited several British West India islands *since* the negroes were emancipated, and have found them idle, insolent, roguish, and more demoralized even than under overseers with masters far away.

"Coming nearer home, I have seen free negroes in our Northern states, and he must be wilfully blind or else a fool who will assert that they are as well off as our Alabama slaves. I remember our free negroes in Virginia and have seen others farther south; I *know* that *they* would be happier with masters. Last summer I traveled on the railroad through the country in which you and I were born. I asked in Farmville how Mr. Richard Randolph's 2 or 300 liberated negroes were doing. I was told that they were squatted on a portion of what was his big estate, called Israel Hill; that their number was reduced to about 80 miserable creatures, that they must in a generation or two become entirely extinct. I have heard that the slaves of Mr. John Randolph of Roanoke were doing very badly in their adopted state. Perhaps you may know something of their condition.

"I have been told by one who was in the confidence of our good brother Edward that shortly before he died he received a letter from one of his emancipated negroes describing the wretchedness of the survivors of all the 28 who were sent to Liberia as being very great. This letter, of course, caused our brother infinite distress, and he then told my informant that he deeply regretted having sent them to Africa. . .

"I have a friend once in the Navy who freed 30 years ago all the negroes he owned (12) and sent them to Liberia. Very lately he told me that he had done a weak thing, for that his negroes had never thriven in the colony and were now all dead! That friend believes now that the reopening of the slave trade would be of incalculable benefit to the entire world, *White and black*, the trade to be conducted under proper restrictions and humane regulations. *This too is my honest and religious opinion.*

"I have given my sons some 24 negroes and have now a dozen of my own. In the language of good old Mr. Woodville, 'if I believed that it was unjust to hold them, or that in doing so I violated God's commandment, I would immediately free them.' I once and until very recently thought that the Liberian colony might afford the philanthropists the opportunity of trying what might be done to improve the condition of the African race, but I have abandoned that scheme as one altogether impracticable. An intelligent officer of the Navy whose father is a distinguished statesman of one of the New England states has lately recorded his honest conviction that the Liberian Colony would not succeed, that the negroes never could govern themselves, and that as soon as the control of the whites was withdrawn from the Colony, the blacks would relapse into their primitive state and in time be again cannibals. This officer had spent two years on the African coast.

"I think you must remember Dr. Savage,[6] who married Miss Susan Metcalf of Fredericksburg in 1836. . . Very soon thereafter they sailed from the United States as missionaries. Dr. Savage is a Northern man, and at that time had all the strong prejudices of his countrymen against slavery, and was as enthusiastically sanguine of the success of the Liberian Colony as was our excellent kinswoman Mrs. Blackford, at whose house we often met Dr. Savage. Well, the Doctor . . . remained 11 years in Liberia, laboring very hard for the regeneration of the Negroes, but *with no good results*. In short, he came away in utter despair. The Doctor has had charge of Episcopal congregations in this state and Mississippi ever since his return from Liberia. I met with him a year ago and had a long talk with him about the Colony. He declared that it was a mortifying failure, that the Negroes were unquestionably a very inferior race of beings, and that their happiest condition was subjected to the will of the white man. . .

"Let me ask you, *What would you have me to do*? Would you have me to free my Negroes and send them to Boston, New York, Ohio or to Canada, there to starve? Or to Africa, there to fall back into the savage state, and it may be cannibalism? Or in your opinion, what had I best do with them?

"My present opinion is that I had best keep them where they are now and *as* they are now, i.e., exact from them reasonable labor, give them 3½ pounds of whale, some fat meat per week, bread without stint or limit, molasses every Sunday, milk every day, butter occasionally, the privilege of raising chickens, two dollars for every bale of cotton they can make for me, one day's holiday and a feast every year when the crop is laid by, liberty to attend meeting every Sunday, several days to themselves at Christmas, and lastly good and sufficient clothing winter and summer." [7]

CHAPTER VI

Mary's Children Growing Up

Thirty years as a valetudinarian had robbed Mary of her graceful carriage and her straight back. Her bones were heavier, but her ever active mind and her wide range of interests had kept her body slim. Fashions had changed the severe lines of the 1820's to voluminous, concealing apparel. She wore only somber colors, usually black; in summer her dress was of alpaca. Past fifty, she considered herself an old lady: she had already donned the white muslin cap of age, with streamers brought together under the chin. The red of her cheeks, it is true, had faded indoors, but her eyes had lost not a bit of their luster. She was still a strikingly handsome woman.

She was tired of spending most of her time in bed: there were so many things she wanted to do. So, in August 1853, Mrs. Blackford, undeterred by earlier failures to regain her health in Philadelphia, decided she must try again. Her husband could not afford to send her, but her oldest son, the only one self-supporting at the time, wrote her on September 4, 1853: "I want you to try the experiment *fully* for I believe you will be benefited by it. Don't leave Philadelphia until you are cured." [1]

Her mother, Lewis, and other brothers chipped in and the way seemed clear. William wrote her again three weeks later:

"You can have no scruples about leaving home now that so few of the boys are at home, especially as Cousin Betty [Hill], who you know you always considered equal to yourself in managing children, will be with them. I shall send you a check for one hundred dollars in the course of two weeks and you must let me pay for your staying as long as you wish to do so. So start at once, if you can conveniently do so, but you must make me one promise and that is that you will not stint yourself nor come away before you are cured. I will not be at all incommoded if I were to pay two hundred dollars more so you may just count on that amount. I should consider three hundred dollars better spent in restoring your health than in any way I could possibly use it. . .

"Remember that your comfort & peace of mind are requisite for recovery of health," he advised, "so don't be in a hurry to come away and, pardon me for the suggestion, don't let the abolitionists nor even the colonizationists have anything to say to you." [2]

En route north Mrs. Blackford visited her brother Lucius in Hanover and her mother in Fredericksburg. She stopped several days with her cousin, Lieutenant Matthew Fontaine Maury, at the Naval Observatory in Washington. She enjoyed these diversions. She finally arrived in Philadelphia and placed herself under the care of a Dr. Hodges. But the new scenes did not keep her from continuing to dole out advice. On October 9, William answered:

"I received your very mysterious letter about a young lady & was a good deal at a loss to know who you referred to at first and I am not sure that I know now. . . I can not imagine who has been telling you that I have been flirting with young ladies. So to make your letters have a proper effect, you will have to give your authority & also the particular case to which you allude."

Mary apparently pursued the subject of her son's affairs of the heart, for on December 4 he confided to her:

"I have read a letter you wrote me upon the subject of choosing a wife over several times, & have read it to one or two of my particular friends . . . all of whom agree that it was first rate. Miss Alice, as was her wont, started or rather carried on a flirtation with your humble servant in a way only Miss Alice could carry one on. I astonished her one evening by telling her that I had gotten a letter from you warning me & advising me about the selection of a wife & then I gave her a general outline of your letter and quoted the lines,

> " 'A violet by a mossy stone, half hidden from the eye,
> Fair as a star when only one is shining in the sky.'

"You may depend upon it," he continued, "she opened her eyes and said, 'I must confess it is opposition from an unexpected quarter!' She asked me if you were alluding to her: I told her you had mentioned no names, but it looked very much like you were. She made me half promise to show her your letter, which maybe I will if you have no objection. She declared she was going to make you love her the very next time she met you, so be on your guard."

None of the many letters Mary Blackford wrote her sons on her favorite theme to them, the important question of choosing a wife, has been preserved. One of her maxims, however, may be learned from a letter of William's after "Miss Alice" had, he thought, treated him badly: "That rule of judging by her conduct towards others & not by the conduct towards one's self is a most excellent one for I defy any one to judge dispassionately when they are one of the actors; vanity always comes in & suggests that you are an exception to the general rule." [3]

The views of Mary Blackford and Abraham Lincoln at this time offer interesting points of similarity and of contrast. She could heartily echo his words of 1837, "The institution of slavery is founded on both injustice and bad policy, but the promulgation of Abolition doctrines tends rather to increase than abate its evils." [4] While Lincoln felt that " 'new free states are places for poor people to go to and better their condition,' . . . his overmastering concern was the welfare of the free poor people of the white race." [5] Mary's heart, on the other hand, while big enough to love the poor people of the black race, beasts of the fields, and fowls of the air, was not big enough to love "the lower class of whites." For individuals of this class she could feel sorry — if they were "worthy" — but there is no indication that she ever wanted to do anything for them as a group except to deny them the privilege of buying alcohol. [6]

For all of her protestations of humility, for all of her glorying in her poverty, for all of her scorn of "attaching too much importance to externals," Mrs. Blackford considered her unquestioned social position in Virginia a thing that mattered. There can be no doubt that she expected her sons to choose wives from the same social level. This aristocratic concept is mirrored in another letter of William's, in which he observed: "I am beginning to think that you think there is no one good enough for me which, you see, is a great mistake." [7] In a letter of January 27, 1854 he expressed his concern about the girls Mary Isabella was associating with, especially his fear that it might corrupt her English. To the child herself he had written earlier:

"It is very hard to speak good grammar when others do not. A young lady who can't speak correctly presents a very bad appearance whatever her other accomplishments are. As I once heard a young lady say while she was playing the piano and looking her prettiest, 'I seed you on the street this morning, Mr. Blackford.' 'Yes ma'am,' says I while my flesh crawled and, thought I, 'where were you raised?' " [8]

Poor little Mary Isabella! She received plenty of advice from her five punctilious older brothers to the day she was married in 1865.

While Mrs. Blackford lingered in Philadelphia, her sons lived the full lives of normal, healthy boys. Her third and fourth sons, now in their middle teens, were enormously pleased by recognition of their increasing position. In May 1853, Lewis wrote his grandmother: "Lanty and I have grown so tall and Lanty's moustache is so black that the good Lynchburgers respectfully call us 'Mr. Blackford,' and ask us to their parties, and the old fogies touch their hats, and a day or two ago an ardent politician begged me earnestly for my vote. You see what important persons we have become. The Hanover folks shan't call us the *little Blackfords* this summer." Lanty added, "Your messages to Peggy are always delivered and she evinces much pleasure at being thought of." [9]

By February 1854 both boys had left home, Lewis to carry a rod for the railroad and Lanty, just before his seventeenth birthday, to teach a half dozen youngsters. A little later Lanty told his mother, "Enthousiasts may say what they please, but my two months' experience teaches me that *teaching* is right down, out and out *hard work*." [10] In April he confessed that he had shot enough birds to make a pie, — "we have been feasting on this excellent dish all spring, so my hunting is not a wanton cruelty as you generally consider gunning, I believe, but I return my enjoyment to good account." [11]

A week later he wrote: "There is a free meeting house on Mr. C.'s plantation, about a mile off, which has no regular appointment for one Sunday in each month, & on this Sunday Mr. Cunningham, Mr. Michaux, young Mr. Dabney and one or two other good people about here go there & hold a colored prayer meeting; the gentlemen reading & the negroes, always, praying. They are well attended by the negroes of adjoining plantations & no doubt are the source of much good. There are a great many negroes in this county, but from my own observation, & from what I hear, they are certainly better fed, clothed and cared for than any negroes I ever saw." [12]

That spring William delighted his mother with the announcement that he had signed up with the Sons of Temperance again, this time for five years; and he was proud of taking six of his friends into the fold with him.[13] In May he wrote her again to describe her home during the Episcopal Diocesan Convention:

"Mary has improved very much in her appearance & manners, & has become fond of reading. I think she will make a handsome woman. I expect you will scold me for giving her some jewelry. I gave her a very pretty little breast-pin and a pair of ear-rings, and bored her ears myself. Eugene is the same little 'scrub' as ever. He is very busy with his mechanical obligations. He is engaged on a boat & a baby mouse. Charly is a wit & Lanty an exquisiter." [14]

Charly exhibited his wit in this account of the Convention: "Here at our sweet University I am again after having spent a *very* pleasant week in Lynchburg, when in addition to the pleasure of the company of all the usual Home folks and all the strangers in attendance, I could occasionally get scraps of the agreeable society of Lanty and William; that is, I slept in the same room with them and saw them dress and undress, and sometimes took a meal with them, — more than that no one did, for they were both run mad about the ladies and were so much taken up with dancing attendance on various and sundry girls that I had little satisfaction in their society. . . When any one made an allusion to matrimony, however indirectly, William joined in the conversation and concluded it by saying, 'Miss Mary is a very fine girl, — a *very* fine girl,' which ejaculatory devotion I consider strong presumptive evidence of his being *non compos* on that subject.

"Lanty, with that aptitude for falling in love and accompanying fickleness which characterizes youths of that age," he added, "was trotting about after every person who wore a petticoat and who had seen more than ten and less than thirty summers — of course therefore you need feel no uneasiness as to his affections being injured. Eugene and myself were the only boys who seemed to be sane. I went to church regularly, paid one or two visits and stayed at Home the balance of the time." [15]

Lewis missed the Convention: he was one of a surveying party in eastern Tennessee, "where the Watauga River bursts its noisy and circuitous way through the great Unaka range. I believe we were the first civilized white men that ever broke the stillness of the place or disputed possession with the bears, rattlesnakes and pheasants." [16]

2

When summer came Mary Blackford, wearying of her lonesome exile, began to long for the sight of her family and for their adulation again. Willy, still her main support there, wrote: "I am truly sorry to hear that you are not much improved by your sojourn in Philadelphia. I can't help thinking the Doctor must be deceiving you about the practicability of your recovery. You ought however, by all means give the thing a fair tryal." [17] But she had had enough for the time, so, after visiting her brother in Brooklyn and other favorite kin on the way home, she arrived in Lynchburg that July. Soon afterward Lewis wrote Lanty:

"I am glad that Mother has come back home at last; she was gone a long time. Give my most affectionate love to her and thank her for her kind but melancholy and foreboding letter. I had intended to write to her now but feel too unwell. Tell her that I am conducting myself like a pattern: go to Church twice on Sunday and am looked upon with admiring eyes by the good old men and women and am *invariably* called upon to head all charitable subscriptions to the exceeding detriment of my private finances for they will take no denial." [18]

Lanty thoroughly enjoyed his respite from teaching that summer of 1854. He spent the vacation for the most part in Lynchburg. Perhaps the town had had as much social gaiety in previous years, but if so he had not been old enough to take part in everything. With a heavy heart he left home in September to return to his little school in Powhatan.

In spite of the lack of improvement in her health after so many months in Philadelphia, the following fall Mrs. Blackford wanted to go back. Willy acknowledged her request for money on October 15: "It is a source of great pleasure to me to think that I am in a situation to respond to your appeal concerning the means for your spending the winter again under Dr. Hodge. If it was the last cent I had in the world, dear Mother, you should have it for such a purpose. I should never feel content, even if you should receive no benefit, if I had not used all the means in my power to restore your health."

But all of the young man's generous contributions to his mother's quest for health did not spare him her reiterated recriminations: he was promptly called upon again to defend himself on the charge of flirting, a charge he vigorously denied. After explaining his side of the case, he continued: "Was your informant a member of the young lady's family? If so, I would caution you against saying anything about it as coming from me. If any information comes from me to one of the family, it should come direct and if they think I have gone too far I shall hold myself in readiness to give the satisfaction customary between gentlemen in such cases." [19]

In January 1855, Mary even attacked Charly, her favorite son at that period. On January 31, Charly tried to defend himself:

"I can not help feeling amused, though at the same time a little grieved to see how seriously you and Pa write to me about my innocent sins." He cites Dr. Davis and Lucy Landon as character witnesses; he asks his parents to inquire of his cousin Ben Blackford, "if I am not one of the leaders among the college moralists at the University. . . I certainly never would go to a place of public resort to play any game because such a course has the semblance of evil, & consequently I never go to Moose's to play Billiards, though it is purely a game of skill at which no one bets. But none of these objections apply when at *very distant periods* I occasionally join some steady fellows in a game of Whist or Chess, the only games in the world with which I am acquainted. The very fact that I do not keep it a secret shows that I do not & never did consider it at all wrong."

Lanty also came in for his share of his mother's scolding. He concluded one letter to her: "Except for the *Southern Churchman*, I abstain in great measure from newspaper & periodical reading which you seem to think so prejudicial." [20] He had been able to send her $20 in the fall, but in February 1855 he made a specific request:

"It is that you go out on Chestnut Street as soon as you conveniently can after finishing this letter and provide for yourself as a present from your affectionate son a handsome set of furs, muff, etc., such as are worn by the ladies generally in the city this winter; I would send you the money enclosed but do not know exactly what it will be. I presume from $20 to $30. Please let them be *handsome* and *à la mode* by all means, and of the *best* quality. . . I know you will be thinking I can not spare it and all that, but on the contrary I assure you that I esteem it a privilege and a pleasure to put in my 'mite.' " [21]

Mrs. Blackford refused to consider her son's request and she was not very gracious about it either. But the boy had been taught to be persistent and he begged her to reconsider: "I could not help [thinking], in reading over your letter where you say 'to show that

I do not indulge myself in unnecessary luxuries,' preposterous idea!!! You may be assured, my death Mother, that it would take a great deal to make me think of you in this connection." [22]

After her return from Philadelphia in 1855, her husband reported, "She looks well but is really no better than when she left home eighteen months ago for Philadelphia." [23]

That summer Mary enjoyed a letter from her brother Lewis, who had just completed a long tour of duty in the Mediterranean. It has a distinctly modern sound:

"At last I have once more reached the so-called New World," he rejoiced to say, "New as it may be and by comparison is, it is in my opinion far in advance of the 'Old.' If we except the architecture, sculpture and painting of Europe, I know of nothing in which our country does not excel that continent. . . That same 'old world' is well enough to visit, but I would not live in it for one of their petty Duchies or principalities. In short, I have come home with a much greater love and admiration for our country than I ever had before." [24]

3

Benjamin Blackford, veteran of the Revolution, was growing old. "By the time he was twenty-one years old he had accumulated a thousand dollars for every year of his life." [25] He accumulated more during the War of 1812. "By 1827 he had turned from manufacturing ordnance to casting instruments more native to peace, especially plough shares, of which at that time he was selling a greater number than were being sold by any other establishment in Virginia." [26] "Though so successful in his business," he had been "noted for his liberality with the large number of workmen he employed and their attachment to him was very strong; many had been in his service over twenty years." It was a heartbreaking blow to him to be wiped out at the age of seventy-three, but he received the blow with Christian fortitude.

After living several years with his older son in Lynchburg, in 1848 he made his home with William. Mary Blackford gave him

a birthday party every October 31, having Dr. Thomas T. Blackford and his family, and any other relatives in the vicinity come in
to do him honor.

"His mind was ever active. . . His life was very regular. He
rose early and read the Bible until breakfast. After breakfast he
read the Prayer Book a while; then the morning papers, especially
the *National Intelligencer* of Washington. This brought him to
about 12 o'clock when he went down town and posted himself
from force of habit in regard to the markets for iron and its products. He then came home to dinner and the rest of the day was
spent in reading, including especially biographies of Washington.
He was an uncompromising Whig and he had been a Federalist.
He regarded Jefferson and Jackson as the beginning and end of
all that was evil. He dressed in the old fashion, and reminded
[Charles] much of Washington in his person, which was striking."
His grandson could remember "no more elegant old gentleman in
his style, and none who retained his faculties to a greater age."

"The Old Master" was "taken with a violent attack of bowel
complaint" on August 10, 1855. Ten days later, according to
Lanty, "there stood around him as he breathed his last: Mother,
Cousin Mary, Cousin Betty, Lewis, Eugene, Mary Isabella, the
servants, Peggy, Ann and Elvira, and I — only." [27]

In December, death also summoned that grand old lady, Lucy
Landon Minor, who had raised six stalwart sons and so deeply in-
fluenced her daughter Mary. She had managed her husband's encumbered estate so well that she had not been forced to sell a single
slave and finally was able to liberate them, sending those who would
go to Liberia; so well that, after securing a college education for her
sons and doing many charitable deeds, she was able to leave to each
of her children a modest fortune (about $8,000).

4

Lewis, who had been "passing his time very pleasantly, hunting,
shooting, dancing and flirting in moderation" [28] while working for
the railroad, was urged by his mother to go to the University.

When he was able to collect his back pay, he was quite willing to accept her advice. He and Lanty, who had saved most of his salary as a schoolteacher, entered the University in September 1855. In the backyard of their brother-in-law, Dr. John Staige Davis, was a small brick building recently vacated by Charly. This little house had been built originally for slave quarters, evidently on the assumption that no professor could ever afford to have more than one or two slaves. Dr. Davis insisted that the boys live there, and also that they eat at his table. Eugene was sent to a boarding school near the University.

Both Lewis and Lanty studied hard; both joined the Sons of Temperance. A new home for that order had been built, and, after the visit of General Cary, the famous temperance lecturer, Launcelot wrote:

"The first evening was occupied by the more commonplace views of the subject, — the evil of Intemperance, etc. On Saturday the address was much longer and a most triumphant and in every way admirable argument in favor of the Prohibitory Law; but I can give you no better evidence of the excellence of Gen. Cary's addresses than by stating that the night after the first speech, *sixty-eight* students joined the 'Sons' . . . Our whole number now is 150, and 'the cry is still they come,' a cry truly melancholy to the ears of the grog shop keepers about College whose trade is certainly languishing just now. . . What a glorious day for this Institution so dear to us all when by some means or other this 'consummation devoutly to be wished' shall have actually arrived! At no distant day, in less than five years, I am sanguine we'll have *the* Law." [29]

Mrs. Blackford's fears as to Willy's flirting were finally set at rest in February 1856, when he married Miss Mary Robertson, daughter of Wyndham Robertson, a former Governor of Virginia. Miss Mary had not been easily won. Two years earlier when Willy had left Abingdon on business, he had written his mother, "When I reached Lynchburg," — not two hundred miles away — "I wrote to Miss Mary & enclosed the letter to her mother with a request, if

she had no objection, to give it to Miss Mary. Was not that right?" [30]
Even in his courtship he deferred to his mother's ideas as to eti-
quette.

Two weeks after Willy's wedding, Charly married Miss Susan
Leigh Colston. Very much to the delight of his mother who, like
her mother, had wanted her sons to have "every advantage" in education, Charly had been graduated in law at the University the
preceding June. The offer of a partnership by a well established
lawyer in Lynchburg seemed to him both a quicker and a surer
way of being able to support a wife than seeking his fortune in a
part of the country where he was not known, so he had accepted.
Sue's parents had long been dead, and Mr. and Mrs. Blackford
welcomed her into the family with so much affection that soon
she loved them like her own parents and she almost made Mrs.
Blackford forget her disappointment over Charly's not leaving the
Old Dominion.

Perhaps the excitement of two weddings in two weeks had exhausted the boys' mother; certainly in the spring of 1856 Mrs.
Blackford was in an unusually captious mood and her letters to
the sons at the University were carping, to say the least. Lewis replied to a scolding on April 8:

"Please don't write in such low spirits, it makes me feel very
badly and I think it is hardly fair, Mother, to us and far from fair
to yourself. You know, you must know, that I love you more than
anything else, and what more can I do? You fear, you say, that
we do not endorse your opinions, that your opinions have been of
none effect. Now in this you certainly do not do us justice. It is
true that we are not everything what you have taught and what
you are, for if we were we would all be Christians, but we love
you and try to act as best pleases you. . .

"Now I know you are thinking about Temperance," he continued in self-exculpation, "well, just ask Cousin John [B. Minor]
who is a wheelhorse of the Un-J Division. His answer will be,
'Lewis Blackford.' Ask him who makes a speech & several motions
every evening & never goes to sleep. His answer will be, 'That

whole team to the cause of Temperance, — Lewis Blackford.'
And, seriously, I do my very best for the cause both in and out
of the Division. I know that when your bodily health is poor and
you suffer so much it greatly affects your spirits but then, Mother,
instead of brooding over what we are *not*, think of what we *are*
and, above all, of how much we all love you."

Even Lanty had to remonstrate: "You say that you have been
deterred from writing to us by 'a sad conviction that what I say
has no effect,' etc., etc., that 'the time when I can be of any use
to you has passed away,' and a great deal more in the same strain.
Upon reading this I was first surprised, then grieved that you
should allow yourself to labor under such a monstrous delusion
and total misapprehension as all this part of your letter shows you
are under. . . *Every day* you are in my mind in connection with
those excellent early teachings of yours which I strive, however
imperfectly, to make the rule & guide of my paths through life;
every day I have to thank that merciful Providence that threw
around my earlier years 'home influences' better and purer and
every way more excellent than which, I believe, no man was ever
blessed with." [31]

Mrs. Blackford returned to the theme of selecting a wife, a
subject she considered of the most profound importance where
her sons were concerned. Lanty replied on April 24:

"Your excellent advice on the subject of choosing a wife was
appreciated duly, — such counsel always makes me feel sad to
think how long it will be before it will be in my power to use
it in my own case. I remember it, & always will until it is no
longer needed."

Mrs. Blackford should not be severely censured for her worries
over the conduct of her sons at the University: she did have some
occasion for concern. In the early days scant discipline prevailed
on the Lawn: even a student brought up before the Board of
Visitors — Mr. Jefferson, Mr. Madison, and Mr. Monroe sitting
on the Board — made no secret of his resentment of its attempts
to curb his personal liberties! [32] In the 1840's drinking was ramp-
ant, duels were occasionally fought, and "student riots" were all

too common.[33] During one of these, shortly before Willy matriculated, John A. G. Davis, Professor of Law and father of Dr. John Staige Davis, had been killed in front of his own home on the Lawn by a drunken student.[34] Conditions had to improve after that. During the session of 1854–55 there was a great religious revival among the young men, and following this the students became much more serious-minded. It must be admitted, however, that there were always some young Hotspurs among their number.

While Mary Blackford was on a visit to her brother in Brooklyn in 1857, she received a letter from Charly in Lynchburg, dated November 27, about a party he was planning in honor of an old gentleman retiring from the bench. "I expect to have a full bar supper next Tuesday night," he wrote, "though the thing is not entirely certain. If I do I have determined, not without a struggle I confess, to have nothing to drink, not even for Judge Leigh, though, in truth, to give him his accustomed toddy was all I ever thought of, but there will still be nothing but coffee and lemonade even for him: it will be the only supper given him which will be strictly on temperance principles."

That missive pleased his mother who replied: "What a very agreeable letter that was that I got from you yesterday, my dear Charly. There were things in it that gladdened my heart to its core. I hope you had the supper you spoke of for the bar. . . I could not help exclaiming when I read that part of your letter, 'God be praised for his goodness.'

"I felt much interested in all you told me of the Christian Association, and the Fair and of your hoping to get a Chapel on Diamond Hill. That plan of the reading room for the young men is a most useful and excellent one. I am particularly interested in all those causes that enlarge the hearts of Christians towards one another, for our blessed Saviour said, 'By this shall all men know ye are my disciples, by the love ye bear one another."

She concluded that letter with, "I hope you go often to see your father and do all you can to make him happy. Children know not the power they have to make their parents happy."[35]

5

After two years Lewis left the University to earn his living again. Lanty persisted: partly to gratify his mother's wishes, partly to satisfy his own ambition, he was intent on securing his Master of Arts, the highest degree the University offered. To do this he taught in Strange's Military Academy near Charlottesville. Eugene, then ready for college, took Lewis' place in the little brick house in Dr. Davis' back yard. Lanty had "more sympathy and intimacy with Eugene than with any of [his] brothers,"[36] so the boys were happy together.

Lanty took exercise in the gymnasium for his health. Once he wrote home: "The Gymnasium is more popular than ever this session. Mr. D'Alphonse has also established *baths,* hot and cold, to be furnished only to subscribers for $6 the session round — once a week, I believe, in winter. This will probably be a very popular thing."[37]

Eugene on the other hand, like Willy, spontaneously loved outdoor sports. He organized a Cricket Club, whose members included: Sandy Pendleton,[38] son of the Reverend William N. Pendleton; and Ran McKim[39] of Baltimore; Frank Robertson,[40] Brother William's brother-in-law; young Dick Maury,[41] Cousin Matt's son; Wash Nelson,[42] son of their mother's old beau; and good-looking William F. Gardner.[43]

Eugene became a "zealous Son" of Temperance, but he was less actively interested in religious matters than his older brother. Lanty wrote his mother in October 1858: "I have resumed my place as Teacher in the Colored Sunday School in town. . . We have just organized a young men's Christian Association[44] among the students. My friend [John] Johnson has been elected the first President, and is much interested in it. I wish Eugene would join. The Final meeting for organization was held to-night and we have started with 60 members. The students seem to take hold of it very readily."[45] And a few months later he told her, "You will be pleased to hear that Johnson has carried out his idea about a Colored Sunday School here at the University."[46]

Charly found his love for his own slaves tending to grow less. On December 31, 1858, he wrote to his mother, again in Brooklyn: "My annual trouble about hiring out my servants has commenced. Ellen is still on hand without a home. Fanny with three children will be on me tomorrow night without a prospect of a home. I sincerely wish she was paddling a canoe on the upper branches of the Niger with Ellen and the children for a crew."

On February 18, 1859, the Blackford's first-born and best loved child, Lucy Landon Davis, after suffering years with pulmonary tuberculosis, died from hemorrhage. It was the first break in the family circle. Even after the death of their sister, Mr. Davis insisted that Lanty and Eugene continue as guests in his home.

That August, Willy wrote his mother to announce the arrival of another baby. He continued: "Eugene . . . started soon after to join a large deer hunting party on the Middle fork of the Holston. He seems to be enjoying himself to the fullest extent. Frank and he seem to get on together as well as any two boys I ever saw and are both fine fellows. It is uncommon now-a-days to see boy-hood prolonged to their age. They have divided their time between Buena Vista and this place. Here they occupy a garret where they make as much noise as they please without disturbing the family. The house has been very gay since Eugene came out. A party of young ladies from Richmond being here, Riding parties, picnics and dancing in the evening have made the time pass very pleasantly for all." [47]

The advanced age of these fine fellows was nineteen! One can not begrudge those young Virginians what fun they had for the times were critical. The question of slavery had been agitated ever more bitterly for thirty years, and the possibility that the Union might be disrupted was appreciated.

CHAPTER VII

Shadows of
the Irresistible Conflict

John Brown's attempt in October 1859, to lead the slaves in a massacre of the white people of the South seems to have made but slight impression on the younger members of the Blackford family. While Brown was awaiting his death, Lanty did note with satisfaction that the clergyman in Charlottesville used the prayer from the liturgy for malefactors under sentence of death.

A few weeks later Eugene wrote home: "Brother Charles' enlistment in a volunteer troop surprized me very much, though I am glad of it. I suppose he rides his war hobby as hard as he does his other hobbies. I am still very much engrossed about my Cricket Club: it occupies much more of my attention just at this time than the Wars at Charlestown and Harper's Ferry." [1]

In spite of Eugene's insouciance, the gathering storm was visible to his elders. Mr. Blackford presided over the fiirst public meeting in Lynchburg concerning the organization of a military company and nominated a captain for it. The year before, although he had not lived in Fredericksburg for twelve years, "when an effort was made to revive the 'Fredericksburg Rifle Grays,' it was proposed to style the company the 'Blackford Grays' in his honor. The advocates of this name cited 'his many years as an efficient and popular company commander.' " [2]

On December 9, 1859, Mr. Blackford gave his views as to the state of the country in a lengthy communication to his wife's cousin, John B. Minor,[3] Professor of Law at the University.

"I am unwilling that you should for a moment longer than necessary suppose that our sentiments on the great question of the Union of these States are not in accord," he remonstrated. "I do not recollect anything in my letter to the *Journal of Commerce* which ought to have led you to the conclusion that I was in favor of disunion, or that I even thought it was inevitable. It is true I expressed the opinion that the election of Seward would lead to the catastrophe, but I am not one of those who hold that his election should be *ipso facto* a dissolution. I maintain on all occasions that we are bound in justice to ourselves to await an overt act of outrage on our rights of so flagrant a character as to leave it no longer possible to submit. It requires some moral courage to hold this doctrine. I am perhaps stigmatized as a submissionist. . . At our meeting the other night I assisted in preventing a resolution about Seward's election from being reported by the committee of which I was a member; also one in favor of commercial nonintercourse and another for the call of a convention, so you see I am not a Fire eater but a conservative. Our resolutions were denounced as tame and pointless. They were intended to let off steam in a harmless way.

"Believing that the north does not appreciate the feeling in Virginia nor the danger in which the Union is placed," he continued, "I seek opportunity of letting my friends in that quarter know the real state of the case. I despatched Saturday last a letter of ten pages to my old friend Charles Davis, former Professor of Math at West Point, in which I have laid the whole case before him and implored him, if there be a conservative party in the North — of which we are constantly assured — to use his influence to make it show its hand. If there be such a party, it must be quite ignorant of the nature of the crisis, or criminally cowardly. We are told that there is a vast majority of the people, even in New England, who condemn John Brown and who think we have been greatly outraged. If this be so, in the name of patriotism why don't they say so? A meeting is talked of in New York this week, after their paltry municipal election for which it has been postponed; and one has been called in Boston. Had such meetings

been called five weeks ago, they would have seemed spontaneous
and have had a fine effect. Now they look too much like the effect
of apprehension of loss of trade.

"I assure you every sentiment of your letter finds a response in
my inmost soul," he concurred. "With you, I believe the rupture
of the Union political death. I have not the nerve to contemplate
the unnumbered calamities which will follow in its train. I have
no idea that there will be a division into two grand sections. The
work of disintegration would be progressive, and before ten years
there would be half a dozen confederacies, or single states playing
the part of independent nations, — then wars of course, — con-
quests, — consolidation and military despotism. I shall battle
therefore for the Union whilst there is the slightest hope of maintaining it. I do not yet despair — the portentous cloud may have a
silver lining and with you I put my trust in God."

Blackford wanted to be sure, however, that his friend understood that he did not favor meek submission to the North. "In the
meantime I go heart and hand for putting the state in military
array," he declared. "I favor — as I have ever done — home
manufactures. I should like to make the marts of commerce, Philadelphia, New York and Boston, feel how essential the trade of
the South is to their prosperity. I would even, if possible, for a
season at least, prevent a shoe, coarse or fine, from Massachusetts
finding its way to Virginia. The non-use for a couple of years of
this single article of manufactory by the slave holding states would
produce such a distress in Massachusetts that to regain the trade
they would stifle abolitionism in the most summary way. There is
no doubt that the cities mentioned will suffer exceedingly the approaching season. I doubt whether one half the ordinary quantity
of goods will be brought into Virginia the coming year.

"I am not disposed to speak harshly of our Governor's conduct,"
continued Blackford. "He was right in assembling a military force
at Charlestown so large as to make the rescue out of the question,
— that rescue was contemplated he has had abundant evidence,
and it would have been successful with a small, or no guard at all,

around the prisoners. . . There is one good thing about him, —
he does not despair of the Union and stands up for it stoutly.

"Charles is very much excited and very belligerent," he admitted. "He is the leading man in the troop."

Mr. Blackford then turned to the subject of his wife's health,
for Mary had determined to seek a cure in Massachusetts. "Your
cousin Mary," he said, "is only waiting an escort. She is suffering
much and if none presents itself in a day or two, Lewis will go to
Baltimore with her. She has had a letter from a lady of Petersburg
giving an account of her sufferings for 25 years. The letter is so
exactly descriptive of Mary's symptoms that, if read to them, her
friends would take it for granted that it was from her pen. She is
now a well woman, able to walk four miles a day and feel all the
better for it. Like Mary she had the best medical advice and received no benefit. It is certain that the faculty never did Mary
anything but harm. . . She is justified therefore on every ground
in trying other means of cure, however empirical. I have, and she
has, very confident hopes of being greatly relieved if not entirely
cured. One thing is certain, she must do something.

"She . . . says you rightly imagine the pain she feels in con-
templating the present state of affairs," he concluded, "and that
like you her great reliance is on that Arm which rules the world
and makes the wrath of man to praise Him. She has suffered a
great deal of anxiety."

2

When Mrs. Blackford went north in December 1859, she left
the housekeeping duties to Mary Isabella, just turned nineteen.
The girl had spent the previous session at a boarding school in
Richmond, Mr. Powell's Southern Female Institute, a session she
had thoroughly enjoyed. At the time of the unveiling of the Craw-
ford equestrian statue of Washington on the Capitol grounds that
February, she had written her mother:

"The girls are in a great state of excitement, the Lexington
Cadets [4] have turned our heads. I see so many soldiers every day

it looks like an army was here. I heard that there would be eight thousand troops here. I wish so much you could be here, you would enjoy it so much, you are so patriotic. The statue is wrapped in the American flag . . . and a platform raised . . . for the speakers. . . I intend to use my eyes that day to see all the big 'wigs'; it will be the first President I ever saw. . .

"What do you think, just now Mr. Powell came down here and gave us permission to receive gentlemen during the holidays," she bubbled over. "It will not do us much good though unless we issue a proclamation, for so many have been turned away, five or six Cadets have been turned away already." [5]

Mary Isabella was ever a dutiful correspondent. By the time her mother arrived in Florence, Massachusetts, she had written, "The servants have behaved very well, — when I say servants, I mean Elvira and Carter. My dear Mammy Peggy always behaves." [6] Elvira, the Blackfords had hired some years earlier from her owner, Cousin Betty Hill. Carter, an adolescent slave boy also hired from Cousin Betty and much spoiled by the Blackfords, did not often rate commendation from the young lady.

On December 22, Mary Isabella, full of the excitement of the season, tried to convey some of it to her mother: "We are all invited to spend Christmas day at brother Charly's, much to my relief as I did not feel like encountering a Christmas dinner, and Sue don't mind much. Papa proposed that I should give the servants a turkey and let them invite a few friends here Sunday. They seemed delighted at it when I told them. Every thing will be cooked Saturday so that it will be a cold dinner. They have behaved so well they deserve some reward. Mammy Peggy intends to invite Aunt Louisa and her husband, and Elvira her father and mother."

The next night she wrote: "Brother Eugene arrived to-day while we were at dinner much to our joy. I was amused at Carter's great delight when I told him he must have a good fire in case he came; he said with great vivacity, 'Yes ma'am, I'll have a good fire, I wants to see Mars Eugene very much indeed.' Mammy Peggy is equally delighted to see her pet. I never saw any thing like her devotion to him. He looks so well and handsome; his complexion is of the clearest red and white, — just what you covet so much for me. I know what you are thinking of, — 'exercise' and 'cold water.' "

From Charly, Mrs. Blackford received the following Christmas letter: "It is the night before Christmas and all through the house not a creature is stirring, not even a mouse, and I can't help thinking how lonely you must be away off among strangers, aliens and enemies; especially as the Heathen, in abolishing every thing else that is good, have laid aside Christmas. Even now I have only a few minutes to write as I am exceedingly tired, first having had a hard day's work, then eaten a Christmas dinner at Kean's with Eugene and the rest of the family, then given a treat to all the neighborhood children and servants in the way of a display of fireworks, — and then after entertaining Father, Mary, Lewis and Eugene until bedtime, I sat at my duties as St. Nicholas and have been engaged for over an hour filling some 14 socks belonging to Nannie and the little darkies.

"It would amuse you and astonish many of your present neighbors [in Massachusetts] to see them in the morning, — not only all living on the lot, but the hirelings are all here and by sunrise will all be dressed, washed and combed, and knocking for admittance at our chamber door to 'catch' me as they call it, without which ceremony they think they would lose all claim upon me. Then Nannie in her night gown will dispense the presents. Our pay is in seeing the boundless joy which pervades their ebony faces. Gerrit Smith [7] nor Giddings, nor any body in Massachusetts, has so keen a pleasure in the whole year.

"Where would the happy little ones have been now if their ancestors had not been rescued from barbarism? Or what would be their condition if they were now free in the Infidel State of Massachusetts? But this is a subject you don't like."

The crisis was developing rapidly. When 1860 dawned even the college students were sensing impending disaster. Lanty wrote from the University, January 26: "We had yesterday in Dr. Mc-

Guffey's Lecture Room the Students' meeting in behalf of the disturbed state of the country. It was well attended, and was conducted with solemnity and interest. The suggestion of such a meeting as yesterday's was received from a circular of the Alexandria Y.M.C.A. and was doubtless responded to in other sections. We expect next month to join in the National Prayer for Colleges by means of a general Students' Meeting on the appointed day."

An important factor in causing this disturbed state was that not all slaves in the South were treated as well as Mammy Peggy, — not even all in Lynchburg. In February, Mary Isabella reported to her mother:

"Uncle Davy is at work in the garden, planting peas and potatoes, — he is delighted to get here again to work — he has been so anxious to come — he has found it difficult to get any work lately — and I reckon he has hard times as his mistress won't give him any thing to eat when he does not get work. I have given him coffy, sugar and molasses — and a meal here occasionally — he is so greatful. I wrote a letter for him a few days ago to his sister in Petersburg.

"To-night after Church was over a bridal party of servants came in to be married. I never saw such dressing, perfect loads of durty finery. I felt so sorry for the poor things, — everybody laughed at them. . . But the servants behaved very well." [8]

In subsequent letters Mary Isabella told of difficulties with the family table, the coming of the spring flowers ("the violets . . . smell like you"), the birth of a calf, the selling of the surplus milk ("I have made $10 by the milk since the calf was born. I gave papa $9. This morning $1.00 I divided between Peggy and Elvira as you desired").

On March 28 she wrote: "I walked up to the College yesterday to see the Home Guard drill. They are brushing up for Friday when there is to be a grand turn out of all three companies. The flag presented by the ladies to the Home Guard is to be given them. Mr. Ribble is to make a speech on the occasion.

"Aunt Minerva came down yesterday to spend the day according to invitation," the girl wanted to be sure her mother had all the news, "and we presented her with the socks. You never saw any thing like her delight. Her first exclamation was, 'Jesus, dese things ain't for me!' and hugged them to her. I then told her my brother sent them to her and she desired a thousand thanks might be sent to him and all sorts of good wishes for his prosperity. I made and gave her an apron, Lucy a head handkerchief and Churchill [9] a piece of meat, and some cake and good things besides a very good dinner — she was delighted. She came down dressed in the alpaca you sent her and a white apron — looked very nice. I asked her why she did not bring down her bucket as usual for butter milk. She said, 'Well, you see, Miss Mary, — I was afraid I might spatter this here nice cote.' . . .

"The roses are all in bloom on the arbor and look so pretty — that one before the kitchen has been blooming beautifully too, it is a purple pea. The servants take great interest in the flowers."

In May, Mrs. Blackford wrote her husband: "I am glad to hear of the increased number of colored people in our church and should like to have heard Mr. Kinckle's appeal to the congregation in their behalf. How does Carter behave now about Sunday School? . . . Pray, my dear, write answers to my letters. Don't write your previous writing, telling me about fights that disgrace the age and country; I had rather hear of the meanest flower that grows in my garden. I wish you would tell me if the roses on the arbors are growing fast and blooming. How does Charly's garden look?" [10]

Gallantly Mr. Blackford responded on June 3: "I seat myself in the back porch to begin my letter to you, though the temperature is rather cool for comfort. The martins are in full chorus and the canary gives an occasional trill — the same rural sounds are heard, together with the manly tones of some one in the back street singing a hymn. Breakfast is just over, though it is later than usual, and there is noise and confusion attending the departure of Sue and the children who spent the night here, together with Charles. I just hear Sue telling Mary [Isabella] that she was never in such health and that she has not had a headache for weeks: she ought to have had one after the supper of waffles she ate last night."

And after many more pages, he concluded, "If you are restored to health or emotionally benefited, I trust our separation for the remainder of our lives will be very brief."

Mary could acknowledge his letters with grace: "There is one pleasure I shall miss, dearest husband, when I get home: it is the delightful letters I get from you." [11]

Mrs. Blackford got other delightful letters in Massachusetts. Charly, never so happy as when telling of his little girl, must have pleased her with the following:

"Nannie . . . is very well and very beautiful, — more beautiful in the gentleness of her disposition than even in her person, — she really weeps with those that weep and rejoices with those that rejoice. During her mother's illness she has been busy in the affectation of housekeeping, — the principal element of which she regards as sitting at the head of the table and lording it over Dick,[12] — who regards her orders with much more reverence than he does mine, I am sure. I heard her tell him yesterday, 'Dick, you so trifling — you worry me to def.' Dick thinks she can do no wrong and would put his head in the fire if she was to tell him to. This evening she had a lot of six or eight of 'the peculiar institution' in the garden 'playing soldier' and it was a pretty fair outcropping of the military spirit of Virginia. I wish some of your present neighbors could have seen it that they might learn what is in store for them. Dick had a pole with a newspaper on the end for a flag — Nannie with her hat decorated with a bunch of pinks for a plume was acting in the double capacity of Drum Major and Captain, and the balance of the company with newspaper hats and stick guns were marching around the flower bed, each to the tune of his own drumming, — it didn't look much like 'oppression.' " [13]

3

In July 1860, Lanty, knowing that nothing interested his mother more than an account of his religious activities, especially if they involved Negroes, wrote his mother from Lynchburg:

"I went last Sunday evening and shall continue to go during my sojourn at home to the colored Sunday School at our church. The attendance was not large, though I understand it would be much better if male teachers could be had. I took a class of some eight boys, Carter among them, and instructed them through the time allotted with pleasure and satisfaction to myself and, I trust, some advantage to them. . . I found them well behaved, intelligent and docile. I am told that there is a very flourishing school at the First Presbyterian Church and perhaps at some of the other churches here. I trust that this is but the beginning of greater and better things. I found the children at St. Paul's Sunday School to sing remarkably well, Carter is their leader. He is gifted in this line. He has a fine ear and voice and a great deal of practice. He sings that magnificent chant *Gloria in Excelsis* admirably." [14]

A few weeks later he was giving her his estimate of the political situation. "The enthusiasm in the Union cause is very strong in this state everywhere," he assured his mother, "and the news from the other states is very encouraging. The whole conservative masses of the American people seem to be roused to endeavor to avert the awful calamity of a Black Republican principle and the election of Lincoln. I can find no language to express my horror for the political sentiments of that traitorous party.

"Brother Charles has been elected President of the Young Men's Union Club here," he added, descending from the general to the particular. "He made a speech Wednesday night last when he was elected which is very highly spoken of. He may perhaps speak at a Ratification meeting in Amherst to day. He is much interested in the campaign and, though not a politician and though we would not have him become such, still papa and all of us are well pleased that he should lift up his voice in so righteous a cause and endeavor to preserve the Union and its Constitution. I would have every man who can lift up his voice in this crisis plead in behalf of Constitutional Liberty and against fanaticism. So far as I am aware, the eleven votes in my father's and our Uncle's family, i.e., all the Blackfords, go for Bell and Everett." [15]

4

Sometimes in Massachusetts Mrs. Blackford managed rather to enjoy herself. On August 24, 1860, she wrote *in extenso* of a drive in "one of the open carriages used here" up the valley of the Connecticut:

"It is the most highly cultivated country I have ever seen, and in some respects the most beautiful. It is not so bold and romantic as western Virginia, the mountains are not so high, but the high state of cultivation, the rich verdure (for the country where not cultivated is covered with grass like that in our yards), the noble old trees left standing in every direction, the beautiful rivers, the ranges of mountains and picturesque country villages make up together the most lovely country by far that I ever travelled in. I think it must be very much like England, particularly in the verdure and in the appearance of the villages. Strange to say, I saw more tobacco than I ever saw in succession in Virginia, and very fine indeed. We passed through Hatfield, Whately, West Farms and South Deerfield. Then crossed the river over a very long covered bridge, and returned through the valley on the other side, passing through Sunderland, North Hadly, old Hadly, and then recrossed the river by the ferry, passing through North Hampton, making in all more than thirty miles. We got here directly after dinner. The roads are very smooth and even, and Mr. F. drove rapidly.

"Their villages are all agricultural, and much good taste is shown in preserving the peculiar character of a country village; in every direction you see what a painter would love to transfer to canvas or a poet to describe. Their noble old trees are standing about, with slopes of the richest turf, the houses standing aloof, many of them with markings of the olden time in the style of building, mouldings handsomely arranged over the front door, something like those that used to be over the front door at Hazle Hill when we lived there.

"The cows are not permitted (as with us) to run out, so that the grass is all like that in our yards.

"I saw great quantities of apples out in orchards carpeted with verdure and some hanging over the road, but no peaches. In one instance I mistook a large handsome barn with a cupola for a church. I forgot to mention the spires of the churches are among the objects of beauty. I could see no marks of poverty at all, every thing looked thrifty and comfortable. We passed close under Sugar Loaf mountain, called so from being shaped like a sugar loaf. The view is said to be very fine from there. We could see a table made of large flat rocks on the summit, said to have been made by Indians. . .

"These villages are different from any thing that I have ever seen before: all of those mentioned (except South Deerfield) have the most secluded, lovely appearance, no taverns or shops; the streets are very wide indeed, covered with lawn grass, except where the road runs, and with rows of trees on each side that look to be at least one hundred years old.

"You see scarcely any one even to ask a question of except when the children come out of the school houses. But whenever there is opportunity of making inquiries of any one in the village or on the road, you are sure of a kind and careful answer for a more kindly disposed people I have never seen. The honesty of the people is remarkable: you can leave your things about in the most uncommon manner without danger of having them stolen. The majority of them have no locks outside or inside their houses.

"The land is in the highest degree fertile, one of the farmers made six hundred bushels of wheat from twelve acres. The year before he had tobacco on it. I hope you read my letter to brother Lucius."

Unfortunately Mrs. Blackford's sense of well-being did not last long. Four days later she was in the depths again. One owes it to the memory of this excellent lady to be scrupulously fair to her: it must be true that she suffered pain in her back, and it probably did radiate down into her legs. It is quite possible, for example, that if she had been born a hundred years later, surgical removal of a herniated intervertebral disc might have given her some relief. But such a formidable procedure would not have made a well woman of her. Unconsciously she betrayed the nature of her major trouble in her next letter to her husband:

"Now (as at home), as soon as my spine is affected my whole nervous system, through my arms, hands, legs, feet and head, I feel the suffering and my mind suffers with it. I scarcely sit in company at all, never go to supper. Have to retire to my room and not ever have any body to talk to in there for, if I am at all interested or excited, I can not sleep much but lie awake as I used to do at home with my mind tossed about like dashing waves, not being able to fix them, only a feeling of horror or distress." [16]

5

That fall of 1860 when Mrs. Blackford got home, she found all of her immediate family still loyal to the Union. Also loyal was her cousin, John B. Minor of the University, who unburdened himself on October 13:

"My soul is afflicted with anxiety for the Country. When I reflect calmly upon our position at present, with the peace, freedom and prosperity we enjoy, I do not know how to believe in the wicked madness which would plunge us into the vortex of civil war for any cause existing or probable, but I have unbounded faith in the stupidity and recklessness of the Belials of South Carolina and the Molochs of Mississippi. I can not tell, between these qualities, what they might not do.

"My warmest indignation is kindled at the factious insolence which leads the politicians of these States to dictate to Virginia and other border states (who alone have as yet suffered anything from northern aggression, and who must bear the brunt of the conflict) when and how they shall resist. . . And then the coolness with which they speculate on the probability that Virginia will not permit federal troops to march to their subjugation. . . They bluster and threaten, safe, as they imagine, behind the intervening tiers of quiet Commonwealths to whose chivalrous feelings and sympathy they design to appeal to support them in a course abhorrent to the principles of these States and destructive to their interests."

Lincoln, with some two million votes out of about four and a half million, won the election.[17] A few days later Dr. James Monroe Minor pontificated from Brooklyn:

"The result of the elections has doubtless startled you and every one else in the South. It is most ominous and distinctly foreshadows what I have been prophesying for more than 20 years: a separation of the states is inevitable, it can only be temporarily stayed. . .

"How painful is the contemplation of millions of people guided by weak, silly, foolish and mischievous councillors! The mistakes which shape the destiny of an individual are painful enough to those who witness them; how much more when a whole people commit a fatal error. It is a most outrageous proceeding on the part of the Northern people to elect a purely sectional president. All things considered however, it is well that it should be so; had it been delayed to another term, the section animosity would have been proportionately agravated and so much the more difficult to stay. As it is, there may be a few more years for the confederacy, but only a few. Had a Union candidate been elected, it would not have lasted beyond a term of four years.

"What are the bragadocios of the 'Cotton States' going to do? Oh, how I long to see calm and collected men at the helm in place of these pernicious braggarts who appear now to rule. The South have the right on their side. For Heaven's sake, don't let them put a cudgell in their adversaries' hand." [18]

Mrs. Blackford, like most intelligent Virginians, was deeply troubled. She appealed to her brother Lucius for comfort and he tried to reassure her with this lengthy philippic:

"I am sorry to see that you are troubled with apprehensions of the evils of war, though I expected you would be. But do not suffer such apprehensions to trouble you longer. There will be much innocent ink shed (such as flows from my pen for instance), but no blood except for the noses of drunken men on the hustings. A revolution may be effected . . . but *pens* and *type* and *tongues* will be the only weapons used on the occasion, or at worst the fists of angry politicians.

"If South Carolina secedes, probably many (or perhaps all) of the Southern States will do the same in the course of a short time. A Southern Confederacy (with much more limited powers and patronage than those now exercised by our present Federal Government) will be organized. In the division of the Publick property the Southern Confederacy will yield the lion's share to the Northern Confederacy, and after a good deal of wrangling about the use of the Mississippi and the Ohio, both parties will settle down to a far more harmonious and prosperous business and social intercourse than ever.

"The Northern Confederacy will however soon begin to assume features of an anti-republican character (and wisely too), approaching (if not reaching) to a monarchical form. The Southern Confederacy will occupy in a short time the immense empire that lies between the Free States and South America, the Atlantic and the Pacific, including Mexico and Central America, embracing the Gulf, with Cuba to guard its gate. Through this gate passes (as Mat Maury tells us) the whole trade of South America with Europe and the U.S. The varied and immense products of such an immense empire will render the combined power of the Southern States far greater than we could ever be under our present organization because more conservative and more congenial. Add to this the command of the transit of the trade across the Isthmus between the two great oceans of the world. The result will be that the alliance and friendship of the Southern Confederacy will be sedulously sought by every nation on earth.

"But suppose that South Carolina be not sustained by the other Southern States and that the Federal Government menaces an attempt to coerce her into submission. Why, she has only to raise one finger and in a short time fifty British ships of the line will be sent to her aid, attended by such other forces as may be desired. The British Government will rejoice at the opportunity of forming an alliance by which British manufacturers would be admitted into Charleston harbor free, or nearly so, and indirectly into all the Southern States.

"When our Federal Government sees that war with South Caro-

lina involves a war with Great Britain there will be *perfect calm.*
Every ocean of the world is white with the sails of Yankee commerce and the freight is too precious to be risked in such an unholy
cause. At the roar of the British lion Yankey valor would evapo-
rate: it would vanish into thin air under the influence of Yankey
cupidity. As for the Southern States, they have fought successfully
two bloody wars with Great Britain in defense of *Yankey interests*
and if they are wise they will do no more in that line.

"But, my dear Sister, if we are to be driven to the dire necessity
of War, can your generous heart that has always pled for, bled
for the oppressed, fail to sympathize with those who fight for their
rights, a small band of bold men who in the name of justice, in
defense of vital political rights, defy the power of a tyrannical
government which they helped to erect, a power which they created for their protection, but which is abused for their oppression?

"And who are the number whom you are taught to vilify as
hot-headed and seditious? Many of them are descendants of the
noble Huguenots, who for half a century courageously fought and
bled for religious and political rights under the lead of the good
old Sully, over whose shameful oppression, cruel suffering and
inhuman butchery you have often wept.

"And for whom is your sympathy enlisted? Why, for a horde
of fanatical, sneaking Puritans, who were too turbulent to be endured at home and being justly expelled from their native land
fled to America, where by dissimulation rather than by courage,
they wrested the tomahawk and scalping knife from the hand of
the fearless savage, far more noble than themselves, and used those
savage weapons upon the heads of the natives of the soil that they
usurped with far more relentless ferocity than the savage himself. . .

"Now was this the crowning curse of their damnable fanaticism.
Fleeing from a pretended persecution, falsely pretending to seek
'an abode in the wilderness' where they could worship God in
peace — worship Him in the mode dictated by conscience! (save
the mark!) they had hardly finished their work of butchery in exterminating the poor savages before they commenced a relentless

and savage persecution of some of their own fellow-citizens on account of *their religion*, emprisoned, whipping and even murdering Quakers and Baptists for *conscience sake* and *by law*.

"Can my dear Sister whose sense of justice is so keen, so feeling, hesitate on such a contrast? On the one hand a little band of bold men who have ever extended to *all* the blessings of religious and political freedom which their fathers found and maintained for them in the wilds of America, after fighting nobly for their king, their country, their religion, their rights, enduring with the heroism that genuine piety inspires the persecution that the Romish church alone knows how to perfect, a sovereign state boldly maintaining her sovereign rights, which 80 years ago were acknowledged by all.

"On the other hand, a nest of sour fanatics, whose fathers 'left their country for their country's good,' ever savagely intolerant of all religious, political or social opinions that were not measured by their own harsh dogmas, ever seeking to substitute some idol in the place of the savior who died for them, compromising with God by giving their money instead of their hearts, out-Heroding the Romish devotee by making the road to Heaven through Hell.

"My dear sister, let not the selfish grasping Yankey come between us to mar our domestic peace. We can not live in peace with them. There is no congeniality, no possibility of assimilation. We have patiently tried it for more than eighty years, and it grows worse each year. As the good old George Mason solemnly warned us in the Convention of 1788 (as if inspired with the gift of prophecy) nearly all of our gifted leading men are *bought up* by the immense, irresistible patronage of a great centralized Federal Government. The Constitution means anything that the majority chooses it to mean. It is a cobweb that catches the smallest flies, whilst the great ones pass through, each leaving a convenient hole for others to follow. Whilst it is a mere rope of sand in *protecting the minority*, it is a mighty engine in hands of the *majority*, for it gives the majority the control of eighty million dollars a year, and in ten years from this time it will be a hundred and fifty millions, if the Yankeys can induce the South to burn brick for their benefit so long. . .

"I feel deeply on this subject and write accordingly. I thank God most heartily that patriotism is not extinguished in my heart, though our present form of government has done much towards extinguishing that conservative — that holy sentiment in the hearts of our people.

"Where is your country? Can you look at a map and put your finger on one single spot and call it 'my own, my native land?' *My* native land is Virginia, and whilst I glory in it, I humbly thank God that he has given me such a nativity. Have you never observed how little of the feelings of patriotism pervades the hearts of our people? . . . Thousands yearly emigrate, they care not where — Mexico, Central America, any where, leaving their native country without a tear. To what condition is Virginia reduced? An insignificant item, an undistinguishable element in making up a great mass of federal centralization. After giving away to the federal union a principality, what is the return? Why, she is sneered at, trampled on by the recipients of her munificence.

"But let not your heart be troubled if the fear of war in Virginia troubles it. Virginians have not the spirit to resist oppression. They will *tamely submit*. The means which extinguished their patriotism have thoroughly evaporated their courage. Half the men I meet are trembling in their shoes. They can not sleep for visions of a great Yankey army — yes, an army of shoemakers and tailors.

"I reckon you think I am very much excited. I was never cooler in my life. I feel too deeply to be excited. The surface of the ocean is lashed into foam by the hurricane, but its depths are calm and unmoved." [19]

November 9, Eugene, teaching in Clayton, Alabama, wrote:
"The people here have been very kind to me and I am very grateful for it, but for all that their ways are not our ways; they are a different people from us, and show it by their living and conversation. They are all violent Fire Eaters, are for dissolution

to a man, and speak of any one who professes the smallest love for the Union as a traitor to his country, namely the South. Up to the 9th inst., every one, old and young, wore the blue cockade (resistance to Lincoln), but now that there are rumors of the success of the Black Republican nominee, they have changed for a cockade of red, white and blue ribbon, which is worn on the lappel of the coat. . . These tricolor badges signify that all parties are now united, and, burying the tomahawk of party strife, are all united in opposition to Lincoln. The cause of half of the violence here in public opinion is their ignorance of public opinion: they never see any papers except the local papers and the *Charleston Mercury*."

Mr. Blackford, gravely concerned both about the country's plight and Eugene's predicament, wrote to Lanty, teaching in a girls' school in Staunton:

"In view of his peculiar situation, a stranger in a strange land, for also Alabama is a foreign state, I have felt it my duty to write often to Eugene. His position is a trying one and may, and I hope will, have a good effect upon his character. He is the only man in the village who is not insane. . . He maintains his principles, refuses to wear the badge. . . There was a grand meeting last Monday in Clayton. The court adjourned and I suppose he gave a holiday. There was speaking from midday till 10 at night. He says he would not hear a word, but sat in his room reading the life of Washington; these madmen were labouring to destroy that Union which was the greatest work of Washington. . . If a dissolution of the Union is accomplished — and I see no way of averting the catastrophe — I shall advise him to return. . . His troubles were carefully kept from his mother." [20]

6

On December 17, 1860, South Carolina seceded from the Union. Mr. Blackford, who had already noted in his diary, "Peaceful secession is out of the question," a few days later observed, "The election of Lincoln is but the pretext, not the cause." About the same time he received the following letter from John B. Minor:

"I need not ask you how you are exercised by the mingled madness and folly, the imports and aspects of which are so bad to the affairs of the country. As I lay lately on a sick bed, my fevered fancy dwelt continually on the dreary prospects before us, and it occurred to me that it would be well to prepare for the flag and seal of the Southern Confederacy the device of a number of falling whims, with the setting sun eclipsed, 'Shedding disastrous twilight,' and the legend, *'in excidio salus!'*

"Indignation and alarm alternate in my breast when I think of wretched little South Carolina, like an insolent and enfeebled reactionary, plunging the whole country into strife and confusion of which others must bear the brunt. I find it hard to suppress my feelings for the spiteful impotent, and when I reflect that the mean desertion of us by the other Southern States compels us to make this the crisis of our destiny, whether we like it or not, I am oppressed at once with indignation and anxiety. And these feelings are aggravated by the consideration that while I think the conspirators in the cotton states deserve condign punishment, our safety makes it necessary that we should interpose to screen them if need be.

"Virginia, I trust, will be mindful of her ancient fame and her historic patriotism, and will interpose a calm, earnest and dignified mediation worthy of her character. Of all things it is important that our people should not be fired with the frenzy which reigns in the cotton State mobs." [21]

The New Year brought nothing to cheer the hearts of those many Virginians still loyal to the Union. In the first month of 1861, Mississippi, Florida, Alabama, Georgia, and Louisiana followed South Carolina out of the Union. In the midst of this exodus Mary Blackford again sought sympathy from her beloved Cousin John:

"I suffer at times such anguish of mind about the ruin of our great Country and the prospect of Civil war that I feel impelled to write you, just to pour out my heart — not that I think it can do any good. No, no one can help us now but God, all our hope

and trust must be in Him. . . Oh! for the faith that can look at
the threatened ruin and see God in all. . . Such faith is hard to
have. . . I know we deserve His chastisement, for we have been
most ungrateful and committed great wrongs, but it falls on me
with a weight that I feel sometimes will sink me into my grave.

"When my Lucy died, though she was the charm of our life, I
felt so sure she had gone into everlasting happiness that it was
a sort of holy sorrow, it seemed to stimulate me to try to meet her;
it deepens as I grow older. . . But Oh how different from this —
To see my sons arrayed against one part of their country, our own
'Star spangled banner,' and *in such a cause*, is a sorrow that makes
me feel that the grave is the only place for me. You did not know,
my dear John, the pains I took to train my five sons in sentiments
of patriotism.

"But the world is too much for me. My voice is drowned, and I
have nothing left but to die. In the war of 1812 I used to hear
from my Father sentiments that sunk into my heart, when he little
thought of the impression he was making, — they were like those
of the revolution, oh, how unlike what are held now. But why talk
any more of my own feelings, but bear with me, it is a relief.
There are *very* few I can talk to." [22]

John responded on January 21:

"I am deeply moved by your expressions of honest anguish for
the approaching woes of our country, and sympathize with all my
soul in the patriotic fervor with which you deprecate them. . . I
coincide with your opinion that . . . help must come from God
only. Madness, literal frenzy, seems to me to possess our Countrymen. The incredible fatuity of the South, — incredible if it were
not exhibited before our eyes, — finds its parallel in an equal
fatuity at the North. It will be solely of the Lord's mercy if we do
not perish as a free, prosperous people and become a hissing and
a reproach to the Nations. I am often reminded of the Latin apo-
thegm, — '*Quem Deus vult perdere, prius dementat.*' Which Mr.
B. will render for you.

"But what a comfort it is to turn from human folly, pride and
wickedness, to the assurance that 'the Lord God omnipotent reign-

eth.' Our dear old Commonwealth, I trust, will not wholly lose the equipoise of her judgement and, I can not help hoping, may be, under God, the means of preserving the Union which she did so much to form and to cement. She has many foolish men and perhaps some wicked ones in her councils and yet, Heaven-directed, she pursues in the main a course of quiet dignity, which I contemplate with affectionate delight."

To Mary's request, "Pray don't show my letter, you know it is treason in the eyes of many to hold the sentiments I do — and I do not want to injure my husband and children," John replied, "I can not prescribe to myself the prudent course you adopt. . . I think it my duty to omit no Fair occasion to express my indignation and disapproval, but I grieve to say that I sometimes 'speak unadvisedly with my lips,' not remembering always that no man does well to be angry!"

The legislature had called for the election the following month of delegates to a constitutional convention to take into consideration the condition of public affairs and to determine what action the State should take. In this Minor found some solace, which he sought to pass on to Mary: "The Convention and its tremendous issues inspire me with an anxious awe, but the *venom* is extracted from the fang by the provision that the result of the deliberation may be submitted to the people, if the people themselves shall so will it, as I take it for granted they will do so. That gains time, and time is everything."

On January 18, the same day that his mother had sent that despairing letter to the Professor of Law, his former student Charly wrote his old teacher in an entirely different vein:

"My delay in answering your long and interesting letter has not arisen from any indisposition to do so, but from a desire to get my feelings into such a condition that an expression of my opinion might not give you pain.

"Ever since the Election I have felt a sensible change going on in my opinions — and a rapid decline taking place in my loyalty to the Federal Government. I date this change from the Election because, though I had become fully convinced that Lincoln would be elected, I had hoped that the vote would be so close as to prove the minority choice even of his section, in which case I should have deemed it expedient to give him a trial and take the chance of breaking his party down during his term. But he has been elected by majorities greater than ever given any man since Washington, and the conclusion is forced upon us that they indicate a complete endorsation of his very obnoxious views by the people of the North — and a declaration on their part to make war upon us and our institutions.

"These facts being demonstrated by the Election, I soon found all my ante-election Union sentiments oozing away and the fires of my National patriotism expiring. But even yet I am forced to acknowledge that the peculiar position of Virginia when she consults the greatest good of the greatest number of her citizens requires her to remain in the Union so long as she can do so consistently with her safety and honour: and hence I should most willingly accept the plan of compromise you propose as it would, I think, give peace and protect us for a while at least.

"But what possible chance is there for a settlement on such terms? There was, it appears to me, never a truer sentiment uttered than that of Seward setting forth the doctrine of the 'irresistible conflict.' How can a union be maintained among a people when the truth of this expression is brought home to every man by the burning in his own bosom?

"I have never been across Mason & Dixon's line (a misfortune for which I am now thankful), and hence speak only from the indications of popular sentiment at the North common to us all; but from them I am forced to conclude that outside of their commercial centers their people are educated to the bitterest animosity to the South. Political excellence is tested by its willingness to minister to that bitterness; their chances for salvation are measured by the warmth of their 'religion of hate' for us: from the cradle to the tomb they are schooled at the fireside, upon the Hustings, in the very house of God, socially and politically and religiously, to hate and spurn every person South and everything Southern.

"Nor is any love lost between the sections. We train our children to despise the very name of 'Yankee,' and so strong is the prejudice in the popular mind that no degree of social intercourse with those who come amongst us can prevent their feelings being wounded by sneers and reproaches. I am, I think, not a very bitter person in my prejudices, but I have never, though I have repeatedly made the effort, yet succeeded in exciting in my heart any warmth of feeling for a person born north of the Potomac.

"With this deep, abiding cleavage of the hearts of the people, how can there be political union? Specially difficult does the answer to the question become when we consider one section, with the gall of its hatred fresh stirred with party triumph, now essays to rule the other, and to rule it upon principles avowedly hostile to all the institutions which it holds most valued and sacred. Thus, I repeat, the two great difficulties in the way of an adjustment of this question are the antagonism of hearts and the fact that the government will be in the hands of a sectional party.

"Could some remedy be devised for the first of these evils it would soon work a cure upon the other. But where are we to look for a remedy? The answer is given, 'to the conservative masses of the people,' and the answer is complete when applied to the North, for with us sectional animosity would soon die out if there was no counter-irritant at the North; but at the North this virulence of feeling toward the South has become a political necessity: their property holders, who generally constitute the conservative portion of any community, feel that the spirit of the agrarian masses around them is already at their gates, and to turn it aside and divert its attention, they point to the power of the Federal government and the rich spoils of the South.

"They have not resorted to this terrible mode of averting the danger until many other expedients had been tried: many sops have already been given to Cerberus, one after another of which have been swallowed and the mouths of the greedy monster are still wide stretched. Magnificent poor houses, costly hospitals, asylums, free schools and other stupendous public charities, have been successively thrown out in the name of philanthropy and religion to stay the filibuster march of the mob, to smother out the kindling jealousy between labour and capital. Their efforts have proved vain: the mob turned again to rend and as a last resort capital at home, for its own safety, in the cloak of religion preaches a crusade against capital abroad. The Cotton King of Massachusetts, to save his vaults from pillage, points the hungering crowd at his door to King Cotton in Alabama. Thus the hope we might have in the conservatism of wealth is taken from us, and this very wealth becomes a source of alarm.

"We look in vain for good influences to the politicians, for the politician there (as he does here) rides into power upon the very passions we ask him to subdue. Who among them will endeavor to check the fell spirit? I see here and there an individual who sees the ruin of his country as the result of its teachings and raises his warning voice, but it is lost in the ravings of fanaticism and the senseless mob moves on its mad career. What the remedy? What the cure? I am unable to suggest. . .

"With these views of the causes of the trouble and this hopeless feeling as to their effects, I can scarcely look for any plan of compromise. . . What stand Virginia is now to take I am hardly prepared to say, but I am inclined to think that prompt secession is the only remedy and the only step which can bring the North to realize the condition of affairs at the South: for if they fully appreciate our position they would be more willing to grant us our rights. The secession of Virginia would bring them to their senses. . . I am not sure what is the sentiment of the people, but I think I speak that of the majority."

7

On February 9, Jefferson Davis was elected Provisional President of the Confederacy. Two days later John Minor of Fredericksburg expressed to Lanty his surprised disapproval of Charly's attitude:

"A passage in one of your father's letters seemed to hint that Charles is a secessionist. I can not tell you how this has afflicted me. That people untrained in the ways of legal investigation should find themselves mired in that bog might be looked for; but that a lawyer who either has studied political law or ought to have studied it, to hold the opinion that the Federal Constitution contemplated the integral parts were to withdraw at their mere pleasure is something unaccountable; it is *mean*: it is beating about the bush for excuses to gain that which they have a right to claim in an open, manly manner when oppression becomes intolerable, and all means of redress of a constitutional character have been tried in vain — Revolution."

And Mr. Blackford, in a letter to John B. Minor at the University, indulged in prophecy: "The Southern Confederacy will not last two years if it ever gets beyond the present Provisional Government. South Carolina is already very much dissatisfied and will in all probability withdraw. She at least has no idea of ever returning [to the Union] and she so unjustly charges upon the other States an intention of mere secession only as a means of re-establishing the Union."

John B. Minor was in for another thrust to the heart: his sister, Mrs. Ann Trueheart on March 5 (Texas had seceded February 1) wrote him from Galveston:

"Yours on Disunion & the cotton states reached me on Sunday the 3rd inst. I did not at all regret yr. having occupied the whole sheet with remarks on that all absorbing Topic, politicks: I desired to know yr. present thots & feelings, & was gratified: they were just what I shd. have expected from 'an old line Whig.' But it does not seem to me that we have become foreigners to each other by the Secession of Texas; you are all there in the N. (all except Abe Lincoln & his Black republicans) still very dear to my heart, to the heart of every true lover of his country; & those who love each other truly must of necessity be reunited; it is only hatred that divides, but 'love overcometh all sins.'

"[Cousin Lucy Byars] & I have both gotten letters from our dearly loved cousin Mary Blackford since Lucy was with us. In that to the latter, Mary copies a part of yr. late letter to her; in both you may guess what the principal subject was, & Cousin Lucy & I cd. only smile to see how totally our views & hers differed. We are staunch secessionists, all of us, from necessity at 1st but now from principle.

"We are glad that Va. is so deliberate in her movements, for secede she must & will at last, with all the other laggard states in her train, & it will give more weight & prestige to the movement in the World's eyes. And then, when we are reconstructed, our Union (with all those elements of black Republican discord cast out) with our own Stars & Stripes, — what a glorious union we shall have!"

Mr. Blackford gave Lanty the lastest news from Alabama on February 17: "Eugene's letters are written with a vigor and simplicity that makes them strikingly interesting. We had one last evening, dated the 11th . . . he explained the difficulties he had gotten into by his joining the military company which was ordered to Pensacola. . . He would probably have been compelled to go had not . . . a fellow . . . intimated he was not 'sound.' . . .

"A chain had been run up on the flag staff in the public square along side of the secession banner and some other subsequent indignity offered: a public meeting was called and death threatened the culprit if he could be found. Eugene says he has no doubt he would have been hanged had he been discovered. He found out that he had been charged as the perpetrator. . . . He took prompt measures to put down the report. But he is evidently suspected of *incivism*, — that undefined crisis of the reign of terror for suspicion of which so many thousands were murdered."

Mrs. Blackford never hesitated to express her feelings, censorious or not, far beyond the immediate family circle. Among her papers was a document on which she had noted, "A letter from Captain V. Moreau Randolph to me in answer to one I wrote him expelling my feelings of strong indignation on hearing he was one of those engaged in taking the Navy Yard at Pensacola and trampling on the American flag. This was before Virginia Seceded." It was dated from Montgomery, Alabama, April 2, 1861:

Mam' Peggy

Private Launcelot Minor Blackford
Rockbridge Artillery

Major Eugene Blackford
5th Alabama Infantry

William Matthews Blackford

Reverend Lancelot Byrd Minor

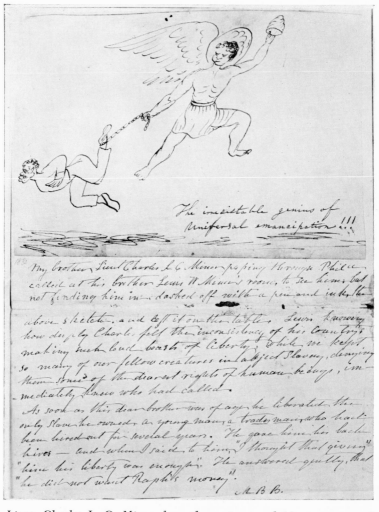

The irresistable genius of
Universal emancipation!!!

My brother Lieut Charles L C Minor passing through Phila
called at his brother Lewis W Minor's room, to see him, but
not finding him in dashed off with a pen and ink, the
above sketch, and left it on the table. Lewis knowing
how deeply Charles felt the inconsistency of his Country's
making such loud boast of liberty, while we kept
so many of our fellow creatures in abject slavery, denying
them some of the dearest rights of human beings, immediately knew who had called.

As soon as this dear brother was of age, he liberated the
only slave he owned, a young man, a trades man who had
been hired out for several years. He gave him his back
hires — and when I said to him, "I thought that giving"
"him his liberty was enough." He answered gently, that
"he did not want Ralph's money."
                                        M B B.

Lieut. Charles L. C. Minor drew the cartoon and Mary commented
upon it (although mistaken about the date of Ralph's freedom —
six years after Lieut. Minor came of age).

"Alas! my dear friend, how it grieves me to incur the disapprobation, if not the displeasure, of one whose good opinion I earnestly desire, my cousin: you seem indignant at my participating in the capture of the then United States Navy Yard at Pensacola. Of course nothing which I might say in my own defence could in the least mollify your feelings, and therefore I shall attempt no extenuation of my conduct. But you will, I am sure, give me credit for honesty of purpose, however much you may deplore what you regard as my unhappy delusion.

"We do not think alike on some subjects and on *one* we have always disagreed widely; but I do not let this dissimilarity produce the slightest estrangement of our friendship; I have ever felt for you the profoundest esteem and have ever loved you as might a brother: and these sentiments have animated the bosom of one who was pre-eminently capable of appreciating what is lovely and lovable in others because she herself was gifted with almost superhuman excellence. My dear wife loved you very much, my cousin.

"But permit me to say that I think you are apt to do wrong whenever your natural good sense is controlled by your tender emotions. It would however, ill become me to insist that I am less prone to err. Yet in *this* case I do think that I am right and you wrong.

"I have favored a political separation from the people of the North even as early as the year 1830. The South Carolinians were in the right *then*, and are entirely so *now*. The Northern people are and have ever been aggressive, intolerant, treacherous, — and we can never live in peace as one people. The South ought to have gone off to themselves in the year 1820. I despise the Yankee character. But what am I about to do? The very thing I had determined I would not do! — argue with my good Cousin. . .

"Dr. Randolph . . . says *I have done right* — and you, my very dear friend, are horror-stricken because I hauled down a piece of old *bunting* which had long ceased to command my respect!

"My cousin, may God indue us both with right judgement and pardon our errors, mistakes and short comings for our dear Saviour's sake."

8

Mary continued to look to Providence for resolution of the crisis but with dimming and despairing faith. On April 3 she wrote to John B. Minor:

"Since my Country has been in such a state of *threatened ruin* . . . if it were not that I could go to Him who rules the destinies of nations, I know not what I should do. But it is hard to believe and trust when the prospect seems to get darker and darker for our country and I see those going off whom I thought would stand firm . . . My own beloved sons, I labored to train them to love their country and to be willing to die (if need be) by her flag, and yet I may live to see them fighting against it. . . I will send you Eugene's last letter to let you see that, though he has been appointed Captain of an Alabama company he is as good a Union man as ever."

Her cousin replied on April 8:

"It always gratifies me to get your letters, and now more especially, because there are not many who sympathize as you do so entirely in my estimate of the Union. To my apprehension its maintenance is a question of no less moment than the freedom of our Country, and I will not consent to part with it while a possibility remains of preserving it on ground compatible with the honor and safety of these border-States. Neither passion nor fear moves me a hair's breadth from my position from which I shall recede only when I must; and when at length it becomes necessary (if it ever should unhappily become necessary) to denounce our separation from the North, I live in powerful hope we shall be able to form, upon the basis of the ultimatum which I trust Virginia will invoke the border-States to propose, — a confederacy of which these States will be a nucleus and the informing soul. . .

"I am glad to see Eugene so firm in his position. . . His situation is doubtless a difficult one, but I should not think he had mended it by accepting the Captaincy. Not withstanding his explanations to his Company, it would be only in accordance with human nature generally and the notions of these people particularly, if they should affect to regard this act as committing him to the participation in their madness. Eugene's friends here amongst the students are much disconcerted at his Unionism. It is a heroism of which very few indeed of our young men seem to be capable. The secession *feeling* is so predominant amongst our youths as practically to have extinguished all Union principles. They hasten 'to follow a multitude' to *folly*, and scarce one but vies with his fellows in frantic ultraism."

CHAPTER VIII

Virginia Must Fight

Delegates were appointed by the Virginia constitutional convention to visit Washington for the purpose of urging upon Mr. Lincoln and the United States Congress a policy of conciliation; others were sent on a like mission to Mr. Davis and the Confederate States Congress, but the calm and conservative counsel of Virginia was rejected by both sides. The convention had not, however, lost hope or given up its devotion to the Union when "South Carolina in the madness of her folly fired upon Fort Sumter." Three days later, April 15, Lincoln called for 75,000 troops to "suppress combinations in the seceded states too powerful for the law to deal with. . . Virginia was thus forced to decide between the two factions. Neutrality was impossible." [1]

The day after Lincoln's call, John B. Minor wrote to Mary:

"I can not but think of you now in this season of National woe, and as we have ever sympathized much in our views and feelings about public affairs, I know not to whom I can pour out my heart more freely.

"I devoutly thank God for the noble, moderate and conservative course so steadily pursued by this dear old Commonwealth in the midst of the wild storm of obloquy and detraction by which some of her unworthy sons have sought to drive her from her course, so that now when Civil War has been inaugurated, it has been by no act of hers. . . I rejoice with great joy that the terrible strife upon which we are now about to enter is forced upon us by Lincoln's administration in ruthless disregard of our protestations and honest attempts at pacification.

"History will visit upon the Cotton States its severest animadversions, and upon the Administration of Mr. Lincoln a condemnation not less emphatic, but we ceased not our patriotic and blessed office of *peace-makers* until the order for 75,000 troops, backed by the prevailing sentiment of even the Conservative masses of the North, sustaining and encouraging the President demonstrated that Subjugation was the object, — Subjugation of all who would not subscribe to the creed of the Conqueror. To tarry longer without the most active preparations for determined resistance is compatible with neither the safety nor the honour of Virginia. Lincoln avails himself of his official position and power and of the power of the Republican dynasties in the several States to precipitate war, notwithstanding the apparent tendencies of the people *seem* to have been towards peace. We are therefore shut up to the necessity of maintaining our rights but as we may.

"*My* preference is for a Confederacy of the Border States, and an alliance only with Cottondom, for which I am obliged to entertain a strong distrust and disapprobation, but I think we can not longer continue in Union with Mr. Lincoln's government, and whether we maintain the war which is upon us independently or unite with the Southern government is an incident only (although of great importance), and not the principal matter.

"These being my conscientious convictions, from which I should be glad to discern a loophole of escape if I could (for Liberty and Union I think are inseparable), I am prepared to make any required sacrifice to give effect to them. I am most thankful that I have not been called to the sacrifice until the cause became a righteous one by the exhaustion of all modes of reconciliation. Nothing remains now to the Christian patriot but to strike strongly for the right, humbly invoking the aid and blessing of our fathers' God.

"The very irregular fact, unparalleled I suppose in the annals of war, of a 30 hours' bombardment *without the loss of a life,* tends to reassure me. It looks wonderfully providential and suggests the hope, faint it is true, that God may have in reserve for us a miraculous deliverance yet. . . I greatly apprehend that one of the ill consequences of the steps Virginia is no doubt about to take will be the premature destruction of Slavery amongst us. My conscience is in no wise anxious on the subject of the institution (except to discharge a Christian master's duty in a more earnest spirit) . . . still to have it rudely and hastily abolished, or indeed abolished at all by *direct* human agency, will be attended, I fear, by very grievous mischief. But that with other more momentous evils we must encounter with such heroism as a religious sense of duty engenders, and, above all, my dear Cousin Mary, with as humble and devout reliance upon Him whose goodness has hitherto so blessed us, and who has promised that He will never leave nor forsake His people!" [2]

Mr. Minor's second wife was the older sister of Sue Blackford who had been visiting them at the University. On April 12 she had written Charly:

"Oh my darling husband, I do wish I could be with you at this moment, I feel as if you were just about to leave me forever. Just now a tremendous shout was raised on the Lawn, and the cry, 'fight, fight.' On inquiry we found that the news that Fort Sumter has been fired on had just arrived." [3]

"Poor Sue left us this morning with a sad heart," continued Minor, "anticipating that her husband might soon be called to the field. It is the province of your sex, in its weakness and its fears, vastly to influence ours in times like these. You women (I'm sure you would not have me say *you ladies*) possess so much generosity and magnanimous unselfishness that you can and do assist in inspiring a high-souled, self-sacrificing patriotism, which diffuses an aroma of virtue through Society which lingers long after the occasion is past which drew it forth. You didn't know perhaps that one of my earliest thrills of Hero's ardour was inspired by your animated recital to me in my boyhood at Minor's Folly, of Sir William Jones' fine ode, 'What constitutes a State?' How often

since have my eyes suffused with no unmanly moisture upon re-
peating the line,

> " 'Men, high minded men . .
> Men who their *duties* know,
> But know their *rights* and, knowing, dare maintain,
> Prevent the long-aimed blow,
> And crush the tyrant while they rend the chain.' "

2

Virginia, once the die was cast, began to arm with all her heart
and soul. Mr. Blackford gave Lanty the news of Lynchburg on
April 20:

"The events of the past week have been so momentous & stun-
ning that it seems a month since the news of the first gun being
fired reached us. . . Our streets remind you of a garrison town.
The Greys and the Home Guard drill three times a day and wear
their uniforms always, and expect orders every day. All were out
yesterday and made a fine appearance. Charles is First Lieutenant
of the troop and is the main spring. He has devoted himself to it
for the past week. Lewis, too, is as busy as possible.

"Our bank today voted $500 apiece to the volunteer Companies,
including the two just raised. The citizens have subscribed
$20,000 and put the Companies on a war footing. I saw a list
just now. Sixteen men gave 500 apiece. We shall have five hundred men ready in a week. I never saw such a feeling. . .

"Your mother was dreadfully shocked and overwhelmed by the
catastrophe of the ruin of that Union to which she was so much
devoted. She has become composed and is now cheerful. The preparation making for Lewis' departure engages her attention and so
far as the danger to which her boys are exposed, she behaves like
a Spartan mother. I hope she will soon be quite reconciled to the
Southern Confederacy.

"So far Virginia has done her duty nobly. She has nothing to
regret. Her skirts are free from the crime of destroying the Union.
I never honored her more than at this moment.

"A young clergyman of our church called just now," he continued. "He was short of funds, being on his return from Havana where he spent the winter for his health. He is the son of the Reverend Dr. Johnson of the Theo. Seminary. . . I gave him the money for his draft on his father and shall take him to my house to stay till Monday." [4] Mr. Blackford took in also the young minister's brother-in-law and traveling companion, the Reverend George W. Bethune.[5] These Northerners needed a haven for feeling in Lynchburg at that time was "at a violent pass."

Letters could still go from New York to Lynchburg without let or censorship. Early in May Mr. Blackford received this courteous, informative letter from the Reverend W. Allen Johnson:

"When I left Washington there were about 15,000 troops in the city, a number probably increased by this time to 25,000; most of them are fine looking men. The New York Seventh surpasses in drill, but is composed of young gentlemen, rather slim and undersized. There would be a good deal of *esprit* and dash about them but little endurance. The Rhode Islanders looked as if they would be the most formidable fighting men of any I saw. The city is not under martial law, nor are there any batteries *visible* to command the streets. Patrols guard all the approaches and public buildings.

"I heard from 'Secession' quarters many wild stories of Mr. Lincoln, as that he drank hard, was in a constant tremor, never slept in the White House, etc. I was fortunate enough, however, to get a true picture from a reliable source. My informant was Mr. John A. Jones, a very gentlemanly appearing man, formerly from Illinois. He said, 'I have known Mr. Lincoln intimately for 25 years. Brought up, as he has often told me, in the roughest way, and having in childhood very few advantages, he yet never learned to drink or to swear, nor did he ever acquire the so universal habit of using tobacco. Every one where he lived, even his political opponents, loved him, and he always bore the character of a *frank, bold* man.' He had seen him ten days before looking much better than when run down a month ago by office seekers, and that a friend told him that he kept a stiff upper lip and seemed to enjoy himself.

"You wished me to give you on my return an idea of the feeling in New York. In doing this, I will remember that you want *the truth,* and do not desire me to conceal the real state of the case because it will necessarily jar your own feelings. I have been anxiously careful while at the South to endeavor to inform myself and possess myself of the Southern side of the great question. This I think I have been able to do to some extent — sufficiently so at any rate to see that this quarrel follows that universal law of all quarrels, — 'There is no quarrel but has *two* sides.'

"You, Sir, know as well as I do that there are hundreds of thousands who, however they may have differed in sentiment, would never have urged matters to the bloody arbitrament of the sword. Now, however, individuals are powerless and all are by the necessities of the case forced to take sides. The very same crisis which drove all you Union men over to the Secessionists has driven every Northerner to support the Government, and to accuse Northern conservatives of dishonesty (as some of the Southern papers are doing) is as unfair as a similar charge would be against Southern Unionists.

"As you at the South feel fully persuaded of the righteousness of your cause and of the entire wrongfulness of the opposing side, *just so* we feel here. . . In the first place, it must be borne in mind that the States Rights doctrine has no existence at the North. We all endorse Henry Clay's doctrine as laid down in his speech in 1850, 'If Kentucky tomorrow unfurls the banner of resistance, I will never fight under that banner. I *owe* a *paramount* allegiance to the whole Union, a *subordinate one to my own State'* . . . The Northern 'case,' as a lawyer might say, would be stated thus:

" 'We had a free and excellent Government which (whatever its defects) had advanced our national interests and made us the happiest people on the earth. No evils existed which did not admit of a constitutional remedy when a conspiracy of designing men broke out in South Carolina, a conspiracy self-avowed, and which unblushingly declared that the arguments it had used to ensure its success were all shams.

" 'The deepest and sternest indignation was aroused against those who were disturbing the peace of the country. The Government however, acts with the most astonishing forbearance. The Secession movement every where scorns all legal forms, and with reactionary violence seizes all the national property it can lay its hands on. At last, when an attempt is made to provision one of the military posts of the nation, it is attacked and reduced by armed violence.

" 'When at last the patience of the State is exhausted and she calls out a force to repossess her property, this action which meets with warm approval in most of the loyal states, (strange to say!) is considered a declaration of war by the border slave states. It turns that great party which had hitherto been apparently battling for the Union into the enemy's ranks. Why should this be, we ask, unless their sympathies with the Conspiracy are greater than their sympathies with that Government which for 80 years has been our greatest blessing? A general belief prevails that the Union men are overborne by the passions of the Crisis. I thought the presence of a Union Army would again give them the upper hand'. . .

"Here there is no mob law or reign of terror as the Southern papers say, — but it is a time of war and the unlimited freedom of public opinion is checked, as it has always been in England and every where under similar circumstances. Men's feelings are high strung, and 'aid and comfort to the enemy' is now treason. Mr. Lawrence Beach, a gentleman formerly of New York and now living at Newport, expressed the wish in the company of Rhode Island people that 'not one of their regiment just sent off would return alive.' One present pulled his nose three times, once for each of his sons in that regiment, — feeling just as you would if some one should express such a wish about your Lynchburg troop. Mr. Beach was afterwards mobbed and compelled to flee. All such things are to be lamented. They never occurred before and are peculiar to 'war' time, but if men will lose all common sense and outrage the deepest feelings of the people among whom they dwell, they must expect them every where.

"I hope you will not take all the 'war articles' of our Northern press as affording a fair index of the temper of the people, or at any rate judge them with the same allowance that you make for similar blood-thirsty utterances in the Richmond papers. But the tempest runs high just now, and I hardly dare speak without incurring a controversy, as my mild peace views are all too far behind the prevailing temper. Nations, I think, have an instinct warning them of danger as well as animals.

"The real root of the matter here is that all feel that if we let the South go in peace we sanction a principle which must at last destroy us. We believe the States Rights doctrine false, we know it to be fatal. Next year New England may secede, the year after the North-West. All that makes us a nation is at stake, and each man's happiness and prosperity is concerned.

"This belief is deep down in the hearts of the people. We deplore the event, we deprecate the sad necessity, but we are going to test the question of Federal and States rights and settle it *once for all*. This you may rest assured of. As an honest friend I dare not conceal it if I would. We live, as we believe, to hold up our Union brethren and restore that free and noble government which traitors are seeking to overthrow, and we are prepared to spend five hundred millions of money and sacrifice 500,000 men if need be to do it."

Having set forth the Northern position earnestly and uncompromisingly, the minister wound up his letter with words of appreciation. "I shall always remember with grateful feelings your kindness to me at the great crisis of excitement and shall always be happy to hear from you," he added. "Remember me to Mrs. Blackford and all your family." [6]

3

On April 23, "amidst the cheers and blessings of the men and the cheers and sobs of the women," Lynchburg sent off three infantry companies filled with raw recruits. The Home Guard, the first one organized, included Lewis, and Dr. Blackford's sons, Dr. Benjamin Blackford and young William H. Blackford. Mary's husband noted in his diary: "There was scarcely a dry eye to be seen. I certainly thought none the less of our gallant young men when I saw their cheeks moistened with tears: I had my confidence in them even increased. Lewis . . . when he took leave of his mother, in regard to her feelings, suppressed his own." [7]

The next day Lewis wrote excitedly from Richmond: "All here safe — quartered at the Old Central Hotel with crackers and decayed beef — raw — to eat. I learn from what seems to be the best authority that it has been decided to take Washington: when, I do not know. Troops arriving hourly. We were formally mustered into service this evening. Lynchburg by far the best troops here next to Richmond. Men in high spirits. . . Companies are leaving here for different points on the Potomac." [8]

Two weeks later Lewis reported from Manassas Station: "Arrived here yesterday morning and have just received orders to go somewhere and do something instantly. Where and what we do not know.[9] I write in accoutrements and surrounded by luggage. To all cartridges have been dealt out." After detailed messages to the family and "Give my love to the servants," he added a word of comfort, "Tell Mother I am *better prepared to fight,* I hope, than when I saw her last." [10]

On April 28 Mr. Blackford abstracted in his diary a letter just received from his son in Alabama:

"Eugene speaks of his Union sentiments, & how entirely they were (like my own) revolutionized by the Proclamation. His company had been ordered to hold itself ready for marching orders for Texas. On learning that Virginia had seceded, he told his men that his first duty was to her and he must return to her soil. They would not accept his resignation and declared that no one else should lead them to the field, and that if he resigned they would disband. He agreed, therefore, to remain. He says his greatest pride would be to bring such a company to the defence of Virginia. He speaks in terms of deepest regret of the anguish he thinks his mother will feel. . . I wrote to Captain Randolph at Montgomery to use his influence to effect Eugene's wishes.

"The ascendancy Eugene has acquired in a village in Alabama where at first he was an object of suspicion because of his strong Union sentiments, is very remarkable considering he is only twenty-two years old. His knowledge of tactics and military training have stood him in better stead than his greek, latin or french. I confess I should take particular pride in seeing him march in at the head of a company which he has raised and made the best in Alabama." [11]

A few weeks later he noted: "Eugene left us at 3 P.M. to go to Alabama to bring his company to Virginia. If he can not get orders from the C. S. Government or an allowance of transportation, he will raise the money there to bring his men to Virginia where their services will be accepted by the Governor. It is a romantic expedition. . . He goes at his own expense 800 miles to place himself at their head and take the chances of getting them here in some way, and he will not fail." [12]

In the meantime, William, eight years older than Eugene, had been active in organizing the Washington Mounted Rifles in Abingdon. He and his troop had been ordered to Richmond to join the First Virginia Cavalry. From a camp near the capital he wrote his mother on May 1:

"If it were not for the terrible work before us, this life would be exceedingly pleasant. Already we are feeling the benefit in hardening muscles, sharpening appetites and unbroken sleep. . . I meet here old college mates from every Section of the State, privates in volunteer Companies, the very flower of the State, the best and bravest blood in Virginia.

"Alas, who are they to meet? the villainous offscouring of the earth; I read from the New York papers this morning that the leaving of the regiments for the South had cleaned the city of every pickpocket, burglar and rowdy, and, adds the paper, may they cut every Southern throat from Washington to the Gulf. Another paper says, 'No need of bounty to soldiers for all know that Southern lands are rich and Southern women fair.' — but I turn from such thoughts. The only Southern land they will ever possess will measure 6 feet one way and 2 the other.

"I think our men are the most orderly, the truest and kindliest I ever met, I mean as a Company. There are 15 in my tent, and I read the Bible to them every night. Moreover, they are always laughing and cheerful. I wish you could see us with a tin cup of coffee, a piece of *fat* (all fat) meat and a hunk of stale bread, sitting on the ground eating ferociously. The [V.M.I.] cadets are here and are of immense use in drilling squads.

"There are 1500 South Carolinians in camp just below us and 500 Artillery close by. The former are terribly worn and dirty, but the men are gentlemen. I recognize many old college mates in the ranks." [13]

William enclosed in his letter the following clipping from a Confederate newspaper:

"In the *Tribune* of May 1st, 1861, that worthy held the following language: 'We mean to conquer them — not merely to *defeat*, but to CONQUER, and to *subjugate* them. But when the rebellious traitors are overwhelmed in the field and scattered like leaves before an angry wind, *it must not be to return to peaceful and contented homes.* They must find poverty at their firesides and see *privation* in the anxious eyes of *mothers* and the rags of *children.* The whole coast of the South from the Delaware to the Rio Grande must be a *solitude!* '" [14]

On receipt of this letter Mrs. Blackford wrote with characteristic impetuosity and virtuous indignation to the Reverend George W. Bethune, who had been a guest in her home a scant two weeks earlier. On May 15 the clergyman replied:

"Your letter of the 4th has only just now come, and it affects me deeply. I remember the kind hospitality to which I was welcomed under your roof with a lively gratitude, and deplore the baseness of politicians and the folly of their dupes which have brought our Country to this terrible war, dividing those who sincerely love one another into hostile bands. . . I continually pray to God that even now He would interpose, but none except Himself can do so.

"No human voice, however beloved or venerable, can prevail here to arrest the determination of our people to vindicate the flag they love so much which has been so foully outraged by the assaults of ruthlessness, and to defend our Capitol so impudently threatened by such Ambitious Conspirators as Jefferson Davis and such insane braggarts as Wise, etc. Dr. Minor will tell you that no man after his ability exerted himself more zealously than I to keep our people at peace with the South. I was only one of countless numbers at the North so disposed, but the first shot at Sumter — the first clearly hostile assault upon the flag which is the symbol of our Nation and our honour, changed this friendly temper in a moment to a determination to defend our nation until death at any cost and by every means of *honourable* warfare.

"But, my dear Madam, allow me on my *Christian Veracity* to disabuse your mind of the monstrous error which you have fallen into with regard to the feelings of our people towards yours. It is true they will not permit us any longer to consider them our Countrymen or fellow Citizens; indeed their words and their actions compel us to regard them as our enemy; but, while reluctantly accepting the conditions of war which have been forced upon us, we have become neither Savage nor atrocious.

"I can not doubt the honesty of your son's statement when he says that *he read from a New York paper* the infamous passages which you transcribed, but I must believe he meant to say that they *purported* to be extracts from a New York paper, for I say unhesitatingly that a wretch who could conceive such thoughts and put them into words *would be hooted and execrated by our whole community as a Monster not fit to live.*

"I read myself seven or eight daily New York papers which comprise all that have any respectability; there are, however, others which are never received in decent families but circulate among pugilists, horse racers and such characters. Of these I can not speak from personal knowledge. I say, however, unhesitatingly *that I never saw or heard of any such expressions being made in any New York papers.* In confirmation of what I say, I enclose an extract from the *New York Express* of the fourteenth, headed,

'The Spirit Arising' — which shows me that the source from which your son derived his impressions was a forgery and lie of the *Richmond Whig* and which will show you the abominable manner in which the Southern people are wickedly deceived by their own political Newspapers.

"The Calumny has not even the merit of Originality. It was charged almost in the same words on the British Army before the battle of New Orleans and I believe with equal falsehood. It was said at the time that the pass-word ordered by Sir Richard Pakenham the night before the assault was 'Beauty and Booty;' pardon me, however, for enclosing an extract from the *Nashville Banner* threatening in so many words such a detestable treatment upon the women and children of Union men in that section of the country.

"Why, my dear Madam, are our troops sent South? Is it not because our flag was there insulted and the safety of the Capitol threatened in the most braggadocio manner by the officers of the Southern Confederacy? We did not make War upon you, — on the contrary, a very large Majority of our people considered such a War as an unparalleled evil — but you made War upon us. I have never seen such unanimity, such enthusiasm, such devotion as the fall of Sumter awakened in all classes of our Citizens; nor is the Spirit lessened by the lapse of time. Our Northern blood, unlike that of the South, is not readily heated.

"A number of a Massachusetts Regiment that had traveled all night from Boston on entering the breakfast room of the 5th Avenue Hotel to breakfast went down upon their knees to make their morning prayer before they touched their meal. Similar things might be told almost without number. We are far from being all Lincolnites. New York, which gave the largest majority against him, has sent the largest number of volunteers. We are all *one for our flag* since seven thousand cowards cannonaded seventy half-starved men for thirty-six hours to strike it down. A Southern man gives his allegiance to his *State*. We Northern people love *our State, but our allegiance is to the Union of which our flag is the Symbol.*

"I join my prayers with yours, my dear Madam, for the mitigation of the evils of terrible War, and that it may please God to unite us all again as a Christian Nation for 'with Him all things are possible,' but we can not forget that outrages on one side will be apt to provoke as cruel revenges from the other, — even as I write, the sending forth of privateers by Jefferson Davis *'with bountys promised for every Northern Man killed and every Northern man taken prisoner'* is rousing our rural and mountain population to an awful degree. Vermont has just sent her first regiment, one thousand strong, scarce a man of which is less than six feet high. Yet the whole of whom will speak fewer words in a month than Governor Wise would write in a forenoon — and drink less whisky in a year than a Southern Company would in a day, and under whose flag one of your Virginia girls would be as safe as in her Mother's Chambers.

"I have written thus long, my dear Madam, to give you as far as possible a true statement of the Case and enclose some extracts from Newspapers for the same purpose — not without fear lest the size of the package may prevent its reaching you as suspiciously large. My special prayers will be offered for you and yours that God may have you in His holy keeping." [15]

Old Captain Moreau Randolph would have enjoyed Mary Blackford's bitter letter to George Bethune: he would have thought that he had converted her to his way of thinking. The minister on the other hand, while he would have thoroughly approved the scolding she had given the sea captain in March, would not have been able to understand why she had completely reversed her position.

These lines to her brother Lucius that spring came straight from Mary's heart:

"I love to think those I loved have died before these sorrows came: My father, my mother, my Lucy, my two brothers and many other dear ones did not live to see these times.

"I have five sons in this dreadful civil war. Lanty is going soon to be an artilleryman. He has been too sick since he came home till now. I have heard of mothers' saying they are glad to have

their sons go; they wish they had a hundred to send. I am not one
of these heroines. I regard it as a dire necessity only. . .

"We hear frequently from brother John. . . He feels the ruin
of his country as I think my father would have done. He makes
us all laugh very much with his caustic remarks. . .

"Will you offer up prayers for my boys that they may be prepared for death, made true servants of Jesus Christ? This is my
highest ambition for them." [16]

4

Much as she loved the Union, Mary Blackford probably loved
Virginia more. Much as she deplored the war then, she was consoled in that her five sons saw service for the most part in their
natal state. Often they ran into each other. Often for weeks at a
time they were in the same neighborhood and several times three
of them were in the same battle. Through mutual friends too they
managed to keep in touch with each other. Sometimes they met in
Richmond and sometimes several of them were in Lynchburg together, for that city after fourteen years was really home to them.
Whenever one could get leave he headed for Lynchburg; even
William would stop over on his way to his own home in Abingdon.
Sometimes one was sent to Lynchburg on a detail. All too often
one was sent home to convalesce from malaria, typhoid fever,
dysentery, or some other disease contracted in the service. But
Mary Blackford had never pampered her sons and from earliest
childhood she had trained them to accept death as a natural event:
it was never necessary for her to provide a haven in which one
might recover from "battle fatigue."

Mary's intense interest in her soldier sons, as well as her reaction
to the crisis which deprived her of their presence, is well illustrated by the following letter which she wrote Lanty, July 13,
1861, shortly after he entered training camp at the University:

"Tell me how the life agrees with your health. I like to hear
all the details, the fatigue must go hard with you when the weather
is so hot. How long do you sleep? I used to think that you spent

too much of your time in sleep, which is as bad as too little. I wish you would write often to your brothers. . .

"Charles did join the church, and he will I hope be a whole souled Christian. He is near the enemy and often engaged in scouting parties when he is exposed to much danger. Eugene's regiment forms the advanced guard of the army. Your Papa thinks the battle may be going on now. And Wm's division of the army in Winchester is in more danger of a battle than that.

"I do not know how I can be so calm — there seems to be a dark cloud hanging over me but my heart seems cold and dead. These are awful times. It seems impossible that such things can be as are daily passing now, and all so rapid, and such horrid uncertainty hangs over us. There was a time when we could say with truth, 'The Lord reigneth, let the earth rejoice,' — What have we to depend on but this? Prayer, prayer, is all we can do, — prayer for faith and His protection."

She and Mr. Blackford were proud of all their sons, satisfied that each did his duty manfully.[17] If they felt a bit of extra pride in the conspicuous gallantry of William and Eugene that made them both lieutenant colonels before it was all over, they may be pardoned for it.

On June 10, 1861, Mr. Blackford recorded in his diary: "Eugene's ambition was at length gratified for he marched into town today at the head of a company, ninety-six strong, brought from a distant part of the Confederacy, to the command of which he had been elected in a manner highly honorable and flattering to him. He was cheered as they went to their quarters in Holcombe Hall. . .

"Eugene was incessantly engaged all day. I did not have ten minutes conversation with him. He tried to get permission to stop here to go into camp to drill and equip his company, but no notice was taken of his application and he has determined to go on tomorrow. The affection and respect of the men for Eugene is most extraordinary. Some of the members, quite ignorant of my relationship to him, expressed themselves in the most enthusiastic terms. They seem devoted to him and think there was never such a captain. . . He understands the drill perfectly, thanks to Murphy's training, and has a quiet dignity calculated in itself to inspire respect. The tones of his voice in giving words of command are such as indicate the necessity of obedience." [18]

Eugene had his hands full near Richmond with "the arduous duty of the Captain of an independent Company," but he was finally able to get his men into uniform and to gather equipment for them. But he complained, "The merchants here charge more than double prices for everything. I have been utterly ashamed of my State, particularly of its capital." [19] His "Company won quite a reputation for drill and discipline" [20] and was promptly placed in the advanced guard of the Army of the Potomac (a term not yet adopted by the Federal forces). In a letter which he wrote to his father on July 12, Eugene added: "Our red and yellow badges were given us last night: we are to be distinguished from the Yankees by them, — a melancholy reflection indeed that we should resemble them so much as to require a distinguishing badge in an engagement." [21]

On July 4, 1861, the diarist lamented:

"American Independence day! Alas! Alas! Alas! that it should dawn on the eighty-fifth anniversary upon States discordant and belligerent. I wonder if, in its celebration today, the yankees will not think of the inconsistency of commemorating a deed of separation from an oppressive government when they are trying to force another people to submit to what is far greater oppression." [22]

Lewis had not had a chance to fire any of the cartridges dealt out to him at Manassas, for he had been transferred to Norfolk to serve as a topographical engineer. (Young Dr. Blackford had also been taken out of the line and assigned to professional duties.) In Norfolk, Lewis, who loved the creature comforts in spite of the austerity of his upbringing, had secured luxurious living accommodations and, though working hard on his maps, was managing as usual to have a good time. He also enjoyed passing on atrocity stories.

"I have seen some fugitives from Hampton!" he wrote in June. "The state of affairs there is truly awful, a vast army of Savages, mostly beastly foreigners, are camped over a ground several miles therearound, and they have committed and are committing every species of outrage . . . I met a gentleman in Richmond just from one of the lower counties of Maryland: he owns or did own a large estate nearly opposite Mathias Pome. He is educated, very intelligent, refined and pious. I heard him tell with streaming eyes of the horrible barbarity of the Federals in his county. They quartered 1500 Yankees (as a punishment to the county) upon them; they don't even go through the form of having a commissary; they live off the citizens, killing their cattle and poultry, insulting the women, hunt down the men like wild beasts; my informant concealed himself for days in the woods before he could escape. They had previously burned his house, killed his cattle, stolen his horses and taken away his negroes by force." 23

But Lewis was also concerned about his less fortunate brothers. "I wish you would send me such of the boys' letters as you can spare," he asked his father. "I am perpetually unhappy about them and if they suffered as much from apprehension of danger as I do for them, they would be very great cowards indeed." 24

The fate of a soldier wounded in that war, as in every previous war, was grim. Before it was over Dr. Jonathan Letterman had organized a good ambulance service in the Northern Army of the Potomac, but the Confederate casualty who had no relatives to look after him was largely dependent upon the kindness of civilians in the neighborhood. William, Charles and Eugene, their father knew, were in the First Battle of Manassas. (Their conduct that day warranted Lewis in saying, "I have bragged absurdly about the boys since the battle." 25) The guns were hardly cool therefore, before Mr. Blackford was on his way to the battlefield. It was the second of many such trips he made. Though he returned exhausted, "he enjoyed the novelty of the scenes, and he was for days the centre of eager listeners." 26 Though he never found a son wounded on one of these trips, they gratified his military curiosity and his first hand account of conditions served to allay in a measure their mother's anxieties.

Soon after Mr. Blackford got back from Manassas, Launcelot came home from training camp on his way to enlist in the Rockbridge Artillery.[27] His health was quite restored and his father was pleased with his looks: "In his neat but simple uniform of gray, with erect carriage, bronzed face and well trimmed beard, he looks the very beau ideal of a soldier." [28]

With the departure of her last son for active duty, Mary Blackford wrote to her Cousin John that she felt bereaved, "yet I keep up a tolerably good heart. I won't think of their being killed or wounded, and there are some bright spots. Charly's conversion is one of them." [29]

After visiting Charly and Eugene and various friends in camp around Fairfax Court House, on September 2 Lanty joined the Rockbridge Artillery. This company, already famous, had been organized in Lexington. Its first captain was the rector of Grace Church, the Reverend William Nelson Pendleton,[30] an old West Pointer and the first rector of the Episcopal High School. Like many of his fellow-townsmen, he was an old friend of the Blackfords. The Rockbridge Artillery attracted a fine group of young men, including many former students of the High School and of the University. Among the University graduates was Clem Fishburne, who remembered Captain Pendleton chiefly for "his long-winded and lugubrious prayers." [31]

In addition to many old college friends, including Randolph Fairfax, David Barton, Kinloch Nelson, Wash Stuart, Joe and Walter Packard, Lanty found no less than six other descendants of his great-grandfather, Major John Minor of Topping Castle, in the ranks of this company during the war, as well as the youngest son of General Lee. The companionship of these choice souls made life bearable to Launcelot. Unlike William and Eugene, he hated the military life with all his heart.[32]

At the time of his enlistment, "the harness of a horse was to young Blackford a complex mystery and one can imagine his preparedness for such service when his first attempt resulted in the gears being put on hindpart first, and the jeers of the veterans and the contempt of the old artillery horse." [33] (Or, as Launcelot himself wrote in after years, "I had to drive one pair of artillery horses and, of course, take care of them, an unpleasant experience and not the more agreeable from the chaff to which my inexperience exposed me at the hands of my friends." [34] For the most part however, he was a cannoneer attached to Gun No. 6.[35]) "While at first they laughed at his finicalness, preciseness, delicacy, and utter ignorance of the most ordinary material things, they soon grew to respect him and admire him, and saw him develop into a cool, courageous soldier who was as religious in the performance of his soldier's duties as at all times he was in his daily prayers." [36]

In a letter of September 30 from the camp of his company, Lanty asked help from home in their housekeeping. "We are not satisfied with the man we have to cook for us," he wrote, "and I wish you would look about and see what you can do for us in Lynchburg now the servants have come home from the springs. . . . I suppose a free negro would be the best chance. It is to *cook,* and if possible to wash, for a mess of 10 or 12 gentlemen; we would pay more, of course a great deal for a man to do both. We would pay, as we have been paying, a very liberal compensation, even as high as $25 a month, for a good hand to cook and wash both."

On October 14, from the vicinity of Fairfax Court House, Lanty recounted a pleasant experience. "Yesterday, being Sunday," he wrote, "we had, as usual, religious services, preaching morning and afternoon by Colonel Pendleton. . . Our services were held in a barn and very well attended, particularly in the afternoon. . . The responses were rendered pretty well. . . There were in attendance officers from Brig. Gen. down to junior 2d Lt., the whole forming a reverent audience.

"Bro. Charles and Eugene rode over before service," he continued, "attended it and then came home with me for dinner. Soon after dinner I heard the fall of horse's feet up the row of tents . . . and looked out to see who came. I descried a fine looking officer in full Captain's uniform, sash, etc., but not recognizing any one I knew, as I thought, resumed my seat and went on talking. Eugene, however, looked out a moment after and with

quicker eye, having seen the officer in question a week ago, immediately recognized brother William. I had not seen him before
since he passed through Lynchburg on his way eastward with his
Co., and a greater contrast you could scarcely imagine, particularly
in respect to costume. His face is much as it used to be, except a
cast of seriousness, perhaps severity, incurred doubtless by habits
of command, added to the stirring and even terrible scenes through
which he has in the past few months passed. His hair is longer
than when you saw him, and his beard and mustaches longer a
good deal and very gracefully turned out. . . His arrival . . .
was particularly acceptable at the time he came, seeing that it
made a complete family reunion of the members included in the
army of the Potomac. . .

"The pleasure I have in my 3 brothers being captains," he
added, "is heightened into a very solid and well-founded satisfaction by the knowledge that their posts have been won by merit,
not given by favour; that they are eminently fitted for them; that
they enjoy the respect, confidence and esteem of their superior
officers as well as subordinates and men; that they are all, last but
not least, as gallant and true men as any the army contains. . .
It is a great privilege, one of God's best blessings I consider it, to
have among one's brothers not one of whom other than good and
honorable mention will be made."

The other three also wrote home of this happy day and it was
long remembered. These four were not all together again for
thirty months.

"Mother wants to know how I stand the hardships of camp,"
Lanty resumed the next day. "I reply that I may say pretty well. . .
I see around me in this co. scores of men accustomed to living
in all the comfort I have, who are now subject to just the same
trials and privations that I am. . . I am quite conscious that as
winter draws on they will multiply, but, by the grace of God,
I trust I shall be enabled to stand them worthily. I trust and pray
the blessing of health may be continued me. I take considerable
pains to use means thereto, e.g., washing my head, neck & face
in cold water every morning, & my whole person whenever I can."

His mother replied on October 20: "How good my dear Lanty is to think of us so much now when our anxieties are so great. May God bless you for it, my dear boy. . . It is enough to make the heart bleed to think of what our poor soldiers suffer. I am glad that you are so explicit in putting so much of your whereabouts in your letters, it is useful information. . . Your letters contain so much that is interesting that I do not know where to begin to answer. That meeting of the four brothers went to my heart. God grant that they, with the one in Norfolk, may meet where parting is no more.

"I am glad that you stand cold so well. I was always troubled to see you so chilly. A good way to prevent this chilliness is to wash your whole person in cold water every day, rubbing a good deal with a coarse towel. I used to be chilly in my youth, but this has cured me of it. I have heard your Uncle James say that after rubbing well in salt water at sea (where you know they are not allowed to have a fire) he would come to his breakfast quite warm while the rest of the Mess would be shivering with cold. . . How does Berkeley stand the exposure? Tell him of the great importance of the free use of cold water.

"I am glad to hear of the prayer meetings, more necessary if possible there than any where. It may be that some of those who join will soon be summoned before God's bar."

She concluded that letter, as she always did, "if you should be ill or wounded, send for me."

The same day Mr. Blackford wrote Lanty: "Though my confidence in the state of our generals and the valor of our troops is unbounded, I have not been a student of military history so long as not to know that the result of a battle very often depends upon contingencies which neither genius nor valor can control, and on public grounds therefore, I can not look upon the near approach of a decisive encounter of the two armies without infinite solicitude. I believe, however, that God will defend the right and favor us as He has so signally done throughout this unhappy war." But to his diary a few days later he confided, "The enemy outnumbers us so greatly, their Army is so much more thoroughly armed and equipped, and they have such vast reserves at their command that my heart sighs at the prospect." [37] His sons though were still sanguine: on October 30 Charly wrote his wife, "I believe Eugene and Willy would be heartbroken if the war were to come to an end. They regard it as a great frolic." [38]

5

In his letter of October 23 to Lanty, Mr. Blackford had said: "The house is now free of company — the first time in months. We all enjoy the reform — especially your mother who of late has suffered a great deal. There has been no diminution of sick in the hospital, in town or camp."

This is the first indication that the Blackfords' hospitality was being abused.[39] The central location of Lynchburg had its disadvantages. Often there were as many as twenty people under their roof. How Mrs. Blackford was able to find food for so many remains a mystery. But the most distressing aspect was that trains and packets usually left Lynchburg before dawn and Mr. Blackford, always the conscientious host, had to get up at three o'clock sometimes four or five times a week to escort his guests to the depot or wharf. As frequently he would get up equally early to meet expected guests; often they failed to arrive and, particularly in '63 and '64, the train might be several hours late. To make matters worse, he never slept well when he had to get up early for he had no alarm clock.

Perhaps the trouble and expense of constant company, relatives, even remote ones, friends and friends of friends, were not realized by Lanty, but he approved of the family's hospitality. He wrote his mother, "It is a source of much pleasure to me that our house has so long been an asylum for sick soldiers." [40]

Mr. Blackford bridled just a bit at this, and perhaps wishing to disillusion his idealistic son, rejoined: "We have no soldiers here now except those in hospital or convalescent. There has been a great deal of old soldiering, and the kindness of families has been grossly abused by men lingering when they were fully able to rejoin their corps." [41]

When late in October, Jackson was ordered to Winchester he succeeded in getting his old brigade, including the Rockbridge Artillery, detached from Johnston at Centreville, and transferred to him. At the completion of the movement, Lanty wrote from near Winchester: "We would be quite content indeed here but for the unwonted and I think absurd strictness about going to town. . . This strictness is in some measure no doubt due to the drunkenness and lawlessness of the Infantry on the way from Centreville here. Some of our men behaved ill too." [42]

Launcelot was evidently careful to spare his mother so far as possible details of the seamy side of war, but his friend, Sergeant Clem Fishburne felt no such inhibitions when he came to write his memoirs.

"One night we encamped in Loudoun County not far from a distillery," Fishburne narrated, "and too many of our boys, the rougher sort of them, got supplied with brandy. They made night hideous to the soberer men and we had great trouble next day in getting enough of the regular drivers who were sober enough to do their duty. Many were hauled along on gun carriages with the prospect of being punished at the end of their journey. The following afternoon we reached the Shenandoah River at Snicker's Ferry in Clark County and had to cross the stream on ferry boats. There was of course great delay on the east bank of the stream, and whilst there some of the tipsy fellows got into a fight. Others joined the combatants and the result of the mêlée was that one man had a leg broken and several had black eyes. At last we got safely over, left the wounded hero of this disgraceful battle at a house and went into camp. . . The broken legged man recovered and afterwards at Malvern Hill was killed by a shell from a U. S. gunboat." [43]

Camp life that fall, however, was not all discipline and drudgery for the young soldier. Three Winchester families were represented in the Rockbridge Artillery, and the members of the older generation had for many years been friends of Lanty's father and mother. On November 22 he told them of his extracurricular activities.

"Thursday evening, by an uncommon indulgence of the Captain," he wrote, "six or eight of us were permitted to spend at Mr. Conrad's. It was one entertainment of a weekly series which are being held in town at different houses. They call them *bees*: the ladies having to work or knit for the soldiers; the gentlemen to entertain the ladies. The refreshments are of the simplest kind and inexpensive, just right these hard times. At Mrs. Conrad's bee I thought the aggregate of knitting done by about three dozen ladies would not have suffered to *sock* one defender of Southern liberty. I saw no other work going on. This *we* attribute to the fascinations of the delegation from the Rockbridge Artillery, whose first appearance on such an occasion it was." 44

Lanty was finally able to announce the solution of the housekeeping problems of Mess No. 10 on December 2: "We have engaged in our mess during the last ten days an excellent servant. His chief function is cooking, but he serves us in other matters and by his presence we find our comfort greatly enhanced. He is a most aristocratic-looking free Negro from Hardy County, and rejoices in the intensely Hebrew cognomen of Israel. His dress is ordinarily better than that of the men he waits upon, albeit his demeanor is as deferential as his efficiency is satisfactory." 45

Lewis was enjoying himself in Norfolk. In the summer he had written his mother, "[Major] General [Benjamin] Huger is singularly polite to me. . . I go a good deal to his house and he never forgets to inquire about you." 46 The North, which had never surrendered Fort Monroe, was landing troops south of Norfolk in December to force the capitulation of the city, but Lewis, nothing daunted, wrote to his mother again on December 10: "I never saw General Huger in such spirits. 'With God's help,' said the old gentleman very reverently, 'We'll lick them like the Devil!' I have been assigned to his staff when the day comes."

The young engineer was very much wrought up. "I have been reading the *New York Herald* of the 7th," he exploded. "It is like catching a glimpse of the fires of hell. I wish all our people could read more of the Northern papers. They would see a malignity which is absolutely fiendish, that sort of malignity that only cowards can feel. The people, the genuine native Yankees, howl themselves hoarse for blood, cry to their army of brutal hired foreigners to push on, give no quarter, to arm the slaves and they offer them unlimited spoiling of a rich empire for reward. Should we be conquered, the world will never have imagined such a doom as they think to make ours. Judging from their papers, they seem to think that we are already at their mercy: how they gloat over the idea of a general slave insurrection! Bathing the Country knee deep in blood is a favourite idea. Probably the true source of hate peeps out in their bitter allusions to 'Aristocracy,' 'a grand rebellion of aristocrats,' and of how they hate a gentleman. The hate that base blood has cherished towards our class for 4,000 years. Do you think I am ridiculous? I feel it (not that I am ridiculous) from my soul. And blood will tell!"

As 1861 drew to a close, Mary Blackford wrote to John B. Minor at the University: "I have more to think of and to do lately, and my suffering always has the effect of confusing my mind and unfitting me for all mental and bodily effort." Concerning the recent death of his brother Charles, she continued: "How much he has escaped too of the troubles that are thickening around us. Oh, my Country! how hard it is to realize that such things can be going on in you, once the happiest the world ever saw. To me, my Uncle's home and family, in their habits, principles and character seemed the very embodiment of the virtuous simplicity of a pure Republic, such as the best patriots of the Revolution imagined, such as my Father hoped to see. Alas! how these hopes have been overthrown. I feel sometimes as if I had no Country." [47]

A year earlier John Minor of Fredericksburg had told his nephew, Berkeley Minor, an early secessionist like his father Lucius, "Don't fight against your country, my boy!" [48] And then, scarce six weeks after Virginia had seceded, his sister Mary was writing that this veteran of the War of 1812, his long, bushy red beard heavily streaked with grey, "belongs to some company in Fredericksburg and is drilled when he can hardly stand up." [49]

When his cousin, Matthew Fontaine Maury resigned from the U.S. Navy ("like all true Virginians")[50] and left his quarters at the Naval Observatory, John Minor offered him his home in Fredericksburg. The unhappy old man moved out to a little "office" in the backyard and there he died on January 12, 1862.

Mary reported the sad news to her boy in the Rockbridge Artillery: "I was summoned by telegraph to see my dear brother as *being very ill*. I packed up immediately to go to him, but had not long done it to have another telegraph come to say he was *dead*! I started the next morning alone. As I travelled along I prayed earnestly to my Heavenly Father for Christ's sake that I might have some testimony left me that he died a Christian, but that if this were denied me, I might have grace given me to believe when I could not see. But blessed be God, when I arrived in Fredericksburg I heard that during his last illness he was much engaged in prayer and was heard calling himself a 'miserable sinner.' . . I humbly trust that the grace of God had been at work in his heart long before that time. . .

"I was in the time I stayed in Fredericksburg (more than two weeks), much engaged in arranging his papers [51] and other things which were in much confusion, — he expressed in his will a dislike of having his matters exposed before strangers and a wish that we would divide them. So we did, but a great deal was left behind and I tried to reduce it to some order and to save out a great quantity of old papers." [52]

Lucius' older sons, who had spent several winters with their Aunt Mary Blackford, did not share their father's affection for her, nor her sons' reverent devotion to her. Charles Minor described to Berkeley his difficulties in trying to help her pack up Uncle John's effects:

"Aunt Mary had taken them in hand and would have the handling of them: after trying one day and part of two others to help her and getting but one box partially packed, I concluded that she could get on as fast with one of her crooked-legged, well-disposed employes, and with much less worry; so, after contriving to let the suggestion come from her, I came away, having been employed eleven days. Dear Aunt Mary, after distributing things as much to her disadvantage as possible, is now going on at a rate that would keep her three weeks." [53]

CHAPTER IX

Battles

By the beginning of 1862 it was apparent to all thoughtful Southerners that hopes for an early cessation of hostilities were unwarranted and that the conflict bid fair to be a long one. William was gravely concerned about the future when he wrote to his father early that year: "Will the 12-month men be allowed to return home or no? My opinion is that this will be impracticable. It is a momentous decision. I feel rather low-spirited when I think of what will be done in the spring. The time between going home and reorganization will be fatal, I fear." [1]

Charles was hardly more optimistic. He wrote from Leesburg on February 2: "The news is very gloomy, but it is stirring up our people afresh and inspiring a new zeal in the Army. All say they are in for the War now, all they want is a short visit home. I told you we are to see some heavy disasters and we will have some more hell, — in fact I look for nothing but losses until July by which time apathy will seize the Yankees and we will be stirred to the heart. And then when we once defeat them in the interior there will be no prisoners taken and few will reach the border to tell the tale."

Lewis was still ultra-patriotic: his confidence in the ultimate success of the Confederate arms was unshaken. Launcelot too at this time had no doubt of final victory. Much as he abhorred the hardships of military life — he was no *"beau sabreur"* [2] — when the Confederate Congress offered not only a bounty but also a twenty-day furlough, he was glad to reënlist. He enjoyed his holiday thoroughly, spending it at home, at the University, and in

Richmond. Eugene had no immediate worries for he had signed up his company and himself for the duration.

Mr. Blackford was in a retrospective mood when he wrote in his diary on February 4, and what he recalled was not pleasing. "This is the anniversary of the election of the State Convention," he mused. "I well remember the patriotic exultation with which this night a year ago I heard the various returns by telegraph showing that the State had gone for the Union. I turn to the entries of that day and the day subsequent and ask myself, Is it possible that so radical a change of sentiment can have been wrought. It makes me question the identity of mind. I then had strong hopes that the Union might be preserved." [3]

2

When Lanty rejoined the Rockbridge Artillery, Jackson was just beginning the Valley Campaign. Three weeks later the Stonewall Brigade was marching down the Valley toward Winchester and everywhere evoking an enthusiastic reception. The young cannoneer wrote home: "When we were passing through country in which the enemy had been but two weeks before, there were indications of loyalty even more remarkable than elsewhere. The enemy had committed no visible spoliations beyond those that a friendly army might make, but the people told us in many cases they had stolen almost everything they could get their hands on. Indeed every one agrees that *thieving* is one of the leading traits of the rascals everywhere they go. The scoundrels will steal, that's natural to the Yankee, 'it's the nature of the beast,' and must be pardoned, but I do not think that they injure the country much more than a friendly army." [4]

Lanty received his real baptism of fire at the Battle of Kernstown, March 23. A few days later he wrote his mother: "I have seen Baltimore and Philadelphia papers this week. The enemy claim it as 'a brilliant victory,' 'a disastrous rout,' and all that. At first they said they whipped the combined divisions of Jackson,

Smith and Longstreet, — in all, 15,000 strong. All their accounts are characterized by their usual and ridiculous mendacity." [5]

His mother did not like those letters and she lost no time in telling him so: "Do not indulge in abusive language against our enemies: remember you are the deciple [6] of Him who prayed for those who were murdering 'This innocent body,' and Who commanded us to 'love our enemies.' " She added, "The servants are most gratified at your kind remembrance of them. We pray for you together every day." [7]

Mary loved praise and did not hesitate to hint for it. Lanty accepted the hint and sent her a eulogy that indicates why he was supplanting Charly as her favorite son: "You express regret that you can not be more useful when your husband and sons are exerting themselves for the country. Does it never occur to you that an influence may emanate from a sick room which may do more to advance the cause than the most constant and efficient efforts in a Soldier's Aid Society? . . . Or does it never occur to you that a long course of careful home education and of instilling of sound principles on your part has given your sons that sense of honour and love of liberty and justice that prompted them to enter at an early day in this glorious struggle?" [8]

The Battle of Front Royal on May 24 will be ever memorable for the capture of the 1st U. S. Maryland Infantry Regiment by the 1st C. S. Maryland! Following this the Confederates captured a train of supplies which must have astounded Jackson's men, hungry for food of any kind. "I wish I could give you an adequate idea," wrote Lanty, "of the immense variety of their contents and of the evidence they afforded of the almost luxurious manner of living among the Yankee soldiery. Lemons, oranges, dates, hermetically sealed fruits and vegetables, candies, jellies, pickles, tea, coffee, sugar, etc." [9]

But Front Royal was merely the prelude to the First Battle of Winchester, Sunday, May 28, 1862, the high point of Launcelot's military career. A few days later he wrote his parents the following detailed account of the fight:

"We took two posts under two hills to await orders for taking position and then were ordered successively from each to the top of third — not hill, but gentle eminence. Here we unlimbered and went to work. Previous to this time we had been under fire. When our battery opened, as it did in short order, it immediately drew the special attention of the enemy's guns, which were enfiladed on us, and not over 500 yards distant. In addition to this, they must have had a corps of their sharp-shooters playing upon us from the number of wounds received from minie balls in our company. . . It was by far the hottest and most destructive fire this battery has ever been under. All of our men stood up to the mark faithfully, though our excessive fatigue and exhaustion prevented the battery from being handled as rapidly as it would otherwise have been. You never saw men so broken down as we had good reason to be. We worked here about 1¼ hours. . .

"The first man wounded was one of the drivers to our gun. Just as the piece had been unlimbered and he was putting the limber in position in the rear, I noticed him quickly dismount and fall to the rear. The sergeant asked him what was the matter. He exclaimed, 'My arm's broke!': he was right and another took his place. Washington Stuart, a very nice fellow and old college mate of mine, who had been a member of the co. but a week, had no regular number but was . . . waiting to relieve some of the cannoneers. Our No. 3 became much exhausted, and Stuart was summoned and went with alacrity to take his place. Poor fellow, he had not fired the gun once when a minie ball ploughed the side of his face shockingly and he was drawn off, speechless if not senseless, to the rear. Another took his place and our furious work went on. About this time I looked to the right and saw my friend, John M. Gregory, Jr. borne off bathed in blood. . . Again I heard some one within 20 yards of me exclaim, 'Help here, McKim is not dead yet!' and I saw Robert McKim borne off the field, insensible and almost lifeless. . .

"A little later a solid shot (or unexploded shell) darted right over my head . . . (having first shattered the wheel of my gun and of course silenced it for the time) and went through and through the two lead horses of our limber within 5 feet of which I was. . . The poor beasts made a desperate lunge around to the left (I was on their right) and were quickly disengaged from the harness — just in time to die. At the same time the driver of the wheel horses of the same limber was wounded, scarcely I imagine by the same ball, though it had that appearance. Our gun was now pretty much *hors de combat*; its wheel shattered, two horses killed and six men of the detachment wounded — two very slightly, though incapacitated for further work. The battle by that time was declining however, or rather the artillery part of it, and fierce musketry had begun. Soon I heard our men cheering and ere long the glad tidings came that our infantry had charged their batteries, that they had limbered up and their whole force was in rapid flight. . . As soon as the enemy began their retreat our whole force joined in the pursuit. The other guns of the battery preceded mine, as it took some time to replace the horses, put on a fresh wheel from the caisson, and get the piece in good moving order. . .

"Our reception as we dashed through Winchester was enough to make a man weep for joy. It was as enthusiastic as could be: no house but what was vocal with congratulations, handkerchiefs waving, Confederate flags flying, etc. The same enthusiastic spirit pervaded every class, condition, age and sex, and the consciousness of being disenthralled seemed to make every one wild with joy and excitement. The effect upon our troops by all this you can better imagine than I can describe: it was the happiest possible. It fitted them with new life and ardor, and fully compensated for lack of food and rest, and the exhaustion of a 24 hour march. . .

"About 5 miles from town we halted & rested by the side of the road," he continued. "We had not long halted when I heard at a distance down the road loud cheering. We immediately exclaimed, 'Old Jack's coming!' — for we knew no one else elicited such shouts — and ran to the road-side. Sure enough a few hundred yards down the road we saw him coming at a canter. As he came the men pressed in shoals to the road-side and waved their hats enthusiastically. It was deafening and the tributes of all troops without reference to Division, Brigade or State. The Louisiana boys were very vociferous. I never saw a more thrilling scene, nor one filled with more interest. General Jackson himself seemed much affected as he rode uncovered, bowing constantly. . .

"Half an hour afterwards I discovered him, having come round by some by-way, in our company talking to Captain Poague. He came to get our two Parrott guns to go on with the cavalry in pursuit of the enemy, and came in person — a high honour to us — to order it. . . The men were completely worn out, but the General's coming for us in person caused them to start without a murmur. The order was happily countermanded afterwards, and our men had not far to go before returning. General Jackson will have us in for it when there is select duty to be done, in addition to the employment of us hotly in general engagements." [10]

Because of recent sickness, Captain Poague allowed Lanty to spend the next day with old friends in Winchester. "I could fill pages telling you of the many incidents they told me of the Yankee occupation," he added. "The Yankees were not content with running off the slaves with the usual incitements during their occupation, but on Saturday and Sunday added to their previous pilfering the most unblushing lies. They declared to the negroes that they were going to burn the town and *that Jackson was cutting the throats of all the Negroes as he came down the Valley,* and that their only safety lay in flight — and many like unblushing falsehoods. In this way they scared off many who had remained steadfast to their masters."

The news from Winchester was agreeable to Mr. Blackford. On June 1 he wrote Launcelot: "I cannot tell you how delighted I was at Jackson's success. I have stood up for him when I was almost alone in his defence and in admiration of his character and merits, so that 'Hurra for Jackson' . . . is very grateful to me." (He had noted earlier in his diary, "I see in him the fighting mania or disease with which most of our generals are not affected." [11]) "I fancied that, Ewell leaving in advance when you last wrote, your corps had not participated in any of the fighting. I was not prepared therefore to hear that you had been in such a serious battle and that your Company had suffered so severely. I am truly thankful to God that you were mercifully saved from harm. I mourn the loss of so many noble young fellows."

To that letter his "ever devoted mother" added:

"I humbly thank God that it has pleased Him to spare my beloved boy and also my dear Berkeley and others in your Company in whom I am interested.

"It was a great loss, 25 out of 80 — Oh, how good God was to us. It is a great comfort to me to believe that my Lanty cultivates his religion in the midst of Camp life. 'Watch I say unto you; I say unto you all, WATCH!' "

The sequel to Winchester was "a bitter pill to all of us, but a stern military necessity." Shields from the northeast and Fremont from the west were trying to effect a junction in Jackson's rear, so he had to retreat with all possible speed back up the Valley toward Staunton. Near Strasburg the unexpected appearance of the enemy caused Lanty to say, "We decamped with rather undignified haste." [12] A few days later he wrote: "In the afternoon a drenching rain came up and wet every one to the skin who was not protected by a (Union) rubber coat, blanket or the like; though enjoying the latter advantage I got soaking wet from the thigh downward. We all bore the wetting with a little better grace however, after meeting a mile or two this side of Edinburg, while the rain was coming down in torrents, General Jackson himself, without great coat or any such thing, riding unattended rapidly to the rear, looking as unconcerned as if the sun were shining. He was in all probability going thither to attend in person to some matter that another general, particularly in view of the storm, would have sent an aide to see to." [13]

On June 7 Launcelot summed up the campaign for his parents:

"Since the 30th April, the morning we left Swift Run Gap, 16 miles from here, 38 days have elapsed. Of these we have been on the march 32 *days*, and have marched about *400 miles*, i.e., an average of 12½ miles a day. Much of this has been done in rain and mud and over very bad roads, though roads and weather have been for the most part good. This marching wears out shoe leather enough to eat up the wages of the time. I am suitably provided however with shoes, of which I found plenty around Winchester and Charlestown and supplied myself.

"Short rations, carrying one's own baggage, and having imperfect shelter from the weather at night have greatly enhanced our trials. One of the greatest is the short allowance of sleep at night. . . We have rarely gotten to camp before sundown or near that time, and then the delay about getting rations from the Brigade Commissariat and mediately from our own commissary, the cooking of supper and next day's rations, generally kept us up until 10 at least, often later. This difficulty was of course increased when, as had often been the case, we have not gotten to our camp until 8, 9, 10 or even 11 or 12 o'clock. The usual time for Reveille on the march is 3 a.m., so this left but a brief time for the rest of men broken down by a fatiguing march. Still more was this quantity greatly diminished to those who were unfortunate enough to be on guard."

He did not think it necessary to name over again to his father and mother the battles and skirmishes they had fought, nor to mention again the dysentery from which he had so constantly suffered.

He looked forward to rest, but the next day, Sunday, June 8, at Port Republic, Shields' men all but captured Jackson, — they did capture two of his staff — and the Rockbridge Artillery fought again. "In Monday's battle our Battery was hotly engaged and exposed to fire scarce less fierce than that at Winchester, but, thank God, suffered much less." [14] Meanwhile, a few miles away at Cross Keys, Ewell had defeated Fremont and Milroy. With the Valley cleared of invaders, the Rockbridge Artillery was sent to a beautiful camp site near Staunton for a month's rest. The next day while standing in ranks Launcelot collapsed. Friends in Staunton took care of him until he was well enough to be sent to Lynchburg. His comrades in arms, however, did not get the rest promised them: the day Lanty left Staunton they went into action at Cold Harbor, where they gained additional laurels.

Launcelot got home on June 27, "very much emaciated," bringing with him Professor B. L. Gildersleeve and three young men of the 1st Maryland — Williamson, Murray, and Laird — whom his father considered "all gentlemen bred and born, and distinguished for polish of manners and high intelligence." Mr. Blackford added in his diary, "In what other service could you find four such men as these three and Launcelot serving as privates in the ranks?" [15]

At this time Charles, equally emaciated, was also at home, impatiently convalescing from one of his various illnesses. But at least Mrs. Blackford had the satisfaction of knowing that these two sons of hers were not engaged in the bloody fighting around Richmond.

3

While the other boys had been in frequent combat the spring of 1862, Lewis had been busy making maps in the very strategic Norfolk area. His letters were always entertaining, though some he sent his mother must have scandalized her. On January 31, for example, he wrote:

"I will tell you a secret and mind, a real secret; *nobody* is to know it but you. The other day, being incited thereto by a little love, a great deal of fancy, & for ought I know by the Devil himself, I proposed plumply and soundly to a certain very sweet and sprightly young lady with whom I have been carrying on a desperate flirtation for some months. She was a good deal astonished and tried to make me give her time on it. I insisted on an answer at once and made some pecuniary statistics (expressed by the way by a minus quantity) and she finally said — No! I told her to be sure she meant it as she wouldn't have another chance. We parted the best of friends and I stole a kiss to make her show she wasn't angry.

"Next day I went to 'Mama' and stated the case; 'Mama' was very sorry and very much surprised (by the way, I was surprised too), but said that there was no accounting for the perversity of young women. The next day we (the young lady and I) met again. She said, 'If you had given me the time I asked, I would have given you a different answer, but I don't think you love me *very* much, and when you refused to wait for my answer, I knew at once what sort of an answer I ought to make.' I don't think we are either of us much hurt. In the main she was right. I loved her *some* and if she had said yes I would have married her — and I dare say we would have gotten on very well; but she said no very sensibly *et voilà tout*! I am going to take her to General Huger's to spend this evening."

A month later he wrote in similar vein:

"My love affairs stand in statu quo. If I were to be put on oath as to whether she loved me or not, I could not tell. I believe I may say the same of myself. I certainly thought I was dreadfully in earnest when I courted her, and I suppose we are both somewhat in love, but I am inclined to think she has got too much sense to marry so poor a fellow as I am, and indeed she treated me to some very sagacious reflections the other day on the convenience of dividends, 'contrabands,' etc.

"I am afraid I shock my dear Mother very much by talking in this way, for I could not speak otherwise without being somewhat hypocritical and I think sometimes I would like to have somebody to take care of me and sew on buttons, and sometimes I get sentimental over 'notions': My beloved widow and fatherless children to lament the irreparable loss should anything serious happen by chance of war, but I dare say there is time enough yet." [16]

That letter also reveals something of what his mother had been writing Lewis, the only one of her sons who ever talked back:

"One thing sure on this subject, all of which is strictly between us: you seem to think there is a manifest impossibility in my making a suitable selection of a wife for myself, and though you know nothing of the young lady (who is really a sweet girl) you speak of the engagement almost with horror. Now I would like above all things for my wife to please you, but you know one will fall in love for himself, and one that would please you might not please me and I think it would be much easier for you to learn to love my choice after marriage than for me to learn to love your choice. However, I say once more I don't think there is any chance of a wedding this time, and we will wait for better times even if we should become engaged.

"So much for love — now for war! Everything looks dark enough, but this I do know: we are as far from subjugation as ever. I have sworn that nothing will ever make me acknowledge myself a subject of Lincoln's. We know but little of ourselves until we are tried, but I believe that I would endure suffering, beggary and death rather than submit to such degradation. My whole soul is occupied in one concentrated hate and detestation of Yankees."

For weeks Lewis had given his father every detail he could learn about the conversion of the *Merrimac* to the ironclad *Virginia*. He was not a witness of the great battle of the Roads. On March 13 however he wrote his father what he had learned in a vivid, highly colored manner. Only a few excerpts can be reproduced. "And I have heard the officers say how tenderly and humanely," he wrote, "the instant the white flags were run up on the *Congress*, he gave orders for the removal and kindly treatment of the wounded, and how that when those flags were treacherously violated, and the *Congress* fired into the little tug that was going out to her assistance, killing & wounding every man on deck but one, he [Capt. Buchanan] rose up in a wrath that was as terrible as his humanity had been tender, and shouted to his crew to send that ship to hell; and so she was burned amid the howlings of the hundred wounded wretches that crowded her decks, by a hot shot." He said further, "But the *Virginia* ran against a snag when she encountered the Erickson Battery; had it not been for this ugly creature she would have demolished every vestige of shipping around Old Point, for the guns of Monroe would have had no more effect upon her than hail. . . What a complete change that battle made in naval warfare! . . . If the *Monitor* had not been ready, we could have destroyed the shipping at Monroe, gone outside, completely blockaded the Point and for aught I know captured the Fortress itself."

A few days later Lewis had to eat his words, at least some of them, to placate his mother: "I made special inquiries for your benefit and found that Capt. Buchanan did *not* use the word previously mentioned: He simply ordered the destruction of the faith-less ship." [17]

Norfolk by then was largely emptied of civilians, so Lewis with three other young officers rented a nice house, sumptuously fur-nished, even including servants. "We are getting along famously with our housekeeping," he reported to his mother, "and you may be sure that there is not a man in the division who would re-fuse an invitation to take dinner at 'the Ranch.' Major General Huger we are always glad to see, but we are studiously cold to the Brigadiers who are rather low people." [18] He had not forgotten his mother's ideas as to social position regardless of military rank.

They had not long to enjoy their luxuries however, for in a few weeks Huger was ordered to evacuate Norfolk. From Richmond on April 30, Lewis wrote home: "I called by to see Eugene in the entrenchments near Yorktown and he came to see me two days before I left the Peninsula. He is hearty as a buck and as dirty as possible, — the very beau ideal of a soldier in spirit. If he has a chance you will hear from him in the next fight. He lost his baggage for the third time this year and did not have a change of clothes. He like the rest of us takes it *al fresco* through moist nights and has done so for more than two months: all the tents were sent away from the peninsula. I would have lent Eugene some clothes but I was pretty nearly in the same fix myself. It really makes little difference however, as he can take time off and have them washed in a few hours, wrapping up in a blanket in the mean time. This better than begging a knapsack with a change."

The future looked dark for the Confederacy that spring. On a day appointed by the President for fasting and prayer, Mr. Black-ford noted without comment: "Mr. Kinckle in his sermon justified slavery on scriptural grounds and concluded, therefore, that it could not be the cause of the Almighty's displeasure against us." [19]

His entry of May 23 indicated that he did not share his sons' often voiced enthusiasm for Mr. Davis. "I dare not speculate on public affairs," he mused, "Nothing can exceed the imbecility of President Davis. His obstinacy and self will are dreadful. He will not have about him men of talent and force. If our struggle shall be in vain and our cause lost, it will not be owing to the people, but to the men they placed at the head of affairs." [20]

While her husband was deploring the political situation, Mary was berating Lewis for his enjoyment of the creature comforts she so much despised. Stung by one of her comments, he retorted from near Drewry's Bluff in a letter to his father of May 29: "Tell Mother not to be too uneasy about my being too comfortable: it's every man's duty to make himself as comfortable as he can, and then not to grumble when he can't. I was sleeping flat on the ground with my head on my saddle when her letter reached me, but I don't know that I ever should have thought of mentioning it if she hadn't seemed to think that sleeping on the ground was a very great hardship.

"Dr. George Tucker Harrison was here," he continued, turning to lighter things. "He has seen much of Eugene: he says that if there was a chicken within 5 miles, it would sure find its way to Eugene's tent, and that he knows every old lady on the route, who admire him beyond everything."

4

As McClellan's nearing Richmond late in May heralded the imminence of bloody fighting, worried apprehension mounted in the Blackford home. On June 1 the father wrote Lanty in the Valley:

"After dinner yesterday we had intelligence of the fighting going on near Richmond. There was great excitement and intense anxiety to learn the fate of sons, brothers, relations and friends. I staid at the office until after 11 — but could hear nothing of Eugene though I knew he was engaged in the fight. . . I went to bed exhausted by fatigue and anxiety and awoke this morning with a most awful headache, which continued all day until a little after 3 when a despatch came from Mr. Gwatkin in these words, 'Eugene was in the hottest of the fight yesterday. He is not hurt. He behaved gallantly.' This ended my headache.[21] I had great foreboding of Eugene's fate as I knew he would be the foremost man in a charge. . . Two of his men have been here in the hospital. It is very gratifying to hear their expressions of admiration and affection for him."

On June 4 Lewis, after noting that "William's bridge built in 3 days over the James river is much talked of: people say it is the only *quick* work ever done in the Southern Confederacy," reported what he had heard of the Battle of Seven Pines:

"The Home Guard, my gallant old company, took 35 men into the fight and brought out 6; 29 were killed or wounded. The closeness of the fight enabled their sharp-shooters to pick off our mounted officers: the slaughter of the horses was fearful. Latham's Battery out of 35 cannoneers lost 19, and 40 horses. Gray Latham himself [our old school mate] had a *bite* taken out of his leg by a shell. I have not seen Eugene. I have heard that he fought as if he bore a charmed life, that he had several balls through his clothes and his haversack shot off."

In the middle of June, business of the bank opportunely required Mr. Blackford to go to Richmond. He wired Charles Gwatkin, husband of his niece, of his coming and Gwatkin assembled William, Lewis, and Eugene at his home to welcome him that Friday. Saturday William took him down to see his bridge, of which he was justly proud, and to inspect the fortifications in and around Drewry's Bluff. Sunday they rode out to see Eugene and called on General Huger and had dinner with Mr. Blackford's old Lynchburg friend, General Garland. En route home he met Commodore Maury and "his own Major Dick," who accompanied him home, where he found, among others, the boys' great friend, Randolph McKim, the cricket star. Cut off from his home in Baltimore, Ran was always welcomed by the Blackfords as one of their own.[22]

Lewis, who followed close in the wake of the Seven Days fighting, drawing maps, wrote his mother on June 12: "I saw horror enough for a century [and] blood enough . . . to swim in, and dead and vast numbers of their wounded all along, and many who were wounded in their flight and crept off in the woods, died lingering deaths from starvation. I myself found a Yankee in a thicket Friday who had been shot through the lungs the previous Monday, and was still alive, lying as he had been shot, without food or drink. I found a surgeon (Yankee, of whom numbers were around) for this poor fellow, but it was no use: the Dr. merely pulled open his shirt and said, 'he'll die, no use to move him,' and went away and he did die while I was looking at him."

Lewis' sympathy for the wounded foe did not extend to the Yankees in general whom he regarded as a brutish, inferior people, though he conceded that some of them fought well enough. "During my survey," he continued, "I picked up and looked over at least 1,000 letters. *Not a single one* was correctly written or spelled, and they were *barely* decent. They *all* instigated those they were written to, to murder and steal. . . The working classes spoke of the negroes with murderous hate as probable competitors to lower the price of labor. They hate us blindly and vindictively; they believe us to be an aristocracy (and so we are, thank God) and they hate us as the French *canaille* hated the *noblesse* in the revolution there."

Of Confederate conduct in the recent fighting, Lewis spoke admiringly: "The desperate courage of our men was beyond any precedent. I have never heard or read anything like it. Tuesday, Magruder ordered a charge on a collection of 36 guns; there was rather more than a mile of perfectly open ground to be gone over; our men were unsupported by artillery and entirely exposed to this awful fire — the charge of the 600 was nothing to it; but they went at it with a yell. Before they had gone ⅔ of the way a thousand men were stretched on that awful field and the increasing darkness was all that saved the rest. Eugene lost 13 of his 25 men in that charge and had his pistol shot away by grape shot."

On July 4, 1862, Launcelot left home to rejoin the Rockbridge Artillery which had won yet further glory in the recent Seven Days. The company was still twenty-five or thirty miles from Richmond, "exactly where nobody knows" [23] when he arrived in the capital. He did learn that they were returning so, the fighting being over for a time, he decided to wait for them. On July 6 he wrote his father: "The general impression here seems to be that McClellan will save most of his army under cover of his guntraps.

"I was at General Lee's this evening. Mrs. Lee told me she had a note from her husband today dated Westover. She says he has not been home since the fighting began last week."

It was but little more than a month that General Lee had been taken out of an office and placed in command of the Confederate Army in Virginia. Lanty's mother saw nothing extraordinary in the fact that her son, a private, had called at the home of the commanding general. Why should she? Her mother, iron-willed Lucy Landon Carter, and General Lee's mother, equally strong-minded Ann Carter, were both great-granddaughters of Robert "King" Carter and the General's youngest son was in her boy's Company.

The Confederacy was hard pressed for hospital facilities. The care of the sick and wounded was difficult enough in Lynchburg, but in Richmond at this time it was worse, and the majority were placed in private homes. After rejoining his organization, on July 11 Launcelot wrote:

"I went to see Cousin Mary Gwatkin Saturday morning. She was very kind in rendering me her hospitality, which I gratefully accepted during a part of my stay in town, less fully than I might have done but for her having a house full. . . I enjoyed greatly several cold baths I got there, as well as other house comforts kindly placed at my disposal by my kind host and hostess. Colonel Withers of the 18th Virginia, who was so badly wounded in the battle of Friday, the 27th ult. [Cold Harbor], is Mr. Gwatkin's guest and is doing wonderfully well, having been severely wounded *three* times. With him are his wife, mother-in-law, daughter (about 14) and, when I left there, his brother and brother-in-law. Both of these are in the army and will return to it soon, I imagine. Besides there are one or two sick soldiers and two more severely wounded.

"There was quite a reunion of the family Wednesday evening at Mr. Gwatkin's," he added: "Brothers William and Charles, Uncle Lewis, Charles and Berkeley Minor (the latter on his way home sick) and William H. Blackford. . . Cousin Mary kindly gave comfortable quarters to Berkeley who was really too weak to move any more than was absolutely necessary."

It was not two weeks before Mary Blackford Gwatkin was able to be of even greater aid to one of her cousins. Hostile fire in the Peninsular Campaign had left Eugene unscathed, but typhoid fever laid him low, and Dr. Lewis Minor had him transported to her home. He became desperately ill and his mother was summoned to nurse him, the only time during the entire war she actually had to leave Lynchburg on such a mission. A month later he was well enough for her to bring him home by canal boat.

After the First Battle of Manassas, Eugene, according to his father's diary, was offered a lieutenant colonelcy in another regiment or a majority in the Fifth Alabama. Out of loyalty to the men he had brought so far from home to the defense of Virginia, he had declined both. However, Malvern Hill left him with only thirteen able-bodied men of the ninety-six of his original command, so when a majority in the old regiment was tendered him again, he was nothing loath to accept it.

5

A little rest after the Peninsular Campaign put the Army in fine fettle. They felt they had just licked the Yankees badly, they knew they had shown magnificent courage, they appreciated the genius of Lee and they believed with all their hearts that, under his supreme command, with Jackson, Longstreet, and Stuart, they were going to win the War.

By August, William, Charles, and Launcelot were heading north. After the Battle of Cedar Mountain, Launcelot wrote home: "I went this evening to see brother Charles at General Jackson's Headquarters, and had the pleasure of meeting there brother William. We three supped together very comfortably." [24]

Five days later he informed his mother: "Orders were received to prepare 2 days' rations. It being my turn to be one of the cooks I spent the whole afternoon laboriously at this duty — the most

disliked of almost all those that fall to our lot in camp. Our cook
Israel went to Albemarle sick early this month and has not yet
returned, nor with our present moves is likely to do so soon." [25]

What Lee was planning the men did not know, but they were
satisfied that what he had planned was great and cheerfully they
coöperated, making forced marches day after day. On August 26
the Stonewall Brigade passed through Thoroughfare Gap and the
next morning Launcelot recorded that they had "the pleasant sight
of a long procession of prisoners, some six or seven hundred in all,
including a large number of 'contrabands,' captured at Manassas
a few hours before by General Stuart. . . About this time brother
William rode by and we enjoyed a pleasant chat. . . When we
reached the depot, we got some refreshments of which we stood
greatly in need. . . I breakfasted on crackers and pickled lobster
and felt much refreshed."

William, Charles, Launcelot, and their nineteen-year old cousin
William H. Blackford were all in the Second Battle of Manassas,
and in the brisk skirmishing that preceded and followed it, going
on up into Maryland. The Rockbridge Artillery was at its best:
the afternoon of the third day of the great battle one feat of the
battery evoked from Jackson, "That was handsomely done, very
handsomely done!" [26]

After their return to Virginia, Lanty wrote home, "I have seen
a good deal of brother William lately. I supped with him and General [Jeb] Stuart Friday night." [27] In October, believing the Yankees would have to lick their wounds until spring, Launcelot accepted a detail as secretary to the Post Surgeon in Lynchburg,
expecting to return for the spring campaign. On his way home he
stopped in Winchester where, as he wrote Berkeley Minor: "I
supped with Capt. Williamson (A.A.G.) and Ran McKim at Brigadier General [George H.] Steuart's Headquarters. Williamson is
a very fine fellow, a private formerly in the 1st Maryland regiment.
I have entertained him at my father's house and once he was my
guest as an invalid for some weeks in my absence. General Steuart
was particularly gracious to me as Dr. Davis' brother-in-law. You
know he was Dr. Davis' patient and for a long time his guest this

summer. My dear friend Ran was what he always is . . . I observe no change in him." [28]

On October 12 Mr. Blackford made another retrospective entry in his diary: "The thirty-seventh anniversary of my marriage!" he wrote. "I believe we have lived together far longer than is allowed most couples, and I believe I have enjoyed more happiness during the many years which have elapsed since October 12, 1825, than falls to the lot of most men. No man was ever more fortunate in every respect than I was in the match I then made. The ill health of my wife is the sole drawback.

"Pride is not the feeling that ought to be indulged in," he continued, "but we have great reason to be thankful for the comfort we have in our children. I think both of us strive to keep off that induration of sensibility which is so apt to be a concomitant of old age and both have preserved in a remarkable degree the freshness of youthful feeling. God grant that we may yet be spared to each other and that our Union may become holier and happier as it increases in duration." [29]

The next day the diarist returned to the contemporary scene with this opinion: "There seems to be no doubt that Lincolndom is in a state of excitement in consequence of the [Emancipation] Proclamation. General McClellan has issued a mild general order cautioning the troops against political discussion. It is a very significant production and goes to corroborate the report that great trouble exists in their camps on account of the war becoming one for the abolition of slavery." [30]

A week later Lanty expounded his views to Berkeley, still and long to remain, a private in the Rockbridge Artillery. "I spend my time chiefly in watching the progress of politics in Yankeedom," he wrote. "Day seems breaking . . . and I am really sanguine that we shall never see another campaign. I think Lincoln 'put his foot in it' in the Emancipation Proclamation. News has just reached us of his party losing Pennsylvania, Indiana and Ohio . . . all gone Democratic in last week's congressional elections." [31]

These two worthy gentlemen completely misjudged the tremendous impact of the Emancipation Proclamation on the North, not to mention that on England and France. One wonders as to its effect on Mary Blackford. She did not commit herself, not even to John B. Minor, but perhaps in her secret heart interest in the success of the Confederate cause waned.

6

Among the many problems confronting the slaveholder was the disposition of a disagreeable one. Bishop Meade's general opinion to the contrary notwithstanding,[32] a Negro slave could be most unlovable, and the more conscientious owner could not sell her down the river just for that. One such was Jenny, who "was very cross and quarrelsome and it was hard to find her a home." [33] In July, Sue Blackford had written Charles: "I am glad to tell you that I have at last gotten Jenny a home. She is hired at five dollars a month and I am to clothe her; not much but a happy riddance." [34] Jenny's daughter, Mary, though, was indispensable.

Maria [35] was even more of a problem. Just before the War, Charles had purchased her to prevent her separation from her husband. On October 23, 1862, Sue wrote him about her: "Maria has behaved so outrageously since I have been sick that I have been forced to ask father to sell her that I may be freed from the bondage under which I have been ever since you bought her. I am afraid of her, and am pretty sure she drinks and is often under the influence of liquor. Father will sell her, he thinks for $1,800, and sell her to remain in town with her husband. I will *give* her away rather than keep her. She is furious at the idea of being sold, and says she only wants to see you and tell you how badly she has been treated.

"When I think of my approaching freedom I feel like a bride about to begin housekeeping, for I am constantly making plans as to how I will keep house and how I will go into the kitchen and see about my own affairs, a thing I have not been able or dared to do for a long time. My conscience acquits me of having done her any harm. What I have done was a necessity, and I feel that my life and that of all the other servants have been in danger ever since she has been here. No one dares to contradict her in anything." [36]

Mr. Blackford did sell Maria to a fellow citizen of Lynchburg that day. He journalized, "I would not have thought of selling her at an auction. I consider I have sacrificed several hundred dollars by not doing so."

Nothing further has been preserved about this Maria, but Jenny was to appear again in the family circle for many years to come. For the most part, however, the relationship between the Blackfords and their slaves was more pleasant. Mr. Blackford recorded on November 26:

"Last night we had 'high life below stairs.' Our colored cook Elvira was married to a man belonging to James Langhorne. The ceremony took place in the lecture room of the Fourth Methodist Church. Hacks and omnibuses were in attendance. The service was admirably performed by a negro minister. The supper was served in our dining room, which we gave her for the purpose, and the viands abundant and elegant. We furnished only a round of beef and the bread. The company was 'select,' and they behaved very well, making no noise to disturb us. It was two o'clock before the house was quiet." [37]

It is surprising to learn that the wedding supper was "abundant" as the South was already feeling the effect of inflation ("hogs are hard to get at $30.00 a hundred") and the pinch of the blockade was beginning to hurt. ("Eugene Davis asked where I got such Java coffee and what I gave for it, and could hardly believe me when I told him it was made of rye. It is better made at our house than any where else that I know. Mr. Wyndham Robertson the last time he was here apologized for taking a second cup on the grounds that genuine coffee was so rare. I did not undeceive him as it would have been folly to destroy the bliss of his ignorance." [38]

On December 2, Mr. Blackford, the family chronicler, recorded his wife's sixtieth birthday. "She does not, when tolerably well, look fifty," he commented. "It is very strange that she should have preserved her good looks under such long-continued and severe suffering." [39]

7

Eugene's convalescence from typhoid had been greatly prolonged by thrombophlebitis of the leg. He had been very impatient to get back to the 5th Alabama Infantry. Having been promoted to major and therefore rating a horse, he could see no reason that pain on walking should delay further his return to duty. A battle was anticipated at Fredericksburg, and this did not diminish his ardor, nor did his father try to detain him. On December 9 Mr. Blackford confided to his diary, "I am glad that three of my sons are near enough to strike in defence of their native town and protection of its people," [40] and during the battle, "I have three sons in the army around town, all likely to be in the hottest of the fray. If it should be the will of God, they could not fall in a better place, defending their native town, or rather avenging its destruction, literally 'fighting for the green graves of their sires.' " [41]

When Charles began this account of the battle on Saturday, December 13, the wooded hills back of Fredericksburg were held in strength by the Confederates; to the southeast a broad plain separated the hills from the Rappahannock. Burnside had crossed the river and seized the town. Mary Blackford was thoroughly familiar with the terrain for she had walked all over it in her younger days.

"Longstreet's corps held the left of our line covering the town of Fredericksburg at Willis' and Marye's Hills," Charles wrote, "and Jackson the right, the right resting on Hamilton's Crossing.

"Just as the mist rose and the sunlight broke through the dissolving veil the magnificent panorama of actual war, still however in repose, was disclosed. I got leave to ride to the top of the hill, not far from the Hamilton house, where General Jackson and his staff were posted. He was on horseback, surrounded by his staff and a number of other generals; couriers and aids were constantly coming and going, and everything betokened that the storm was about to break, but that all was ready and that there was no anxiety about the result. It was a historic group and made a lasting impression on my mind; but I was more interested in the wonderful sight presented on the broad savannah below me, over which I had so often roamed in boyhood, and with every square foot and every pathway I was so familiar.

"From the town of Fredericksburg, several miles to my left, to a point considerably to my right, the long blue lines of the enemy were drawn, in many places doubled, and everywhere interspersed and flanked by battalions of artillery, all in frowning battery. The hills on the Stafford side of the river were crowned with numberless guns which, when the battle was opened, belched their sulphurous roar to cover the advancing lines in the plane below. . .

"As I stood looking down from my temporary post near General Jackson upon the grand but quiet scene, suddenly there was a terrible outburst of artillery fire from the other side upon our left near the town, followed in a few moments by the deadly rattle of musketry, which announced to the whole line that the battle had begun and that the enemy were charging our left at or near Fredericksburg. In a few moments the batteries all along the line from the opposite hills and some down in the plain opened upon our lines. I was close by Col. Lewis Minor Coleman's battalion and saw the enemy's line of battle in beautiful order leave the cover of the river road and begin the advance with the purpose of attacking Jackson's strong position. Coleman permitted them to move out into the open field and then opened a rapid fire, and I could see the shot and shell plough through their ranks. Of course, as soon as the advance began it was my duty to return to my company. . .

"The enemy advanced along our line, most of which was behind breastworks, and were driven back with great loss — leaving the field over which they had so gallantly charged blue with their dead and wounded. This first charge was about eleven o'clock in the morning and was repeated time and again, but with the same result every time. Once they broke through at the point of our line which was weakened by the depression in the rising ground made by the headwaters of Deep Run, but the troops under General Maxcy Gregg of South Carolina . . . drove them back with great loss, but at the cost of poor Gregg's life. The heaviest fighting was on the plain at the foot of Marye's and Willis' Hills, near Fredericksburg, where all day long Meager's Irish brigade and others charged our lines and recharged in vain, leaving some of their dead and dying within twenty feet of our works. I am very sorry I could not get up near that point, as of course the nearer I could get to my old home the more interesting it would have been. . .

"Our brigade maintained its same position all day and took no active part, though under desultory cannon fire all the time. Its loss was small. It was, however, a very trying position and active work would have been much less trying upon our nerves. We stood all day with our horses in line ready for a charge, but none was ordered.

"Late in the evening, as the enemy was being repulsed in Jackson's front for the last time, a staff officer rode up in haste to General Fitz Lee and said: 'General, General Stuart says charge the retreating enemy in their flank with your whole brigade!' Lee was on the ground, but sprung to his saddle in an instant and the brigade was ready for the move in less time than I take to write this. The order was given and we started in a column of regiments five deep. I commanded the right company of the front regiment and was therefore riding with General Fitz Lee and Colonel Munford. I knew the ground better than any man in the brigade and knew that the instant we reached the top of the little hill which protected us and commenced to move on the plain we would come under the fire of a hundred cannon from the opposite hills, to say nothing of the small arms. As we struck the trot I said to General Lee: 'This will be a second Balaklava.' He replied, 'Yes, I know it, but we must obey orders.' It was a solemn moment which I will never forget.

"Just as we were nearing the top of the hill and were to take the gallop, we saw an officer coming from the direction of General Jackson's position making frantic demonstrations with his sword and riding at full speed towards General Lee. The whole front line checked its speed and the officer rode up and with great excitement said that General Jackson wanted to know where he was going. General Lee replied, 'I am about to charge the enemy under orders from General Stuart!' The officer replied, 'There is some

mistake, General; General Jackson says go back to your first position or you will not have a man left alive.' We went back of course.
I do not know how others felt, but knowing the topography as I
did, I knew the countermand saved the lives of most of us, and
it would have been idle to say I was not glad. It would have been
an historic charge and would have been most gallantly led by Lee
and Munford, but I believe I would rather have been spared to
narrate the incident of the countermand than to have been sung
of by some future bard who would have made immortal the charge
of the three thousand." [42]

Of course Mary Blackford was vitally interested in everything
about the town where she had lived forty-four years, where her
parents and many of her ancestors were buried. Her youngest son
appreciated this and he took particular pains to give her details
of the battle as he saw it. Eugene wrote:

"At four o'clock Monday morning, December the 15th, we
moved silently to the front and relieved Jackson's old Division. At
daybreak the grandest sight I have ever seen broke upon my view.
Our line extended along the railroad which ran parallel with the
edge of the woods for two miles, and was raised about four feet
from the general level of the ground, thus affording fine protection
to our men. The country in front stretched out in one unbroken
plain for a distance of a mile or more. In this vast field the army
of the enemy was drawn up in battle array, presenting a magnificent sight. They also had three lines which were dressed as accurately as if on dress parade. These lines glittering in the light
of the rising sun presented a sight which was grand in the extreme.
In front of either army were the skirmishers lying on the ground,
not more than 150 yards apart, the first lines of battle being not
more than 500 yards distant from each other. So near were they
that the buzz of conversation was distinctly heard. The picquets
did not molest one another at all, though their aim at that distance
would have been sure.

"At 10 o'clock I was sitting with General Rodes when a man
was seen advancing from the enemy with a white handkerchief
fixed to a stick. The General sent me forward to our picquet line

to receive it. The bearer of the flag of truce introduced himself as a Lieutenant, sent by a Brigadier General, asking leave to enter our lines for the purpose of attending to their wounded who lay between our first line and the picquets in great numbers, and whose cries were piteous. Upon communicating with General Rodes, I was sent again to refuse the demand, but with authority to grant it if it was made a general truce and came in due form from Burnside. With this answer he withdrew, saying that he would communicate with his commanding officer.

"About 3 o'clock, P.M., a very handsomely dressed officer, accompanied by a mounted escort, rode slowly down to the front, having a lancer with him bearing a white flag. I went forward to meet him, mounted also, taking an escort which I left at our line and advanced alone to meet the flag. The officer accompanying it and myself immediately exchanged cards and we commenced our negotiations. He was an aide to General Franklin, 'commanding left Grand Division, U. S. Army,' and was authorized by General Burnside to treat for cessation of hostilities. I went in again to report to General Rodes and was referred to General Jackson, who said the proposal must be in writing. When I returned the Yankee Officer presented the written authority required, and we were arranging the matter when one of the enemy's batteries a few hundred yards off opened on our lines. Hereupon I broke off the business very abruptly and refused to proceed until this firing was stopped and a suitable apology rendered. The Yankee Major, for such was the rank of my interlocuter, seemed much mortified by the accident and soon returned making the required apology.

"I allowed his ambulance corps to advance to our picquet line where our men met them bearing their dead and wounded, I paroling the latter as they passed. I had much pleasant conversation with the Yankee officers, many of whom advanced to the front. Our men came forward in crowds and mingled with the enemy. It was curious to see the difference between them. The Yankees were all nicely dressed but had a cowed look. They all seemed ashamed to look our men in the face, whereas our poor dirty fellows went about them with uplifted and defiant looks. When they took leave, our men expressed the hope that they might 'meet tomorrow in battle,' at which the Yankees gave a ghastly smile, and but faintly echoed the sentiment. They all, without exception, men and officers, professed themselves utterly sick of the war, and declared their desire to see it end in any way. I gave them my views very plainly and they were obliged to acknowledge I was right.

"I never was in such spirits for a fight in my life as during the three days we faced the enemy, being as I was in sight of my native town. The steeple of St. George's Church was plainly in view. I had many newspapers given me by the Yankee officers, several of whom offered to exchange cards, with which I am fortunately provided. I have rarely met a more pleasant fellow than the Yankee Major with whom I negotiated. I had a good deal of conversation with him and the ubiquitous correspondent of the Associated Press, who was of the party. They all offered to send me papers containing an account of the affair. The Yankee Major was a great friend of Major General Stuart, who soon came down to see him and hailed him very cordially as 'Bob,' the other in turn calling him 'Jeb.'

"Our time was now out and both sides withdrew; the men ceased their trading and went to their posts again and I, left with the Major, took leave with an *au revoir*.

"Altogether I never enjoyed anything more than I did the whole day. . . I was convinced that these men would never trouble us much more. Their spirit is broken, and a more dejected set of wretches I have never seen. The immediate cause I did not fully know until the next day. At daybreak, Tuesday morning, the 16th, the sun, instead of revealing the Yankee lines, showed merely the vacant field. It had rained furiously during the night and, availing themselves of the additional concealment this afforded, they had decamped.

"As soon as their departure was well ascertained, General Rodes directed me to push forward his whole line of skirmishers and discover the whereabouts of the enemy; so on I went with my line, nearly a mile from flank to flank. Upon reaching the heights overlooking the river we saw the last of the villains crossing and re-

ceived a few shots from their artillery on the opposite bank. In
my advance I picked up about two hundred prisoners. In one tent
we found a full band of musicians, with their instruments, who
asked us *if it was reveille!* They were aghast when informed they
were prisoners.

"Later in the day I got leave to accompany a brother officer to
Fredericksburg, whither we cautiously advanced without a shot
from the enemy, still on the other side of the bank. Just about the
Gunnery Spring, and in front of Mr. Marye's house, was the principal scene of battle near town.

"There were thirteen hundred and fifty dead Yankees in a two-
acre field. My horse could not make his way through them. I have
seen battlefields, but never anything to equal this. Our loss in the
same quarter was but small. Our artillery was posted on Marye's
hill; our infantry at the bottom in entrenchments.

"Fredericksburg is completely sacked. Every house left standing
has from five to twenty cannon shot holes through it, and many
are consumed. Every one, without exception, has been broken open
and pillaged. The furniture has been all broken up and much of
it lies in the streets. We went through every street and saw the
same thing everywhere. There is positively no exception. A great
many of the doors were split to pieces. Dr. Herndon's house was
ruined inside, though there were not many shot holes in it. You
can imagine with what emotion I witnessed the ruins of our old
home. It had been used by the Yankees as a hospital, and there
was a large pile of arms and legs lying under the cut-paper mul-
berry tree in the yard, and six of the scoundrels were buried in
the grass plat. The lot was strewn with books and papers, and the
whole house defaced. No fencing whatever remained about the
premises, either in front or behind. In the steeple of the Episcopal
church alone I counted twenty cannon shot holes. More were in
the main building. Some houses have fifty to seventy holes in
them." [43]

While the havoc of Fredericksburg and of her old home caused
Mrs. Blackford heartache, she was thankful to God that her three
sons had come through the battle whole. Mr. Blackford worked

out his feelings by raising a large sum, more than $4,000, for the relief of the civilian sufferers. He also managed to make a trip to the old town to get answers to some of Mary's questions and to satisfy his own military curiosity. The victory was a great boost to Southern spirits.

Christmas that year was pleasant. Charles was able to get home. Lewis was also there a few days and managed, as usual, to brighten things up. Lanty was still on duty in Lynchburg.[44]

8

In December 1862 the Confederate Congress had provided for a permanent military court to be set up at each corps headquarters. Charles, appointed judge advocate of the court of the First Corps, recommended to the court that Launcelot be made its clerk, a recommendation that was promptly accepted. In February 1863 Lanty left home on his new assignment. His mother, who always enjoyed an exquisite faculty for seeing the morbid side of everything, mourned to John B. Minor: "I have thought much in my intercourse with Lanty lately that he seemed ripening for Heaven and that thought depresses me now. I can not help fearing it may precede death." [45]

In January Lucius had sent his fifteen-year-old daughter Thomasia from Edgewood to spend some months with her Aunt Mary in Lynchburg. Thomasia wrote to Berkeley in April that things were proving a little dull for her, "for you must know that Aunt Mary says she wishes the time I spend with her to be sacred from all novels and stories. I am expecting every minute," she explained, "to see Aunt Mary come in and say, 'Now, my dear, go take a sweet walk.' You must know that I have taken no less than three sweet walks to day, so you may imagine that I dread a fourth. As for the walk, however, I feel pretty safe for this evening as Aunt Mary is in her room, deep in Bulwer's 'Strange Story.' It does me good, she seems to enjoy it so much." [46]

Both his parents were worried over Lewis that spring, his father writing on one occasion: "He is said to be much in love with Miss

P. of Richmond, though he professes vast love for Miss C. of Norfolk. I hope he will come out of this duplex affair honorably. He ought not to think of marrying now." [47]

Lewis did not take his parents' concern very seriously. He wrote home on March 11: "I had a long and most interesting letter from Eugene some time ago; he believes all the girls will be married before he can get a chance at them and as a devious resort, encloses me power of Attorney, humorously drawn up with a redundancy of legal verbiage, empowering me to act for him in all affairs relating to the disposal of, and the acceptance of a proper Equivalent for his heart, affections, etc. I at once proposed in his behalf to Miss J. P. (who is the sweetest, prettiest, most refined and purest girl in Richmond) and he was graciously accepted under certain contingencies, of which happiness I have not yet informed him." [48]

Eugene, though, was quite capable of handling his own affairs. He never even caused his mother to worry over his flirting: there is nothing to indicate he ever made love to any girl other than the one he married when the War was over. There is reason to believe, however, that at least one girl fell seriously in love with him.

That spring Lewis, while map-making in Louisa County, narrowly escaped capture by an enemy patrol, which did get all his belongings. "Among his losses was his note book in which he kept copies of poems and other clever things he had written various girls, all of which were published in full subsequently in the *New York Herald* to whom they were furnished by the captor." [49] His mother's mortification at this may better be imagined than described.

In early April, Eugene, home on a three-day leave, was described by his father, always proud of him, as "well and hearty, brown and weather beaten." Mr. Blackford continued: "He belongs to a fighting regiment in a fighting division in Jackson's corps, and must therefore be actively engaged in the hottest of the fray. His danger is enhanced by his commanding a battalion of sharp-shooters." [50]

When two weeks later he was sent home again with "cholera," his father noted: "Dr. Minor says varicose veins have developed in Eugene's leg, which will give him much trouble. To be laid up during the summer campaign would be dreadful to him." [51] But the youngest Blackford would not consent to being laid up that spring. After Chancellorsville, General Rodes wrote his father: "Your boy Eugene deported himself gallantly. He had his extra trials, severe ones after the battle was over, besides opening it. He had to 'feel' the enemy for us after the battle." [52]

The victory at Chancellorsville was dearly bought: Stonewall Jackson was killed at the peak of his career. Not even General Lee himself was at that time a more famous captain or a more beloved leader. After ceremonies in Richmond, Jackson's body was brought up the canal to Lynchburg, accompanied by Sandy Pendleton, among others. As one of his early admirers, Mr. Blackford was invited to join the escort on to Lexington.

9

William under Stuart, Charles and Launcelot under Longstreet, and Eugene under Ewell, advanced into Maryland that June. Concerning the reception of the invading army in Hagerstown, where he met "a very pleasant bevy of Southern sympathizers, including 4 or 5 of the prettiest girls in the place," Launcelot wrote on June 28 from Chambersburg:

"The excitement became greatest and the smiles, nods, waving of handkerchiefs, etc., most striking when towards noon Gens. Lee & Longstreet, followed by their respective Staffs and Corps of Couriers, rode gracefully by in twos. The two Chiefs both courteously rode uncovered a few seconds in acknowledgement of the welcome, but did not stop. The beautiful majesty of Lee's whole person and the lion-like serenity of Longstreet seemed to make a profound impression. It was hard to determine which enjoyed this view of the commander-in-chief most, the Hagerstown ladies who saw for the first time the renouned general, or the officers and others of his command who stood near and witnessed with undisguised pride and satisfaction the sensation his passage produced."

Lanty recorded too: "Last Sunday the Rector of the Episcopal Church (a Yankee) with commendable independence said the usual prayer for the President of the U.S., though the house was full of Confederate soldiers. The only notice taken of it . . . was one officer leaving the Church."

On July 4, 1863, not knowing of the great battle going on at Gettysburg, Mr. Blackford soliloquized, as he had done two years earlier: "We ought to celebrate the day and the Yankees ought not. They cannot read the bill of indictment in the Declaration without being conscious, *nomine mutando*, we might apply it to them, with this difference in our favor, that the wrongs of the colonies were, for the most part, *in esse*, whilst ours were actual and tangible. It is a day of Virginia's making. I hope we shall continue to celebrate the day for all time." [53]

Eugene was the only son of the Blackfords actually engaged in the Battle of Gettysburg. On July 16, after the return to Virginia, he wrote the following detailed and critical report of the campaign:

"Carlisle was the most distant point reached by our Division, which constituted the Advance all the time; we spent 3 days there very pleasantly, some of our Brigades being in the Barracks, and one in the College grounds within the City limits. I never saw a more beautiful place than this; the population too seemed somewhat more refined than the almost God forsaken people we had encountered all thro' that beautiful valley. From Carlisle we moved towards Baltimore and passed through Papertown, the site of the Mt. Holly paper mills where a great deal of the paper we use is made. I sent forward our A.Q.M. with orders to buy some for me, which the agent scornfully refused, whereupon the Q.M. seized two or three reams, of which I fell heir to two. There was an immense supply on hand, but our empty wagons passed the door and nothing was disturbed.

"That day we marched to Heidlersburg and there learned that the enemy's Advance was at Gettysburg. Arms were inspected, & all put in order for a general engagement, which every one could see was right at hand.

"July 2nd [54] (the next day) we moved on the town, and Rodes' Division reaching it first attacked at once, without the smallest concert of action with the other Division Commanders. He drove the enemy's three Corps very handsomely thro' the town, capturing

3 or 4,000 prisoners, but losing heavily himself. In this battle I was more exposed than I have ever been in any engagement as my peculiar duties as commander of a whole Battalion of sharp-shooters required me to expose myself very much. I was frequently obliged to move along my lines when the mere raising of my hand would be the signal for a dozen Yankees to fire at me. The men would constantly urge me to take care, but there was no help for it. From this time until the night of the 3rd inst. we were incessantly engaged in picking off the enemy.

"On the last day I advanced my men to within 300 yards of the enemy's lines, and poured in a constant fire from day break until dark. I myself shot about 80 rounds directly at their lines, and I am considered the best shot in the Battalion. I do not know what number the men fired, but the firing was so incessant that it could not have been less than 200 each. The cannoneers could not stand to their guns and finally abandoned them.

"We were (some of us at least) posted in homes in the suburbs of the town. My Hd.Qrs. were in a fine brick house which had been deserted, larder and all, the latter fortunately well stocked with every delicacy of the season. I have never lived so high since I have been in the Army as we did those two days. My buglers, 4 in number, are all good cooks and, being perfectly devoted to me, you can imagine how I fared. They had nothing to do so I made them keep under cover, thus giving them ample time to prepare all manner of edibles: we have some five or six meals a day. If my conscience had been tender on this point it might have been quieted by the reflection that it was absolutely necessary, as no rations could reach us from the rear, there being nothing to protect the bearer from the fire of the enemy.

"From the first day reason seemed to have deserted our generals: the fighting of the men and regimental officers was magnificent, but Division after Division was hurled against an almost precipitous mountain without any supports. Each Division General acting on his own hook, the works were taken each time, but for want of support, the men were regularly driven down the hill again. So lamentably conspicuous was this want of concert that the privates noticed it and when ordered to charge did so with misgivings as to the result.

"Beyond a doubt, it is the most bloody battle of modern times. Our losses can not fall short of 25,000, while the enemy admitted a loss of 40,000, — their forces being massed on the mountain, our Artillery mowed them down by thousands.

"On the morning of the 4th Gen. Lee moved his line back to the hills . . . and left the town full of the enemy's wounded in their possession. Of course all knew we would fall back as soon as it was possible, so I was prepared for an order received by me on the night of the 4th directing me to hold the outposts until day and then rapidly withdraw. This was about 10 p.m. Soon after I went up the heights in my rear and not a rebel was to be seen, all had been quietly withdrawn. Thus we kept our lonely watch until just before day when I assembled the skirmishers from the whole front of our Division and commenced retreating sullenly towards the mountains. The enemy did not disturb me however, until late in the evening after I had overtaken the main body, so I had nothing to do with fighting them, but was complimented for having withdrawn so quietly and without loss. The next day Gen. Rodes had the rear, my corps was slightly engaged but lost nothing, tho' we encountered great fatigue.

"Finally after being half starved, we reached Hagerstown where the appalling news reached me that our private wagon had been captured and burnt by the enemy. Thus all my purchases in Penn. for myself and friends, & they were innumerable, are lost. Besides, all my clothes and entire cuisine are gone, and our mess, from being one of the most elegantly equipped in the Division, is now reduced to one tin cup. My servant who was with the wagon at the time escaped & brought me the tidings. I have no prospect whatever of getting any more clothes, and am almost in despair. Visions of the elegant top boots & gauntlets and fancy cassimir shirts will intrude themselves upon me even now when all private troubles are swallowed up in my grief over our common disasters.

I had bought all the shoes, gloves, hair pins, hooks & eyes and everything that I thought . . . a rebel lady might want, so you too are a sufferer. . .

"Among other things we had a large quantity of the finest white sugar & 25 pounds of coffee, which is of course all gone. In consequence of this loss I am living like a dog almost, being all the time hungry, for, as the Commissary wagons have gone far to the rear, nothing is issued to us, and if it were we would have nothing in which to have it cooked, so I am living on charity. I have to day made my dinner of dew berries, & breakfast I had none, as we marched at daylight. Where supper is to come from I don't know nor care. If my men had any idea of my wants they would gladly share with me, but they have nothing but bread and not enough of that for themselves. I don't complain of this at all, but merely mention it as a matter of interest to you. . . It seems strange that a gentleman should be reduced to the necessity of almost begging his bread here in the Old Dominion.

"I wish that General Lee had seen fit to stay in Maryland until he had lost every man in his army rather than come out of it in this disgraceful manner. His army was not demoralized when it reached Hagerstown, but crossing the river had caused that disorder to spread among its ranks fearfully. A. P. Hill Corps is said to be in a terrible condition. I keep up my spirits where the men are, and am considered the most sanguine man in the Brigade, but it is a miserable farce. I tried it in this letter, but have signally failed and may as well confess that I am utterly miserable. Fool-like I went into Maryland & Penn. in the most buoyant spirits, fancying that I could see the end, and only doubting whether or no I should live to see our entrance into Baltimore. Nor were these hopes groundless at all: the destruction of Meade's Army would have given us Baltimore, Philadelphia and all south of N. Y., — and to think that in less than 3 weeks we should be ignominiously retreating Heaven knows whither.

"But worse than all, my blind confidence in Gen. Lee is utterly gone: if possible I will never more put any trust in any thing human, but we had every reason to anticipate success, the movement was so splendidly planned & so secretly carried out that the enemy knew nothing of our whereabouts, but finally, of all places in that broad level country, to hurl his Army against an enemy entrenched on a mountain top, it exceeds my belief. How men can climb with one arm and fight with the other is more than I can comprehend. I had fondly hoped that Nemesis was to be our goddess for a while, and that our poor suffering people in Virginia were to rest for a season. Thank heaven, however, I have done my duty: never after any battle have I had so clear a consciousness of having done my whole duty, and I have endeavoured to do it in all.

"But excuse this outbreak I pray you. I could not help it. I am obliged to tell it to some one, and it is best not to say any thing of these matters in the Army. May be these are mere clouds, this fall of Vicksburg and our retreat, and that yet a smiling face will beam upon us.

"The day may now perhaps be coming when we will have to take to the mountains and swear eternal vengeance against our enemy. When that time does come, if I am alive I have men who will follow me to the grave and whose lives are pledged to the bitter end.

"Alas, if old Jack was but here we would have been in Baltimore this day. 'Tis sad to hear the men longing for him." [55]

On receipt of Eugene's Gettysburg letter, his father remarked; "Like an old soldier, he grumbles a great deal over Gettysburg, and with some reason, I think." [56]

Eugene's small comfort in the belief that his wagon had been burned was short-lived. "When the Yankees re-possessed Hagerstown it was determined that the family of Dr. Macgill, whose Southern sentiments were well known, should be sent home. Mrs. Macgill was sick in bed. A yankee officer called to announce the sentence. Throwing himself into a large rocking-chair in the parlor, he addressed Miss Molly Macgill saying:

" 'Do you know Major Blackford of the 5th Alabama Regiment?'

" 'Yes; I do.'

" 'Well, these nice pants,' slapping his thigh, 'were once his and this fine field glass, and perhaps you would like to hear what he says of you?'

"Here he pulled out a small note book in which Eugene had kept a diary of the campaign and read the notices of the family he had made. Of course they were very complimentary, as he was grateful to them for much kindness shown him. It is to be hoped that these notes were not the cause of the proceedings against the family. The girls are now in Charlottesville and Miss Molly relates the story." [57]

The people of Virginia for several days were led to believe that Lee had achieved a decisive victory at Gettysburg. After considerable crowing in his diary, on July 8 poor Mr. Blackford wrote:

"In the midst of my labors I was shocked — the word is not too strong — by the unexpected announcement of the capitulation of Vicksburg, and shortly after the news that Lee had been forced to leave Pennsylvania and had his army about Hagerstown. The retirement of Lee I think the greater calamity of the two. My personal anxiety about my sons is overridden by the sense of disaster to the cause. All the reports we had of a grand and crowning victory were false. They came, too, from our own people. There ought to be some means of punishing those who circulate false news." [58]

John B. Minor sympathized with him on the 10th: "The news of the day has oppressed me also, — and the more because the reckless lies with which our credulity has been taxed for some time have made it difficult to estimate the value of intelligence, favorable or otherwise. A gloom pervades our whole community in consequence of tidings received of so many of our 'unreturning brave.' "

The death of John Davis Minor in 1852 had deprived Mr. Minor of a son to bear arms, but in the field he had many young kinsmen and former students he loved like his own sons. It was natural therefore that he should be one of the committee of civilians to go north to look after Confederate wounded. Mrs. Blackford, who never pretended to be a heroine, wrote to him on the 12th:

"Mr. B. says he knows you will look after our sons without my asking you, but still my anxiety urges me to entreat you to inquire

particularly after them. If my health and infirmities would permit
I would go myself. . . We have no information about William or
Eugene. . . Will you, my dear friend, pray for their conversion
and then, come life, come death, (in one sense) it is all the same."

10

Sunday evening, July 26, 1863, an ambulance drove up to the
Blackford door in Lynchburg bringing William home. He had
been sick at the Bower, and when the Army fell back he was sent
further into the zone of the interior. He had been "fortunate in
escaping from the care of a very presumptuous and ignorant young
surgeon who had charge of his case at the Bower." Dr. "Turkey
John" Minor thought he was suffering from "camp fever" but his
father thought, with considerable justification, "The truth is he is
worn out by hardship and exposure." [59] Stuart and his command,
though not in the great battle, had been through a very active
campaign.

With the Army of Northern Virginia south of the Potomac
again, General Longstreet gave Charles a few days' leave before
rejoining his corps in Fredericksburg. Here Lewis, engaged in a
topographical survey of Stafford County for the use of General
Lee, had already established his own comfortable headquarters.
On August 5 Mr. Blackford outlined a recent letter from Lewis:

"It was dated at our old house . . . which he and his party
now occupy. . . He confirms the rumor of the death of Mary's
aunt, Mrs. McFarland, who fell a victim to the ill usage of the
Yankees. Her daughter Elizabeth performed the last sad rites for
her, and she says she did so without sympathy and without aid
from any Federal soldier. Yankee women, affecting to be the wives
of officers, entered their house and took their dresses out of their
wardrobes and gave them to negro women.

"Charles, Sue and Lucy Minor came to tea," he resumed, telling
of scenes he had himself witnessed. "William for the first time
got into one of his talking moods and related many incidents of
late battles and skirmishes in his usual graphic style. He has been

under fire as often as any man in the army and has had many remarkable escapes." [60]

The next day, shortly after William, accompanied by his wife and Mary Isabella had departed for Abingdon, his father noted: "Letter from Eugene. He gives a bad account of his leg. He can not ride with the leg pendant and has to put it across the pummel of the saddle. He is in bad spirits. It seems strange that *our* house should be empty. There is no one here now but Mary and myself. The respite is agreeable." [61]

When Charles rejoined his command near Orange on August 12 he took with him a load of fresh vegetables. Nothing was known of vitamins then, but hungry soldiers in wasted country have ever loved fresh vegetables. Charles charged Lanty with the responsibility of a dinner for the military court of the Second Corps (recently Jackson's).

Lanty's "chief cook as well as headwaiter on the occasion was Captain Cochran's servant Tarleton, an elderly man of sedate and gentlemanly appearance and courtly manners, who, with all the colored staff entered as much into the success of the dinner as we did." At the table were five colonels, including Richard Henry Lee who had spent several months with the Blackfords recuperating from wounds received at Kernstown and who was accordingly "always particularly polite" to Charles and Launcelot. He was a cousin of the General's. Major Eugene Blackford of the 5th Alabama and Captain James Pleasants, son of an old beau of Mrs. Blackford's, were also among the commissioned personnel at the party. The clerk of the court of the Second Corps was Lanty's old friend of the Rockbridge Artillery, Clem Fishburne, and these lowly young gentlemen completed the group. Lanty was very proud of the success of his famous dinner party *al fresco*, which he described in minute detail to his mother. He also painted a bright picture of the resilience of the Army of Northern Virginia: "The *morale* of the army is from all accounts that reach us from the rear, far better than that of the people back home in view of the present dark aspect of our affairs." [62]

The boys' father commemorated his birthday, August 19: "I complete my sixty-second year. It is hard for me to believe it, but I know it from the record, from sons and daughters, and four grandchildren, some fifteen years old, that it must be so. . . My sons, in the midst of great dangers, have all been spared and are unhurt, and have *all done their duty* manfully. I have been entirely relieved from debt and have accumulated almost an independence. The relief from the obligation of debt is a special blessing, — a blessing which is doubled by the satisfaction it gives my wife. I literally owe not a cent to any one. The future of the country is gloomy and I suffer much from it, but I can not believe the Lord will forsake us. Our fate will be decided before my next birthday." [63]

The preceding year Mr. Blackford had speculated most successfully in tobacco, clearing more than $23,000, and the bank raised his salary frequently. His "independence" he invested largely in Confederate bonds. It is still hard to understand how he made out so well, how he was able to feed his family and their many guests, for food was becoming increasingly hard to get in Lynchburg. When obtainable, brown sugar cost $1.00 a pound, eggs $1.50 a dozen, flour $40.00 a barrel and wood $35.00 a cord. Coffee and coal were practically not to be had.[64]

Peggy was ailing that summer, and that was a serious matter to the whole Blackford family. On August 11 Lewis wrote home: "I sincerely hope that Peggy is better, — tell her (with my love) that no Yankee shall steal her away while she has five tyrannical young masters to oppress her!" [65]

Meanwhile Launcelot had arrived at Fredericksburg whence he wrote his mother the following detailed account:

"The first place we went was to the Masonic burying ground where we dismounted for a time to examine the tomb of my grandparents which I did closely. . . The tomb is totally uninjured.

"Our next visit was to the old homestead. As I rode down Commerce and Main Street, I was surprised to find my recollection of the localities so vivid, considering that I had not been in Fredericksburg for about 14 years. There was 'Hall's Drug and Medicine

Store' at the corner, 'William Allen's' family grocery, with the 3 sugar loaves for a sign in front: the only store where really fine tea could be bought, if I remember Grandma's tenet on this subject aright; the ruins of where the Post Office used to be and of where Chester B. White used to sell books; the shop where Kate used to sell toys and confectionery, now deserted to the owls and bats; Dr. Herndon's house (occupied by some poor family) and William B. Pritchard's Coach Maker's Shop opposite; Mrs. Neal's, with the old lady herself in the white turban of yore sitting on the porch; — and last though not least, the old stand (a little wooden house at the corner now closed) of weasen-faced Mrs. Roberts, who used to sell one horse-cake or two 'gal' cakes for a cent. All these and many more of the places with which so many early and happy associations are connected, challenged my attention before I reached the house where I was born.

"The front of our old house is so much altered by the destruction of all the fencing that I was not quite sure of its identity, nor was I at all certain that Lewis was still there until, riding in between the next house and ours, to the back door, I inquired of a man standing there whose quarters these were, and was told, 'Captain Blackford's.' Lewis himself appeared in a few minutes and gave me a most cordial and affectionate welcome. I found him in the parlour, which he uses for his own chamber and as an office, with 3 or 4 assistants at work on maps. Shortly afterwards the rest of the party, from which I had gotten separated at the grave yard, came in, and it was soon arranged we should all stay and dine with Lewis.

"I had not been above 10 minutes on the premises when I made a rapid survey of the whole. I went in every room and examined every accessible nook, closet and corner. The chamber, used now as a sleeping room by several of the party, is, save in being bare of furniture and far from clean, much as you last saw it, down to the convenient presses and shelves in the closets which bear the unmistakable impress of father's handiwork. . . Upstairs and down, every room is occupied by the luxurious members of Captain Blackford's party as sleeping apartments. I went into 'grandma's room,' 'Uncle John's room,' 'the little room,' and even into the little porch off the upstairs passage (now bare of railing), where we as children used to sit and hear Maria tell stories while the ladies' prayer-meeting of the neighborhood was held at grandma's on Wednesday afternoons. . .

"Uncle John's room is the nicest looking one in the house and reminded me most vividly of its beloved occupant now no more, His study looks somewhat dilapidated inside, old books and papers thrown about, presses open, etc. The door is made fast but I looked in through the window. On the front of the house and between the study door and the one next are the names of Yankee soldiers scribbled inside; on the wall fronting the door is scribbled in large letters, 'Sam. I. Morrison, 7th Maine Regiment.' What a contrast this and all its surroundings to the long years of even quietness that characterized the life of the last occupant of that room!

"The only sign however of the bombardment about the whole place that I discovered is the track of one large shot (say a 20 pound Parrott) from one of our guns in the rear, which entered the kitchen window next Mrs. Ames', took out 2 panes, tore a hole in the brick partition wall between the kitchen and sleeping room adjacent, and went out at the door of the latter, carrying a panel with it. I understand the shot subsequently ricocheted and tore the roof of the house across the street.

"After sitting a while with Lewis at home, [we] took a walk. We went first down to the old 'Sentry Box' [Colonel Mercer's home]: the most dilapidated of all the houses at all left standing that I saw, and of course abandoned. It is literally torn all to pieces with shot and shell. A trench runs diagonally across the front yard, ruthlessly bisecting that incomparable grand walk that was perhaps never before disturbed. The houses in the vicinity of Colonel Mercer's are all much torn up, among them Hazle Hill,[66] where a sailor and his family are residing. We went there and reclined for an hour or two in the shady grass plat before the door." [67]

They returned after a little while to the old home on Main Street where Lewis gave them a good dinner and then Charles and Lanty moved out to their camp a few miles away. All five Blackford brothers remained in or near Fredericksburg for a time. These brothers were always friends, and they enjoyed each other's society. In September, Charles and Launcelot were ordered to Tennessee with the rest of Longstreet's Corps and Lewis was sent to Wilmington, North Carolina; William and Eugene remained to take part in the raids, skirmishes, and battles in northern Virginia that fall.

CHAPTER X

Yielding Place to New

In October 1863, Mary's brother, Lucius Minor, became seriously ill. Ignoring the inconvenience, discomfort, and actual dangers of travel across war-torn Virginia, again Mrs. Blackford hastened across the State, arriving at his bedside a few minutes before he lost consciousness. His wife had died in 1858; Charles and Berkeley, the older sons, were in the army; the girls had their hands full managing the farm with the aid and protection of their faithful slaves. When Mary left Edgewood, therefore, she took Robert, the youngest child, home with her: Lynchburg was still considered a safe place. In November, however, the enemy advanced from Lewisburg to within fifty miles of Lynchburg, and apprehension was felt as to the fate of the city.

Further to the southwest the Yankees were making constant raids. These caused grave concern to the Blackfords for William's wife and babies were living at the Meadows, Wyndham Robertson's home near Abingdon. It was then with great relief that they learned on November 11 that their newest grandchild had come safely into the troubled world. Mr. Blackford that day abstracted a letter from his daughter-in-law in his diary: "She says Pelham [1] was born a soldier. The enemy within five miles, our troops drawn up in line near the house and every thing in wildest confusion so that no assistance could be had. She says she remained perfectly calm and never had an easier or safer confinement. The child is healthy and very handsome." [2]

With Charles in Tennessee, Sue had rented their house in October and had moved in to live with Mr. and Mrs. Blackford. She

brought with her Nannie and her nurse, Mary, "a slave girl of
ours who was honest and faithful, and, while not clever, a lady
in her instincts and manners." [3] The grandparents completely lost
their hearts to the little girl; indeed everyone who came in contact
with Nannie Blackford succumbed to her charms. The child was a
great comfort to them all that dreary fall.

On November 13 Charles returned from the neighborhood of
Chattanooga, ill with malaria, his last sick leave. His father realized "It will take some time to put Charles in working order." [4]
Over his parents' objections, he, who had also profited from tobacco, insisted on paying board for himself and family. Eugene
turned up the same day, "broken down with recent hardships and
exposure," [5] and crippled with pain and swelling in that leg.

On December 5 Mr. Blackford confided to his diary: "I long
for a quiet household. We have had a great deal of company all
the summer and fall. *I want rest.* But it could not be helped, and
the hospitality was necessary and much appreciated by its recipients, I think." [6]

On December 8 Dr. "Turkey John" Minor performed an operation on Eugene's leg for varicose veins, which his interested father
explained thus: "It consists of injecting into about two inches of
the vein, cut off by pressure above and below, a solution of per-
sulphate of iron, which has the property of inducing the blood to
coagulate immediately. Inflammation ensues and the vein is obliterated after a few days and the coagulum sloughs out and the blood
finds or makes a new channel or channels of circulation. The operation was painful. It is new in these parts and is said to be the best
remedy. I have great confidence in Dr. Minor, but of course feel
much anxiety. This is only one of the operations Eugene will have
to undergo." [7]

Little was going on in Longstreet's Corps in Tennessee, so Lanty
was able to get a month's furlough to spend Christmas at home.
Around the table that day the Blackfords had three sons and Mary
Isabella, Sue Blackford and Nannie, and Lucy Landon's son, Willy
Davis. If Mrs. Blackford did not thoroughly enjoy the family re-
union, the others did. Christmas night "sixteen whites and six or

seven blacks" [8] slept under their roof. New Year's Eve William showed up on his way home to inspect his new son. That day Mr. Blackford refrained "from any reflection on the close of this eventful year." [9]

2

While other members of the family in Lynchburg were worrying over the problem of food and other necessities, Lewis was spending a rather pleasant winter in Wilmington, "living on sweet potatoes, hogfish and oysters." [10] He was very much interested in the success of the blockade-runners, and this suggested a plan to him: with Commodore Maury in London on business for the Confederate government and his affluent uncle, Dr. James Monroe Minor, in Brooklyn, it seemed a perfect setup. He wrote his mother:

"The clothes and things I got from Europe brought me in debt to Uncle Jim about $35.00, but I would not hesitate on that account. But you must be very cautious, and ought to send your letters as I did via England. Mail from Nassau to New York is all inspected by Yankees. Write to Cousin Mat to purchase what you want and instruct him to draw on Uncle Jim for the money, — that will be perfectly sure not to compromise Uncle Jim in any way. Enclose to Cousin Mat a letter to Uncle Jim stating the circumstances, and get Cousin Mat to forward it with the draft for the money. Cousin Mat can forward the goods very readily to Wilmington to my care. Surely an advance of two or three hundred dollars to his own kin ought not to seem a hardship to a man as rich as Uncle Jim." [11]

But Mary Blackford was no more willing to owe money to her brother James than she had been to borrow from her brother Lewis eleven years earlier: her lifelong horror of debt put a prompt stop to her son's scheme. After that Lewis used what money he could scrape up to have his blockade-running friends bring him shoes, gloves, and other things his mother and sister might need, as well as other merchandise which he retailed at a profit. (His father was paying $60 for a pair of shoes in Lynchburg at this time.)

Though thus disappointed in getting many things for his mother, the success of the blockade-runners appealed to Lewis' hedonism. He wrote home later: "This port averages an arrival and departure every 24 hours. When these schooners arrive safe the officers like to celebrate. . . The finest ship that comes here is the *City of Petersburg*, owned altogether in Virginia, and her captain and Purser are very pleasant fellows and of endless hospitality. They give breakfasts, lunches and dinners every day while the ship is in port, and seem to take great delight in having as many ladies and gentlemen as the cabin will accommodate at the table," serving choice wines, cheeses, and other "rarest delicacies." [12] (By this time flour was bringing $100 a barrel in Lynchburg and corn had gone up to $11 a bushel!)

Lewis fell desperately in love that winter with a girl of Northern parentage and, in spite of her father's vehement disapproval, they became engaged. Mr. Blackford wrote that he would welcome her with open arms, but Mrs. Blackford was still very skeptical about Lewis' being able to pick out a suitable wife. Both discouraged his getting married until the war was over.

3

In January 1864, Charles and Launcelot returned to their duties in northeastern Tennessee. About the same time Mr. Blackford recorded a rumor that Louis Napoleon was about to propose help to the Confederacy provided all slaves were emancipated in thirty years, and he observed: "Virginia, Kentucky, Tennessee and Missouri would be glad to make such a bargain. At the beginning of the war I repeatedly said that, terminate as it might, slavery would be practically at an end, for with it the end and the beginning of the end would be much the same." [13]

Thirty years later Charles commented on his father's words: "Long before the end of the war there was a belief, certainly amongst the Virginia soldiers, that in Virginia at least, slavery would be impossible even after we gained our independence. Such sentiments were openly expressed by the privates and much conned by the more thoughtful and prudent officers. . . I remember a declaration by General James L. Kemper (at a dinner attended by some high-ranking officers in Tennessee, February, 1864). He said that he believed our only chance of success lay in our at once declaring the slaves all free, and proclaiming to the world that we fought only for self-government and independence. In this sentiment most of those present, much to my surprise, concurred. The difference was only as to how that end could be accomplished. Kemper held that if such a proclamation was made by President Davis and General Lee, it would be approved by the people and that foreign nations would at once recognize our independence and interfere in our behalf." [14]

On February 2, 1864, Eugene underwent a second operation for varicose veins, but the severe pain and the risks involved were all in vain.[15] March 29, believing further fighting imminent, he returned to his regiment.

Meanwhile from Russellville, Tennessee, Launcelot announced to his mother on February 5, "the safe arrival of Sister Sue, Nannie and Mary." Like many a bachelor since that day, Lanty knew all about bringing up children, and he disapproved of the way Charles and Sue were raising Nannie. Perhaps forgetting that they had lost three babies, two from diphtheria, he wrote the little girl's grandmother on March 3: "Nannie has of course had more than the usual of the constant spoiling to which she has long been accustomed, but gives the best evidence of her many excellent natural traits by showing it so little. She is, I think, a very fine little girl, clever, amiable and generous, and needs nothing but careful training to make her a superior woman, if one may express an opinion at her early age. I do not think I ever knew people of character who had less idea of properly training a child."

Like many other Confederate officers, Charles had a body servant to relieve him of much of the drudgery of camp. The Tennessee sojourn so debilitated this servant, a free Negro of literary tastes, that Charles had to send him home on March 30. He carried with him this note from Lanty to his father: "John Scott, Charles' tried and faithful servant and mine to some extent, goes to night to Lynchburg on leave of absence of several weeks to recruit his health which has for some months been feeble. Any kindness or service you or mother may have it in your power to do for him he will highly appreciate, and Charles and myself will be grateful for. He is deserving of your consideration." [16]

The coming of spring found the Blackford household in Lynchburg reduced to Mary, her husband, and little Robert Minor. This situation was not displeasing to Mr. Blackford who was working twelve to sixteen hours a day on the latest funding operation, being responsible for very large sums of money.[17] He was looking forward to being able to take things a little easier when the operation was completed at the end of March. The record for more than a year, read in the light of modern knowledge, shows that his blood pressure had been soaring. His brother, the Doctor, had died of cerebral hemorrhage a year earlier. On April 1 he did reduce his working hours but a few days later he had to take to his bed, suffering with a stroke. Dr. Davis and Dr. Ben Blackford were in attendance, so "all that medical skill could do was done." [18]

Longstreet had just been ordered back to Virginia. The train from Tennessee with the headquarters of the First Corps, Sue, Nannie, and the ever faithful Mary, arrived in Lynchburg the afternoon of April 12. Learning of their father's critical condition, General Longstreet gave Charles and Launcelot leaves of absence. The other three sons failed to arrive before his death two days later but they were in time for the funeral, the last time all five were to be together for almost thirty years. Charles was able to remain at home another ten days, but the rest had to return at once to their commands.

A few days later Eugene, acknowledging the sympathy of a cousin, wrote her: "Mary [Isabella] writes in very poor spirits: I fear the worst for Mother. Knowing her as I do, I was not surprised to see how well she bore up (apparently) at the time of the funeral, but it was just what I expected. She suffers most when others begin to forget. It was so in regard to Sister's death, and Uncle John's. His memory is just as fresh with her as if he had died yesterday." [19]

Launcelot tried to console his mother on April 23 with these words: "I trust that the recollection of how much you are to your sons and of the fact that you are now the sole surviving stay of the old homestead, will serve to divest your mind from a despairing tone, and to stimulate you in every way to preserve the health and lengthen the life on which so much of the happiness of your children depends. Your work on earth seems, in my eyes, my dear mother, as yet far from complete."

Mrs. Blackford wrote her cousin at the University on May 3: "I am very grateful for your two letters to me, they contained the best comfort I could have. But I have [suffered], and still do suffer so much from that dreadful sickness of heart; even when I enter for a while into what is going on around me, the feeling of desolation returns with greater force afterwards. There was so much to love in the exceeding sweetness of his disposition and every thing that makes home delightful that it is scarcely possible to miss any one more. In every thing around me I see proofs of his ingenuity and love, for many of the things were made to please me. His love was the charm of my life. I often used to tell him, 'You keep me young in feelings.' "

4

Those first weeks after her husband's death Mary Blackford helped the younger women to prepare bandages. What made life bearable to her was her interest in the wounded soldiers. They seemed to "arouse her more than anything else." [20] There was plenty to do for, in the spring of 1864, Lynchburg was taking care of more sick and wounded Confederate soldiers than any other city in Virginia but Richmond. Important, too, in sustaining her will to live was little Nannie, who spent most of her time with her grandmother, and whom she declared "the best child" she had ever seen and "the most affectionate and amiable."

It was fortunate that Mrs. Blackford did have something to divert her mind for, that May, William and Eugene were in the heavy fighting in Spotsylvania. On May 8, Longstreet [21] was again severely wounded: he and other wounded officers of his staff were sent to Lynchburg. Sue took especial pleasure in showering little attentions on her husband's friends. The enlisted men of the First Corps too were cheered by hearing she had been with them in Tennessee.

In June, Hunter, that "renegade Virginian . . . traitor to his blood and home," [22] advanced on unprotected Lynchburg. Mrs. Blackford had the family silver hidden under Peggy's bed.

General Breckenridge with a handful of fit men reached Lynchburg the night of June 15. Two nights later General Early arrived with a few more, but he bluffed the Yankees by running a locomotive in and out of town to make the enemy think that reinforcements were arriving in large numbers. [23] By the evening of Saturday, June 18, additional troops really did arrive. Among them was Eugene. He made straight for his mother, but he could not be with her long, for soon, as he narrated some days later:

"A cousin came in and said the attack would be made at day light. I therefore went out at once. At 2 A.M. we moved, & marched through Spring Hill Cemetery within 50 yards of my Father's grave. At dawn Gen. Early discovered what I had been all the while convinced of, that the enemy had retreated, & then commenced the race which I shall remember to my death as being the most miserable two days of my existence." Early pursued Hunter through Liberty. "Every where the country was desolate, homes burnt, stock killed, barns burnt, and every species of outrage inflicted upon the people which a devilish ingenuity could devise. Woe to them if our soldiers could have overtaken them, cries for quarter would have fallen upon deaf ears. For once I was sufficiently worked up to have been able to refuse the most direct appeal." [24]

He described Early's further course through Buchanan on the James, via Lexington where the home of former Governor Letcher had been destroyed by Hunter, Staunton, down the Valley Pike to Winchester, to Harper's Ferry, Shepherdstown, Sharpsburg, the bivouac on the Antietam, to Rockville on the outskirts of Washington. "We could have gone into Washington with a loss of a thousand or two men from their Artillery. What then? The men would have sacked the City — and have been drunk and unmanageable in an hour. Meanwhile heavy re-inforcements would have come up and have destroyed us in that fix. No private in our ranks ever had any idea that 'Old Jubilee' really intended to attack the place. Forts were as thick as blackberries around the town, — with plenty of Artillery, but no men."

From Lynchburg on June 20, Sue wrote Charles: "Mother stood [the perilous excitement] remarkably well. She was of course very anxious about Eugene as she could hear the booming of the cannon, but she kept up her nerve and her spirits." [25]

Launcelot expressed his feelings in a letter to his mother on June 24. "It is with . . . devout thankfulness to God," he wrote, "that I hear of Lynchburg's being relieved from the prospect of invasion, a feeling greatly stimulated by hearing of the outrages of the enemy elsewhere in that quarter, particularly at Lexington . . . It is my deliberate opinion that Hunter and his crew are outlaws and should not be taken prisoners, but slain wherever and however found. . .

"I am glad to know you had an opportunity of seeing Eugene," he added, "though but for a few hours. It is always cheering to meet him and brother William: they take such cheering views always of the aspect of our affairs, a good antidote in this respect for the contrary temper just now in Charles whose heart seems to be failing him, though this is not the usual tone of his sentiments. For myself, I am glad to say I can ordinarily maintain an even and cheerful temper as to our prospects."

Charles' comment for once was pithy: "I suppose Eugene was perfectly charmed at the chance of fighting at home and for his home. I wish I could have had the same chance." [26]

5

James Churchill Cooke of Dewberry, Sergeant of Company C, 4th Virginia Cavalry was severely wounded on June 16. He had "addressed" Mary Isabella before the war without success, a fact that repressed young lady had confided to no one. Undiscouraged, Churchill had continued his suit and she had finally accepted him. As soon as she heard of his wounds she hastened to Dewberry to help his mother and war-widowed sisters nurse him back to health.

Charles and Launcelot spent a monotonous summer in and around Petersburg. On August 25 Lanty wrote his mother:

"I had a letter yesterday from Eugene, dated Strasburg, Aug. 15. The Major (for Eugene is Major still, I am sorry to say) writes somewhat fully and in good spirits. . . In two months he has marched 1000 miles. In that time he has seen but 3 Richmond papers & knows, he says, little or nothing of what is going on in other quarters than the 'Valley District.' . . .

"Raw onions and tomatoes are the staple vegetables of our diet," he went on. "The latter I do not eat, but I am very fond of the former, which I eat twice a day. I think onions must be a very healthful diet and am inclined to attribute the uninterrupted and excellent health I have enjoyed this summer in this lower country to their free use. Notwithstanding this, it is an essentially vulgar vegetable, and should never find place on a gentleman's table except in camp."

In August, Lewis, whose health had been "miserable on the North Carolina coast" [27] (he was to suffer from malaria for several summers to come), succeeded in getting transferred back to Virginia. Soon he was comfortably ensconced once again in the house where he was born, and from there he wrote on September 20:

"Indeed I believe that so far as I can observe, Fredericksburg is the cheapest place that I have been to in the Confederacy; and I know it is the case in Stafford that the people, especially the poorer citizens, are better off than they have been during the War. I am very glad to be able to offer Willy Davis [28] a good place. He is with me now, and seems to be a handsome, manly, intelligent fellow: I can hardly realize that Sister's son should be old enough to be in the Army." (Willy was sixteen.)

In August too, Colonel Dick Maury of the 24th Virginia Infantry offered the adjutancy of his regiment to his cousin Launcelot. Lanty had a sense of having performed well a necessary duty, but after twenty-two months he was becoming increasingly uncomfortable in a noncombatant role. Not wishing however to enlist again as a private, he accepted the post immediately. He informed his mother that "the change would go hard with me, but the very hardship and danger of the new position would add honour to it and in no eyes, I am sure, more than those of my dear mother." [29]

The adjutancy of the 24th Virginia had the added attraction to Launcelot of throwing him again with its chaplain, his old college and army friend, William F. Gardner, who had been ordained as an Episcopal priest while convalescing from wounds incurred at Second Manassas. In his new role Lanty soon found opportunity of renewing his social activities. On January 4, 1865, he wrote his mother:

"I called twice on the Misses Lee, one of whom I knew before. I went first with Charles Minor and next with Gardner. The General happened to be in town, and when Gardner and I entered the parlour Monday evening he was the first person we saw. He received us with the courtesy which is natural to him but which is always somewhat stately, though simple, towards young gentlemen, and shortly afterward he withdrew. He looked grand: almost the only man I ever saw to whom it did not seem natural to extend my hand; though he relieved me of the embarrassment by offering his first. General Early had just left the parlour and it was to bear him company that General Lee was there, I supposed. The Misses Lee are very clever and agreeable and perfectly free from any trace of assumption on their father's fame. Miss Agnes is pretty, but her older sister the more agreeable."

6

The sands were running out fast. All the glamour, all the joy of the struggle had long since disappeared. By February 1865 the approaching end of the conflict was all too clear. Unsettled condi-

tions afterward were anticipated, so the Blackfords were quite willing for Mary Isabella to marry immediately her invalid fiancé
they had all known so long. It is to be hoped that the many letters
of advice the girl received from her rigidly formal older brothers
were terminated with the long letter Lanty wrote her as to her
approaching wedding. Lanty's communication contained this striking item:

"Be sure to let Churchill's *regiment* appear on the card. I would
not have it appear that you married any body but a soldier, particularly now. Men that ain't soldiers may be very well in their way,
but I prefer not to have any such in the family." [30]

The hopelessness of the last days and the tragedy of the surrender have been told over and over again. The course of the Blackfords during this period may be stated briefly:

Launcelot was captured at Sailor's Creek just before the end:
he was paroled after Appomattox and walked home, arriving on
Easter Sunday, April 17. William had just passed through on his
way to rejoin his wife and children in Abingdon. Sue had been
sent from Richmond to the University when the fall of the capital
became imminent, and she was staying with her sister, the second
wife of John B. Minor. Charles joined her there: June 10 he too
walked back to Lynchburg to take up again the practice of law,
but it was some time before the railroad bridges were sufficiently
repaired to allow Sue and Nannie to travel home. Lewis divided
his time between Richmond and Hanover. Eugene tarried at the
University, where he was soon engaged in tutoring his former
comrades-in-arms, impatient to continue their interrupted educations. Their only clothes were their battle-stained uniforms.

7

Although Lewis had declared in the first year of the war, "nothing will ever make me acknowledge myself a subject of Lincoln's
. . . I believe I would rather endure suffering, beggary and death
than submit to such degradation," [31] when he received an offer of

employment (at $1,600) under General Michie of the U. S. Topographical Engineers within a month of the surrender, he changed his mind and hurried to New York in pursuit of his fiancée.

On May 21 Lanty described to him conditions at home. "For the first time since you left us," he wrote, "the town was re-occupied by the Enemy in small force about ten days since. On the 18th the command of this 'Military Subdistrict,' one of the five into which the state of Virginia (exclusive of the so-called West Virginia, I believe) is divided was assumed by J. Irwin Gregg, 'Bvt. Brig. Gen. Volunteers,' with Lt. Col. A. P. Duncan, 4th Pennsylvania Cavalry, as Provost Marshal. General Gregg has already made a very favourable impression upon the community by his demeanor as a gentleman and his apparent dispositions as an officer. . . Of the Provost Marshal too I have heard only favourable estimates. . . Excellent order is preserved here and few if any collisions between soldiers and citizens have occurred. Indeed the entire period between the two Federal occupations was as quiet as could be.

"Citizens generally are taking the 'Amnesty Oath' — the most prominent setting the example. Though it is exceedingly repugnant both to my taste and feeling to assume any such obligation, as there is no longer any better reason against it, I expect to succumb in a week or so and take the oath in good faith. It is impossible to do otherwise. . . Mother sends her love to Miss K." [32]

On his return to Richmond May 30, Lewis reported to his mother: "Uncle Jim has suffered so terribly on account of the South that his hatred and abhorrence of Yankees amounts to a monomania. I can not in a letter convey to you the remotest idea of the fierce condition of his emotions.

"Now for Sue: I found her perfectly radiant in her beauty and dazzling in the triumphs of her dress; I could hardly recognize her as the pretty girl I left in Wilmington in a brown calico dress and straw hat. I have so much to say of her and her kin and their disposition towards me, etc., that I must postpone it to another letter. Suffice it to say that she is as true in the sunshine of the vanities & splendor of New York as she was on the beclouded sea-coast. . . There are heavy & threatening clouds in the air though, of which I will tell you in my next. She is a darling.

"I commenced operations here yesterday," he added, "and feel somewhat amused at being in command of Yankee soldiers. I am going into Camp near town. I am furnished with ambulance, saddle horse and obsequious orderly."

His conscience was none too easy however, and he asked for moral support from his family. Charles came through magnificently with the statement: "I don't for my part see the vast objection to your conduct and to the contrary I approve of it highly. It is far more honorable to go to work for whoever may pay for it than to eat other men's bread in idleness. And I admire the determination you showed in at once going to work and incurring the odium which may be expressed by a very few foolish people, all of whom are actuated more from jealousy than any other motive. So far as I have heard any expression of opinion, it has been that you are perfectly right. All the business men here think so and so do your friends at the University." [33]

His mother added her endorsement in these words: "We are very glad you have such a good situation, at least Charles, Lanty and, I have no doubt, William. Eugene, who is *distracted* by our failure, does not like it. When his mind recovers its tone, he will, I hope, feel differently.

"We have had many conversations," Mary Blackford could never refrain very long from preaching, "about the beauty & excellence of economy when it enables us to be just and generous, — and in these times it assumes a higher character than ever before in our time; it is nearly allied to integrity & honor — and so far from being connected with closeness, I love and cherish it because it keeps me from having to use meanness.

"Did you know that Charles L. C. and Berkeley are working daily in the fields," she continued, "and so is Col. Nelson of Oakland and his brother Robert who was a missionary? And I hear that one of Gen. Lee's sons does the same." [34]

On June 22 Mrs. Blackford chided Lewis again for epistolary neglect with these words: "The affection and attention of my children, since I lost the dearest and best of husbands has been my greatest earthly comfort." Six days later however, she wrote to him as the comforting mother of a heartbroken boy:

"I can not express, my beloved son, the sympathy I feel for you, and the indignation at what I know to be your unworthy treatment. It makes my heart sick to think of it. . . Oh! my darling, when I think how this girl has made you suffer my whole heart rises in strong indignation. She certainly has trifled with you. I do not blame any one for discarding my son, but to do so as she has done is quite another thing. I will tell you *now* that I distrusted her, there was something a little overstrained in her letters to you, or rather expressions in them, a departure from what Shakespere calls 'the modesty of nature.' She seemed to me to express too much, like the French novels. Yet I kept it to myself, thought that I might be wrong, and was ready to receive her to my heart. Yet, my beloved, I do not expect you to feel what may be true, that this apparent misfortune may turn out to be a blessing."

Mrs. Blackford in July accepted her brother James' invitation to come north. She was accompanied of course by Peggy. From his country place she wrote Lewis again on August 1:

"My mind dwells often upon your bad treatment by Miss K., and though I feel so deeply for the wrong done you, I am more and more convinced that you have made an escape from a union for life to an unprincipled woman. Her conduct would have been so even if she had not engaged herself *immediately* to another man. But *at once* to turn (after all her professed love to you, her caresses and tears) and engage herself to another man because you *were poor* — showed her to be such a woman that I shudder to think you might have married her. . . I wish you would confide all this trouble to your excellent and faithful friend and brother Launcelot. . .

"I shall be extremely anxious to hear from you. Pray write yourself, and if not well enough, get some one to write for you and if you continue ill send for me, my Son, and let Peggy and me nurse you."

The depth of Lewis' hurt was revealed by his unwillingness to confide in any of his brothers for, contrary to his mother's opinion, he did love them. Launcelot was not informed until August 27. Promptly he replied:

"I write now for the joint purpose of assuring you of my sympathy in your grief and of entering my most earnest protest against the plan it has put into your head of self-expatriation. To this there are so many objections that I can not decide which most to urge. Indeed it seems to me that all the arguments that relate to it are on one side, i.e., against it. If you are in sorrow, what worse remedy can you devise to render it tolerable than going to a country where you will be remote from every individual who sympathizes with you. Things are bad enough in this country now to suggest the idea of seeking another I know, but they must improve and, I believe, they certainly will. But great as are the evils incident to remaining here, can you be at all sure they are not less even now than those you would incur in Mexico [35] or Brazil for example, where the moral, political and religious atmospheres are as far as possible from what we have been educated to like and admire? May you not plunge into another Revolution, or may you not find yourself in a community where negro-suffrage and equality are more imminent than the most apprehensive consider them to be in the South?

"For my part, if I left the South my first thought would be to seek a home among the Yankees, either in New York City or in one of the North Western States; and if the idea of remaining any where in Andy Johnson's Dominion was intolerable, I would go to some of the British possessions — they are large enough, thank God, to admit of a very wide range of selection. After this I don't think there is very much choice.

"But my preference for myself, and my most earnest counsel to you, is to *stick by old Virginia* where we know the people even as we are known of them, where our ancestors have lived under three different governments, where their bones rest and their names live and are respected, where we may even yet live to enjoy a fair share of national liberty and help transmit it to those who are to come after us. This I conceive to be *equally to our interest and our duty*. Any other course I believe must result in unhappiness and discomfiture.

"You have a good place and a good profession. Why not stick by both, and determine not to let misfortune cast you down? Continue to serve where you are until you can do better." [36]

Charles again was brief. "I hope you will think well of it before you give up any sure place for an uncertainty," he counseled. "So many are now out of employment that $150 a month is very handsome pay, — *many, many* times more than I expect to get for some years to come." [37]

8

Among the unhappy Confederate veterans at that time was William. He sent his mother this gloomy account of conditions around Abingdon that summer:

"My life now is a perfectly idle one and can not be otherwise until something more of the future is known. Reading and fixing up such little things as I can find for the amusement of the children together with an occasional ride on horseback make up the sum of my daily life.

"The country out here is in a very unsettled state, subject to forages from bands of robbers who infest the borders of Tennessee and Virginia. Many horses have been stolen and houses robbed in broad day light by them. . .

"Mary was much surprised and distressed by Phoebe's announcing her determination a few evenings ago to leave the next day and thus on a few hours' notice she broke the connection of a lifetime, plunging into 'freedom' with the blind infatuation that it is a state of freedom from cares and troubles. She and her husband have set up for themselves about eight miles from here and are in as fair a way to starve to death as any people I know. He is idle and thriftless. She is lazy and delicate. Mary thought she was ruined, but we now have a little girl of twelve, who does very well and we get along much better than we expected, & I think in more comfort than before. Phoebe had become much spoiled." [38]

After four years in war-torn Virginia with constant anxiety about her five sons and her many young kinsmen, Mary Blackford enjoyed the luxuries of her brother's home near Scarborough, New York. But she was glad to receive news from home in a letter by Charles on August 30:

"We all feel much pleasure in the thought that you are enjoying your trip so much, and that Peggy is too, and that you both are in better health. We hope that you will not shorten your stay on account of any of us. Sue is keeping house for Lanty, Eugene and myself. Lanty's work at Mr. Cabell's school does not begin until October so he will be here another month. I regard him as the best teacher in Virginia — if I had a boy to educate, I should rather have him under his care than that of any one I know.[39] He is teaching Nannie now. Eugene will have a very fine day school, and his gross income, I think, will certainly be as much as $2,000. It is a great pity he & Lanty did not go into partnership & open a school. . . Lewis is still in Richmond. I have only lately heard of his troubles in regard to that tar-heel girl, though I suspected something was the matter a month ago. . . It was infamous conduct on the part of the girl. Blood will tell, — her Father is a Yankee & she was born in N. C.! . . .

"There is no improvement here in business. . . I am really now so hard up for money that some days I can not go to market. I have been steadily in my office for two months. Thus far my professional earnings have only amounted to $60, which is only a dollar a day. I am, it is true, doing as much business as any one else — but that reflection is not comforting. The last five months I was in my office before the war I made $400 a month, and that in gold, & in addition to that I had an income from my property of near $2,000. The difference is very great. I find it hard to keep up my spirits — sometimes they sink so low I bend over my books & cry like a child. . . William, I suspect, is as bad off at present as I am. He is going to rent a farm near Abingdon & go to farming. We seldom hear from him."

In September, Charles announced to his mother the birth of Charles Minor Blackford, Jr. He went on: "While we are in great

delight over it, we are in other domestic affairs in 'doleful dumps.'
. . . A few days ago Jenny came up with a petition that Mary
might be allowed to go to a party in some alley on Main Street,
which I knew was not a decent place for her. I refused and told
her mother that so long as she was under my care she should not
go to any such place. Jenny went off in high wrath, saying I would
not let Mary see any pleasure and as soon as the baby was born
she sent Mary with a message to Sue informing her that she would
not let her remain with us any longer, that she wanted her at
home to help her. I told her to go when she thought fit.

"She has not left yet, nor do I know when she will go; when
she does the baby will be without one human to nurse it. I could
stand that as we can get any body who would be more efficient
than Mary, but I do much grieve that she should be carried to
Main Street to be made a prostitute by her own mother. The de-
bauchery here among the servant girls exceeds anything that I
have ever known, — freedom and the Yankees have demoralized
them all. Mary cared nothing for either — she has always been as
free as she knew how to be and was too well trained as a respectable
negro to associate with Yankees — but now under her mother's
teaching she will be taught that freedom consists in street walking
with Yankees." [40]

Late in October Mrs. Blackford returned to Lynchburg. A few
days later she received a gratifying letter from an old friend in
Staunton, Maria West Campbell, the long emancipated Negro
woman who had taken such good care of her mother in Lucy
Landon Minor's declining years:

"Dear Madam, It have bin a long time since I heard from you
or any of your children and allway feeling interested in the wel-
fare of all your family makes me anxious to hear from you all. I
have written diferent times but I thought the letters did not come
to hand. Has any of the gentlemen imbided religion. I heard Mr.
C had and I know Mr L M had but has any of the others in the
midst of all my difficultys I prayes for them all my prayers are
weak yet I must try. where is Mis Mary Isabelas do you ever here

from Fredericksburg do you ever think of going there again to live
O When I think of the happy times that I have seen there and
now see and feel the changes it makes me feel very sad please
remember me humbly to all your family.

"Lucindia sends her love humbly to you and your family. She
have not bin out doors for near two years her health is very deli-
cate pleas give our love to Peggy tell her she must write to me
I have written to her but got no answer if it had not been for
Lucindia ill health I should have bin to see you all long since
Farewell and God bless you and all yours is my prayer." [41]

A few days later Mrs. Blackford wrote to Launcelot who was
teaching boys, many of them veterans, in Mr. Cabell's school in
Norwood: "The kind of life they led as soldiers was a good preparation, teaching them first, obedience to orders, and making them
feel sensibly the great advantage of education from which they
were forced to be debarred during war time." [42] A visit from a
Confederate hero and kinsman drew from her a rare expression of
happiness. "Night before last Gen'l Dabney Maury stayed all night
here on his way to New Orleans," she continued. "I enjoyed his
little visit immensely, he is so affectionate & fresh in his feelings,
has such a playful humour, and is so free from pretension that
his company is charming. I have not for a long time enjoyed any
one's company so much."

The first postwar autumn seems to have stirred her to unusual
activity for when Dr. Lewis W. Minor, practicing in New Orleans,
wrote her a few days after General Maury's arrival there, he felt
constrained to reprove her: "Dabney told me of a piece of your
imprudence in climbing the hills or mountains of Tobaccoville. He
says it was enough to break him down. You should be more careful, sister mine. If you would let the hills and the Churches alone
you would, I think, find yourself benefitted." [43]

That same month, November 1865, she received an impersonal,
almost curt, letter from the Reverend William McLain, President
of the Colonization Society. The rapid transit of letters from beyond the Potomac had not long survived the outbreak of the war:
Mr. McLain had written on January 5, "I have this moment re-

ceived letters from the Colony dated Oct. 22 and am informed that *Abraham* is well and is doing well."

About the same time she was happy to get an answer to a letter she had sent her old friend and co-worker, the Reverend R. R. Gurley. "Great changes have occurred since we met," he wrote on November 14. "But such are to be looked for in our changing state. I rejoice that your Christian Faith is unchanged, & your confidence in the Divine Love to our race, & especially toward our colored people. Liberia has on the whole prospered greatly & she has room and can obtain it for any number of our emancipated people." [44] Mr. Gurley never lost his faith in the colonization project.

"I can not but think," he continued, "this great & terrible war will prove in the end an incalculable injury to both races that inhabit our southern states. Many of the colored people will live and die among us and many others will emigrate to Liberia & perhaps other countries. But the civilization & moral and Religious renovation of Africa through His love enlightened by our most blessed Faith, is an object vast enough to warm and animate all hearts imbued by the spirit of the gospel." But even Mr. Gurley's hope and enthusiasm were not great enough to persuade many Negroes to embark for Liberia after the war, and many of those who did regretted it.[45]

He closed that letter on a very personal note: "You have indeed lost one of the best husbands, & please accept my cordial sympathy. We are passing rapidly toward a land where the sound of war is unheard and death is unknown."

That winter in Lynchburg passed uneventfully. Peggy kept house for Mrs. Blackford and Eugene. Charles and Sue lived in the neighborhood. Lewis and Launcelot got home from time to time, and occasionally William came over from Abingdon.

A year after the war Mary Blackford brought to an end her *Notes Illustrative of the Wrongs of Slavery* in glorious triumph:

"March, 1866. A new era has dawned since I last wrote in this book. Slavery has been abolished!!! Too suddenly for the real good of the Slaves, as they were not prepared to enjoy and appreciate the great boon of rational freedom after beng kept so many years in abject Slavery and in profound ignorance. . .

"5th June, 1866. I have been this morning to witness a procession of nearly a thousand children belonging to colored Schools. It is the anniversary of the first establishment of schools here where colored children could be taught to read, exactly one year ago. The procession was swelled by different societies, benevolent and literary, the parents of the children and a vast number of colored people beside. I suppose it extended half a mile. It was a great picnic occasion, and the procession marched out to a wood near town where an abundance of good things were prepared for the children, and I believe there was enough for all. There was great order and propriety observed and they had speaking, and then returned quite early in the evening, there being a threatening of rain.

"I only saw the procession from Dr. Payne's porch. It was to me the most interesting public occasion I ever witnessed. For when I thought that this was the anniversary of the day when the little ones were no longer shut out of the light of God's truth, that the fetters of ignorance were at last broken, and that they might not be forced from their parents & sold at public auction to the highest bidder, my heart went up in adoring gratitude to the great God; not only on their account, but that *we white people* were no longer permitted to go on in such wickedness, heaping up more & more the wrath of God upon our devoted heads.

"As my mind reviewed such thoughts, there appeared more of the moral sublime in what I then witnessed than I ever knew of before in any other scene. It was a sight I am sure that angels rejoiced in; and had I given way to the emotions that filled my heart and eyes, I should have shouted,

" 'Praised be the Lord!' "

Epilogue

About the middle of the eighteenth century a wealthy Virginia planter selected for the site of his country home a hill three miles west of the newly founded town of Alexandria. There he erected a mansion he called Howard. It still stands. The thickness of its walls suggests that he feared Indian raids; the lofty ceilings of the two large rooms on the first floor with their beautifully carved woodwork also indicate that he built soon after 1750.

In front, a little to each side of the great house, connected to it by a picturesque covered corridor, he put a square, one-story cottage, divided into two rooms. At the beginning of the twentieth century a very old willow tree was rotting between the mansion and the south "office": tradition has it that this willow sprang from a riding switch that young George Washington had thrown away when he came over from Mt. Vernon one day to call on the young lady of the house. That story may be pure fantasy, but it is true that the northern boundary of the farm was the road taken by General Braddock on that ill-fated expedition against the French and Indians.

The Episcopal Diocese of Virginia had founded a Theological Seminary in Alexandria in 1823. Perhaps thinking the city life too distracting for the divinity students or perhaps unhealthy for them, the Trustees of the Diocese moved the Seminary out to the country and, while they were about it, decided to open a boarding school for boys next door, so they bought the Howard estate. Behind the residence they added a large building to house the boys and provide class rooms: the Episcopal High School was opened in 1839.

Its first Rector was the Reverend William Nelson Pendleton, a graduate of West Point in 1830, and later Chief of Artillery of the Army of Northern Virginia. The Reverend John P. McGuire, formerly of Fredericksburg, was in charge when the War began. Only eight miles from Washington, the place was seized by the Federal forces in the early days of the War and soon it was utilized as a hospital. Remains of old forts and breastworks for the protection of the capital may still be found in the neighborhood, but in the past forty years suburbanization has obliterated most of them.

The School was reopened in 1866 under the Reverend William F. Gardner, an "Old Boy." He resigned after four years to go into parish work and the Trustees, violating the precedent of having a clergyman as Rector, appointed Launcelot M. Blackford Principal. He borrowed $3,000 from Charles (whose fortunes had improved in five years) to make necessary repairs and opened his first session September 21, 1870, with thirty-one boarders and nine day scholars, two of whom he had inherited from Mr. Gardner. Among those Launcelot early chose as his assistants were Berkeley Minor, kinsman and fellow veteran of the Rockbridge Artillery, Frank Page of Oakland and George Washington Nelson, Jr., of Mont Air; all three had been friends of his long before they entered the Confederate Army.

Launcelot Blackford liked the place. Next door the Dean of the Theological Seminary was the Reverend Dr. Joseph Packard, whose two sons had served in the Rockbridge Artillery, and the Seminary was still thronged with old army friends. Not least among the attractions of Alexandria to Launcelot was Christ Church, the church of George Washington and of Robert Edward Lee, and its Rector was his dear friend, Randolph H. McKim. Launcelot promptly transferred his membership to Christ Church.

Satisfied that his mother would also like the place, Lanty invited her to come and live with him. Lewis was in Georgetown across the Potomac, Eugene in Baltimore, and William in Louisiana; Mary Isabella was on her husband's farm near Richmond. Only Charles was left in Lynchburg. Mrs. Blackford may have felt that in Alexandria she would be more conveniently located for visits from her children. She may have thought that Launcelot, still a bachelor, most needed her counsel and guidance; that was probably the reason she assigned to herself. Perhaps she realized that he would be most patient with her demands for attention, which did not lessen with age. Perhaps she loved him best. Whatever the reason, she declined the invitations of her other children to spend her remaining years with them, and came to the Episcopal High School with Peggy. They were installed in the north "office."

Mrs. Blackford brought with her the massive mahogany four-poster [1] that her father had had made in England for his first bride whose name she bore. The old lady spent most of her time in this bed, receiving like a dowager empress the homage of her children and their children, and of her brothers' grandchildren. She required each of them to read the Bible to her and Peggy, and to join them in prayer. She particularly liked to have her granddaughters get down on their knees around her great high bed to pray for good husbands: one used to sneak out on all fours and, her sister maliciously recalls, she never did get a husband of any kind! [2] The grandchildren still remember however that she used to reward their piety with quarters, and that Mam' Peggy was often able to find oranges in the wardrobe for them too.

She never considered the training of her children complete but, after 1870, she had little opportunity, save by letters, to supervise the lives of any but Launcelot. He of course called on her every day and often spent hours reading aloud to her, but that was not enough. Somehow, even in her nineties, when the spirit moved her she would, with the help of Peggy's right arm and a cane, manage to hobble up to her son's study. If she found nobody, she would rattle her stick across the balusters of the stairway to the second floor until she received attention.

If she found the Principal in his sanctum, regardless of what he might be doing or of whoever else was there, she would go in to demand what she wanted. If she found him smoking she would wait till he put down his cigar, and then pounce upon it to destroy it. The presence of a schoolboy never deterred her in the least: though her attitude might appear *lèse-majesté* to the boy, none ever saw him betray impatience.[3] In 1876, however, Mr. Blackford decided to go abroad every summer to enrich his culture and broaden his outlook, but especially to study the methods and traditions of the famous old English public schools; at least such were the reasons he gave. His diaries on such trips show that he received many letters from his mother, even that time he got as far east as St. Petersburg. She wrote innumerable letters after she went to Alexandria but none, it seems, has been preserved.

In 1884 Mr. Blackford achieved his greatest happiness: he won the hand of Miss Eliza Chew Ambler, a young lady who met with the approval of his mother. It particularly pleased her that the bride was descended from that archenemy of slavery, Colonel George Mason of Gunston Hall.

To celebrate the wedding of her best beloved son, Mary Blackford had to produce a gift worthy of the occasion, her most precious possession. She gave him therefore a book that she had kept wrapped in a towel safely locked up in the little trunk under her great bed all during the War. On the flyleaf she expressed the hope that by that time he was old enough to appreciate "this work of genius," *Uncle Tom's Cabin*.[4]

Mary Blackford was an exigent mother-in-law. Except for short periods the wives of the other four sons were never required to live on the same premises with her. Fortunately a certain amount of protection was afforded Eliza Blackford: as well as the old lady could travel through the corridor, the great parlor and the entrance hall, to reach the Principal's study, she could not climb the long flight of stairs to Eliza's rooms. By the time four robust little boys [5] were living in those rooms, Launcelot's wife stood high in the affections of her mother-in-law.

Mary's hair had long since turned white. It was always crowned with a white chiffon cap; its streamers were caught under her chin with a mourning brooch. Her skin was of a transparent, otherworldly pallor, and this pallor was emphasized by her nondescript black clothes. But if the infirmities of age had somewhat damped her internal fires, they had left a serenity of expression that made her really a beautiful old lady.

Although her children often came to see her (and each time for thirty years they were warned never to expect to see her alive again), the first time all six were together after the funeral of their father in 1864 was on the occasion of her ninety-first birthday, October 12, 1893. They enjoyed each other so much they decided to make it an annual reunion. On these visits William loved to tell her, "Mother, you have never been really happy since the slaves were emancipated: your pet hobby is gone." [6]

She gradually grew feebler. In her last days her mind wandered far. She could be brought back to reality only when Launcelot's baby namesake was allowed to play on her bed. Or perhaps she mistook him for her own Lanty.

On September 15, 1896, the brave heart of Mary Berkeley Minor Blackford ceased to beat. Her body was carried back to Lynchburg to rest beside that of her husband in Spring Hill Cemetery where her youngest son had fought in 1864.

Mam' Peggy succeeded to the matriarchal position of her mistress in a way incomprehensible to any one but a Virginian. In her declining years she had her own maid and was supplied with everything she wanted. While her wants were few, she did want an ornate, shiny brass bed. Between the foot of this bed and the head of her maid's white iron bed was room for a small wicker chair: in this chair, her head swathed in a red bandanna that allowed her gold earrings to show, a dark shawl around her shoulders, a clean gingham apron over her knees, she spent most of her waking hours gazing into the open fire. In her extreme age this fire was never allowed to go out. Except that sometimes on very hot days in summer she might sit a while on her back stoop, it is doubtful if she ever left her room after Mrs. Blackford's death. The other half of the cottage was soon occupied by growing Blackford boys.

Every day Dr. Blackford — he was now an LL.D. — dropped in to see Mam' Peggy. If any child she had nursed or his descendant was on the place twelve hours without calling to pay his respects, woe betide him! Indeed no relative of the Principal's wife dared to visit the School more than twenty-four hours without paying a ceremonial call. And if any of the clan left the School without making his formal adieus, though he stayed away five years, his dereliction would be thrown at him on his next visit. She continued to enjoy having the Bible read aloud to her, but she did not require her visitors to pray with her.

Mam' Peggy was a most remarkable person. She had an excellent sense of humor (which she most certainly had not assimilated from her mistress). She never learned to read or write, but she could quote freely from the Scriptures. She had a goodly store of aphorisms and she was a font of wisdom. When her advice was asked, as it often was by the young wife of the Principal, she would give it freely, and it was good.

Her dignity was immaculate. She taught manners to more than one generation of Blackfords. She was however always a bit of a snob: if a child deserved her severest reprimand, she would caution him, "Don't behave like no po' white trash!" She contemned a colored girl who would sleep with a white man, but the man in the case was beneath her contempt no matter how blue his blood; and if she ever learned that a man who was received at the Blackford home was guilty of such conduct she would see to it that he never set foot in the house again.[7]

Mam' Peggy received payment for her services after the War and her visitors often made her little gifts. She never spent anything so in time her savings account exceeded $5,000. A few years before Mrs. Blackford died she led Peggy to her son's office:

"Lanty, Peggy wants you to make out a will for her, leaving everything she has for the benefit of the missions in Africa."

Peggy did not look pleased at the idea but she dared not dissent audibly so Lanty, still in the habit of obeying his mother's commands, dropped what he was doing and duly drew up such a will, to which Peggy affixed her mark. Later that day, however, Mam' Peggy stole back to the office alone:

"Marse Lanty, please tear up that air ole paper. Hit ain't my will at all. Them niggers ain't never done nothin' for me." [8]

After Mrs. Blackford's death Mam' Peggy employed a lawyer

to draw up a second will: this divided her estate equally between Launcelot and Mary Isabella.

We long wondered how old Mam' Peggy was. For years all she could say was that she remembered when she went to live with the Blackfords "An' I growed after I got thar." Finally one day she remembered that she had been born the same year as "Miss Kate Berkeley" (Mrs. Lucius H. Minor). That fixed the year of her birth as 1813.

One day in the early nineties when Mr. Blackford was very busy in his study — and on such occasions there was only one person on the place who would think of disturbing him — "the thump, thump of the old lady's stick was audible as she moved along out in the hall. He knew no power could keep her from coming right in and staying as long as she pleased. He clutched his head with both hands and murmured in the most refined and reverent and pleading tones, 'My God! My God!'

"In came his mother, one hand grasping her cane, the other clutching Mam' Peggy.

" 'Launcelot,' she announced . . . 'I have decided that when Peggy dies she is to be buried at my feet.'

"Up spoke Mam' Peggy . . . 'I done tole her and done tole her I ain't gwine to be buried at nobody's feets.' "

The Principal's prayer was heard. His inspired answer was:

" 'Perhaps you had better decide that between yourselves before you take it up with me. I shall do my best to see that your wishes are carried out.'

"That appealed to both the ancient women and they tottered out, each convinced that she had won a round in their unending but devoted battle." [9]

Mam' Peggy, however, was not convinced for long: she knew too well her mistress' iron will. She had seen many desolate, abandoned Negro graveyards, so she had an equal horror of being buried among colored people. She sought out the Principal's wife and explained the situation to her, concluding with,

"Law, Miss 'Liza, I don't want to be buried at nobody's feets."

"Miss 'Liza" promised her that, provided she outlived old Mrs. Blackford, she would not be.[10]

When in 1911 Peggy passed on to her richly deserved reward at the age of ninety-eight, her body was reverently placed in Dr. Blackford's lot in Ivy Hill Cemetery, Alexandria. When he died three years later, it so happened that Launcelot's body was laid at the feet of Mam' Peggy.

NOTES

NOTES

C M B Memoirs. Unpublished memoirs of Mary's son, Charles M. Blackford. A copy in R F B Collection.

B M Recollections. Unpublished Recollections et Alia of Mary's nephew, Berkeley Minor. These holograph volumes are in the possession of his son, James F. Minor, of Charlottesville, Virginia.

Fox, *Am. Colon. Soc.* Early Lee Fox, *The American Colonization Society, 1817–1840.* (Johns Hopkins University Studies in Historical and Political Science, 1919.)

Lanty's Diary. The boyhood diary of Mary's son Launcelot. The original volumes are in the Southern Historical Collection, University of North Carolina.

L Congress. The files of the American Colonization Society preserved in the Library of Congress. Some letters there are copied from Fox's paper; others were copied for the author by Margaretta Douglas.

L M B Sketch. The autobiography of the first thirty-three years of Mary's son, Launcelot M. Blackford, "Sketch of my Life." This is in the author's possession.

M B B Notes. Mary's "Notes Illustrative of the Wrongs of Slavery." This holograph work is in the author's collection.

R F B Collection. The collection of Mary's grandson, Rev. Randolph Fairfax Blackford, of Talladega, Alabama. Most of this collection is on deposit in the Southern Historical Collection, University of North Carolina. Only typescripts have been consulted by the author.

S L B *Memoir.* Susan Leigh Blackford, *Memoir of Life in and out of the Army During the War between the States,* 2 volumes. (Lynchburg, 1894–1896.) Her husband Charles M. Blackford (Mary's son) had thirty-five copies of this work "printed but not published." Charles Minor Blackford III edited and abridged this work, which was published as *Letters from Lee's Army.* He has given the author permission to use what was left. In addition to the copy in the author's possession, two copies are in the Jones Memorial Library in Lynchburg, a copy is in the Library of Congress, in the Virginia State Library, the Library of the Virginia Historical Society and in the Confederate Museum in Richmond.

W M B Diary. Diary of Mary's husband, William M. Blackford. The first volume, 1843–1847, is in U Va. Many excerpts from the period of the War were given in S L B *Memoir,* and of those not presented in *Letters from Lee's Army,* many are used in this book.

The last seven volumes of the diary, terminated two weeks before Mr. Blackford's death, were considered lost, but in November 1953, they were discovered by Mrs. Spencer Nauman, of Harrisburg, Pennsylvania, among the effects of her mother, the niece of Mrs. C. M. Blackford. Mrs. Nauman, who plans to place the last seven volumes with the first in U Va, graciously placed them at the disposal of the author, who, having checked the quotations in S L B *Memoir*, feels impelled to insert a few more.

Mr. Blackford's comments on his children are frank and interesting. Lucy Landon was without spot or blemish in his eyes and he adored her. His references to her continued after her death.

Perhaps dating from their lonely exile in Bogotá, he always cherished an especial intimacy with Willy. He considered him "the handsomest man in Virginia," though Willy's lack of interest in things cultural sometimes bored him.

Charly, "the most impulsive of my children," had a quick temper, but was the most intelligent of the lot, indeed, to his father, brilliant.

Mr. Blackford was sensible of Lewis' wit and charm, but thought him lazy and often worried over his fickleness.

Lanty was "one of the purest-minded men I ever knew," but, though he rejoiced in his religion, erudition, and capacity for making friends, he apparently did not love him very much.

Whatever faults Eugene may have had, his father did not see. He loved him unreservedly and was intensely proud of his exploits. On December 20, 1861, he wrote: "Got off another box for Eugene, containing a rundlet of Whiskey [about 15 gallons]. Though a teetotaler himself, he felt bound to treat his men at Christmas. I send it with great reluctance, and his mother is very much distressed. But on the whole having promised it to his men, he would be much embarrassed were our scruples to prevent it being sent. The best article costs now $3.00 a gallon. . . A year ago it would have cost 25 to 30 cts. Those who have distilleries are making fortunes."

Mary Isabella's comings and goings are duly recorded but she rated no particular remarks.

It may also be noted that, in spite of his attitude toward secession as long as Virginia was in the Union, "the palladium of our liberties," long before his death, William Blackford had become a thoroughly loyal Confederate.

W M B *Address*. William M. Blackford, *An Address Delivered at the Request of the Board of Managers before the Fredericksburg Auxiliary Colonization Society, Feb. 23, 1828* (Second Edition. Published by the Fredericksburg and Falmouth Female Auxiliary Colonization Society. Fredericksburg: Printed at the Arena Office, 1829). Commander Charles Minor Blackford III, U.S.C.G.R. lent the author his copy.

W W B Memoirs. Unpublished memoirs of Mary's son, William W. Blackford. A copy is in R F B Collection.

U Va. Alderman Library, University of Virginia.

Chapter I

IN OLD VIRGINIA

1. This letter was quoted in Early Lee Fox, *The American Colonization Society, 1817-1840*, 167. The original letter is in the Library of Congress.

2. Mary Berkeley Blackford began her journal, "Notes Illustrative of the Wrongs of Slavery" in 1832. She added her observations and comments from time to time until 1866, though infrequently after 1835. She also included stories she gathered from friends and relatives she considered credible, and she copied many extracts from the Bible and jingles by Abolitionist writers. In time the original became time-worn and she transcribed it with her own hand, probably before 1861. The original she destroyed; the second draft is in the author's possession. In her old age she copied important family letters and added recollections of her childhood. The extant version is destined for the Alderman Library of the University of Virginia.

3. "Seperated" was one of the few words she habitually misspelled.

4. Colonel Landon Carter of Cleve was the grandson of Robert "King" Carter of Corotoman and of Colonel William Byrd II of Westover. Both are familiar to students of Virginia history.

5. Mildred Washington Willis was the granddaughter of Colonel Henry Willis of Willis Hill, founder of Fredericksburg, and of Mildred Washington, aunt and godmother of George Washington.

6. This quotation, the background of this section, the letters from General Minor and his wife are from B M Recollections.

7. This anecdote came to the author from Mary's son, the late B. Lewis Blackford, through his daughter, Mary Berkeley Sawtelle. Lewis attributed it to Mam' Peggy. However, since Mam' Peggy was only three when General Minor died, it is improbable that she originated it. She may have quoted it from Mrs. Minor's old nurse, Mammy Betty, who, until she died at a ripe old age, lived on in Fredericksburg in the home of Lucy's sister, Mildred Ann Byrd, who married successively Robert Mercer and John Lewis. Or perhaps Mam' Peggy got it from Aunt Lyddy, a privileged old retainer of the Berkeley family of Edgewood; a similar story attributed to Aunt Lyddy is given in B M Recollections.

8. Kenmore, the home of George Washington's sister Betty, the wife of Colonel Fielding Lewis, has been restored and is the showplace of modern Fredericksburg.

9. W W B Memoirs.

10. Paul Wilstach, *Tidewater Virginia* (New York, 1929), 280.

11. Peter Minor of Fredericksburg to his nephew, John Minor, September 25, 1783, from a copy in M B B Notes.

12. From the will (1677) of Maindort Doodes, in the Virginia State Library. Maindort Doodes came from Holland to Virginia about 1650, bringing with him his son, Maindort Doodes, Minor. When they were naturalized in 1673 the father retained his original name, but the son

adopted the name of Doodes Minor. His son Garat Minor was the father of the first John Minor, who married Sarah Carr of Topping Castle. Their son, Major John Minor of Topping Castle was the father of the third John Minor, Mary's father.

13. He so signed his will, which is preserved in the courthouse in Fredericksburg. His spelling of "Hazle" is preserved throughout this book. The property on which he built his home had been used by Colonel Fielding Lewis for the manufacture of munitions during the Revolution.

14. "Why this plain old wooden house was called Topping Castle no one has ever explained, unless because it was so little like one," said Berkeley Minor in his Recollections.

15. December 2, 1808.

16. February 3, 1811.

17. April 20, 1811.

18. December 23, 1813.

19. Mary to John B. Minor, December 28, 1861. MS. in U Va.

20. April 12, 1812.

21. December 16, 1813.

22. August 19, 1814.

23. August 19, 1814.

24. Mary's daughter, Mary Isabella, in B M Recollections. On a recent visit to Fredericksburg the author was surprised to learn that Hazle Hill is still known as "the old haunted house," but he could find no one who knew why.

25. In Rev. W. C. Andrews, *Memoir of Mrs. Ann Randolph Page* (Philadelphia, 1844) is a touching account of Mrs. Page's tribulations under similar conditions. She was forced to sell some of her slaves, but fortunately they were bought by her neighbors. When her fortunes improved she was able to send a number to Liberia. A copy of the *Memoir* is in the possession of Mrs. J. Houstoun Johnston of Atlanta. The story is also given in Fox, *Am. Colon. Soc.*, 152–153. Both as an ardent Colonizationist and as a sister of Bishop Meade, Mrs. Page was unquestionably well known to Mary Blackford.

26. M B B Notes.

27. The exact date of this letter from Mrs. Minor to John Minor IV is not given in B M Recollections.

28. March 3, 1825.

29. The quotation is from L M B Sketch.

30. This mansion at 214 Caroline Street (after the Revolution the good citizens of Fredericksburg thought it unfitting to continue to use the names of the royal family on their streets; more recently the original names have been restored) is now the home of Mr. and Mrs. William B. Braxton, who graciously showed the author through it. It has been tastefully modernized.

31. From a note in *The Monthly Chronicle* of the Episcopal High School, April 1892.

32. Bath is now Berkeley Springs, West Virginia.

33. As he reminded her from Bogotá, October 12, 1844, the nineteenth anniversary of their wedding. R F B Collection.

34. This remark was also handed down from Lewis through his daughter.

35. B M Recollections.

36. The original of this letter was mislaid while R. F. B. was in World War II. It is impossible to supply the day of the month. Appointed by President James Monroe, Charles L. C. Minor was at West Point from July 1, 1822 to June 30, 1826.

Chapter II

Dragon's Teeth

1. Helen Hill, *George Mason Constitutionalist* (Harvard University Press, 1938), 202–203.

2. *Ibid.*, 218.

3. Albert J. Beveridge, *Abraham Lincoln, 1809–1858* (Boston, 1928) II, 50.

4. "Reverend John Orcutt, of Connecticut, a traveling agent of the Society, reported January 16, 1861: 'Not only are free negroes forbidden to come into Indiana by express statute, but it is made a penal offense for a white person to induce such immigration. . . When a State constitution was adopted in Oregon, four-fifths of the electors said by their vote we will not have slavery! and they also said by about the same majority, "we will have no free negroes!" Illinois, too, has a similar prohibitory law against free negroes. . . Already in the Eastern States, the black man finds himself on equal footing with the whites *nowhere*, except in the State prisons, where he is on the same level, and fully represented! No wonder that some of the free colored people at the North should begin to inquire with solicitude what they shall do. I saw several at the West who said, "We must go somewhere!" ' " Fox, *Am. Colon. Soc.*, 37.

5. W M B *Address*. The paper also appeared in the *American Quarterly Review*, IV, 396–426, 1828.

6. Mary added to her copy of that letter in M B B Notes: "What gives more weight to these expressions is that he said little about his feelings, never making a parade of any sort. Much in this like my brother Lewis, brave, sincere and quiet. Those were the opinions of that day among our best patriots. We learned after that to call Slavery a blessing!!!"

7. W M B *Address*.

8. "Almost all masters in Virginia assent to the proposition that when the slaves can be liberated without danger to ourselves and to their own advantage, it ought to be done." J. B. Harrison, 1828, in Fox, *Am. Colon. Soc.*, 15.

9. W M B *Address*. A year later Henry Clay, for many years a strong advocate of Colonization, said: "Both objections cannot be founded in truth. Neither is." Fox, *Am. Colon. Soc.*, 141. On page 144, Fox editorial-

ized: "To the Colonizationist the difference between gradual emancipation and immediate emancipation was not equal to the calamity of the dissolution of the Union, or an American Civil War, or both."

10. Fox, *Am. Colon. Soc.*, 14.

11. Lt. Charles L. C. Minor to his mother, April 16, 1828. This and other letters from Charles are from B M Recollections.

12. But Mary had noted he was a humane soul. She wrote to her son Willy, March 23, 1843: "I always thought spurring a cruel custom. I never saw your Father with spurs, even in his courting days when gentlemen are often anxious to make their horses cut capers." MS., U Va.

13. Fox, *Am. Colon. Soc.*, 84. MS., L. Congress.

14. October 25, 1828. The originals of all the letters quoted from W. M. or Mary Blackford to Gurley are in the Library of Congress. Those not taken from Fox were copied for the author by Margaretta Douglas, M. A.

15. December 26, 1828.

16. The first part of this letter to Gurley was written September 1, 1829, the last lines, April 30, 1830.

17. September 18, 1840. Fox, *Am. Colon. Soc.* 152.

18. Mrs. Ann Randolph Page, March 26, 1831. Fox, *Am. Colon. Soc.*, 24.

19. Beveridge, *Lincoln*, II, 17.

20. Mary's report of the Nat Turner insurrection is from M B B Notes. A fuller and more recent account will be found in Joseph C. Carroll, *Slave Insurrections in the United States, 1800–1865* (Boston, 1938), 129–151.

21. The Reverend William Meade earlier in his career had been the first agent of the American Colonization Society in Virginia, and a liberal contributor to its funds. Fox, *Am. Colon. Soc.*, 48.

22. M B B Notes.

23. An old copy of this letter is in the author's possession.

24. This and the following quotations through Lt. Minor's letter are from M B B Notes. A copy of the letter is also in B M Recollections.

25. B M Recollections.

26. February 18, 1832. B M Recollections.

27. James Monroe to Lewis W. Minor, July 13, 1830. B M Recollections.

28. On large-scale Federal maps of the Civil War it is labeled "Dr. Anderson."

29. Marquis James, *Andrew Jackson, Portrait of a President* (Indianapolis, 1937), 311 ff.

30. February 18, 1832. B M Recollections.

31. This letter was copied from the *African Repository and Colonial Journal*, 1835, IX, 126. Mr. Gurley prefaced it with, "The letter is given with scarcely an alteration or correction."

32. W W B Memoirs.

33. M B B Notes.

34. This account of Mary's missionary brother is (unless otherwise

specified) based on Mrs. E. Hening's book, *History of the African Missions of the Protestant Episcopal Church in the United States with Memoirs of the Deceased Missionaries and Notices of Native Customs* (New York, 1850), 122–208. A copy is in the author's possession.

35. W W B Memoirs.

36. Hening, 192.

37. This section is almost verbatim from M B B Notes.

Chapter III

MISSION TO BOGOTÁ

1. Mam' Peggy's own statement.

2. C M B Memoirs.

3. *Ibid.*

4. Vice President Tyler sent Blackford a copy of his letter to Secretary of the Navy George E. Badger. This copy is in R F B Collection.

5. The original commission is in R F B Collection.

6. L M B Sketch.

7. *Ibid.*

8. William's letters from Bogotá are in R F B Collection. **Only when** the date is not in the text will there be a footnote.

9. June 12, 1842.

10. June 25, 1842.

11. June 27, 1842.

12. July 2, 1842.

13. July 11, 1842.

14. July 23, 1842. Compare the statement of Henry Clay in 1830: "The adult slaves will, in process of time, sink in value even below $100, I have no doubt." Fox, *Am. Colon. Soc.*, 24. And John Randolph of Roanoke: "The disease will run its course. It has run its course in the Northern States; it is beginning to run its course in Maryland. The natural death of slavery is the unprofitableness of its most expensive labor." George Mason, already quoted in Chapter II, also realized this.

15. August 11, 1842.

16. October 9, 1842.

17. October 30, 1842.

18. November 6, 1842. In the nineteenth century "faculty" was often used to denote the orthodox medical profession. William so used it later.

19. This letter of July 3, 1842 from Mary to her son Willy, the others quoted, and the one letter to her husband that has survived are in U Va. Notes will be given only when the date is not given in the text.

20. July 21, 1842.

21. December 9, 1842.

22. February 19, 1843. Mary's ideas as to the basic cause of overeating are quite abreast of those of modern psychiatrists.

23. The original of this letter of February 8, 1842 is in U Va. Dr. James M. Minor was not the first doctor to disregard his own advice. On November 13, 1865, his brother Dr. Lewis W. Minor, on hearing that Jim had sailed for England, to recuperate from the strain of war, wrote to their sister Mary: "I hope Jim's trip will result favorably to his health, but I fear his imprudences in diet will mar his success. But for these, he must, with habits of persistent & laborious exercise, have long since become a strong, robust & healthy man." This MS. is also in U Va.

24. January 1, 1843.

25. February 16, 1843.

26. On March 23, 1843, Mary wrote her son: "This is my dearest Willy's birthday and the children are to have a little party. They are all highly delighted and have dressed themselves nicely for the occasion. Their usual supper (since the cow has stopped giving milk) is a slice of dry bread, so the addition of sweet cakes and buttered rolls is considered a great indulgence. It would do you good to see them sitting around their little table in my room."

27. Letters of April 13 and June 25, 1843, have been run together.

28. March 23, 1843.

29. September 17, 1843.

30. September 29, 1843. The original of this and of her other letters to the headquarters of the Colonization Society are in L Congress.

31. One such slaveholder was the Reverend Churchill J. Gibson, who wrote Mr. Gurley on January 26, 1844: "I have belonging to me two families of servants whom I am anxious to emancipate if by any means I can settle them in Liberia. The duties of the Holy Ministry render me utterly unfit to be a faithful Christian Master & incline me to desire this step for the benefit of my own highest interests and those of my sacred office. At the same time, I feel bound to consult the best good of my servants, and in releasing them from my care to place them in a situation where the blessings of freedom may *really* be enjoyed. This, I am very sure, can not be found in my own country, and I am therefore determined not to set them free unless they can be sent to Africa." Fox, *Am. Colon. Soc.,* 38.

32. June 30, 1843.

33. July 14, 1843.

34. August 11, 1843.

35. August 31, 1843.

36. September 17, 1843.

37. Jefferson Davis was not in the army at this time.

38. October 27, 1843.

39. December 19, 1843.

40. MS., U Va.

41. W M B Diary.

42. Mr. Blackford to his son Lewis, October 11, 1844.

43. Lawyer, writer, editor, temperance orator, Lucian Minor (1802–1858), son of Mary's uncle Lancelot Minor of Minor's Folly, older brother

of Mary's Cousin John B. Minor, wound up his career as Professor of Law at William and Mary University.

44. Lucian's *Letters from New England by a Virginian* were written to W. M. Blackford; they were first published in the Fredericksburg *Arena*. Lucian edited them and republished them in *The Southern Literary Messenger*, I, 84–88, 166–169, 217–220, 273–278, 421–426, 1834. He thought Abolitionism was already dying out, and he aimed to draw the attention of his fellow-Virginians "to some traits of Yankee life and character which we may advantageously copy." The concluding sentence of the series was, "*The North and the South need only know each other better to love each other more!*"

Lucian's original journal fell into the hands of James Russell Lowell, who thought it fresher and more entertaining than the published works. Prefaced with a highly laudatory note about Lucian as "a Virginia *gentleman*" and with an additional note by John B. Minor, Lowell published it as *A Virginian in New England Thirty-Five Years Ago*, in *The Atlantic Monthly*, XXVI, 162–179, 333–341, 482–492, 739–748, 1870, and XXVII, 673–684, 1871.

45. Dr. James M. Minor to his brother Lucius, February 8, 1843. MS., U Va.

46. In this long letter of October 13, 1844, Blackford discussed politics and philosophy at length. He was sure that his idol Henry Clay, who did not want to admit Texas to the Union or to fight Mexico, would be elected.

47. W M B Diary, February 15, 1845.

Chapter IV

MARY'S TRAINING OF HER CHILDREN

1. L M B Sketch.
2. *Ibid.*
3. W M B Diary, February 16, 1845.
4. *Ibid.*, March 29, 1845.
5. *Ibid.*, March 6, 1845.
6. *Ibid.*, March 10, 1845.
7. The original bill of sale is in the possession of Commander William M. Blackford, U.S.N.R., of Seattle, one of Mary's great-grandsons.
8. W M B Diary, March 18, 1845.
9. *Ibid.*, July 16, 1845.
10. *Ibid.*, April 10, 1846.
11. Lanty to his grandmother, December 29, 1847. R F B Collection.
12. L M B Sketch. Among these choice young men was William E. Peters, who became a distinguished colonel of cavalry in the Confederate Army, and then for thirty years Professor of Latin at the University. Another was Junius Fishburne, who left Lynchburg to become Professor of Latin and Greek at Washington College. In Lexington, Fishburne and Major T. J. Jackson of V.M.I. became intimate friends and married two

daughters of Rev. Dr. George Junkin, President of the College. Fishburne and the first Mrs. Jackson died before the Civil War.

13. C M B Memoirs.

14. The data on the boys' forensic activities are from Lanty's Diary. The beginning of the diary in May 1847 was brought to an abrupt stop by a serious case of typhoid. Lanty began again February 23, 1848, and continued it until he entered the University in September 1855. The original volumes are in the Southern Historical Collection, U N C. The author has been content with typescripts prior to January 1, 1853. This diary is a remarkably mature and polysyllabic document for a boy.

15. The six days in 1847 are not counted. Lanty's Diary has been freely drawn upon, more times indeed than it will be cited.

16. Lanty's Diary, March 26, 1848. It is strange that the boy did not mention their entertaining another hero of the Mexican War, severely wounded, twice brevetted James Longstreet, who came to Lynchburg to marry General Garland's daughter. His father noted the fact in his diary.

17. *Ibid.*, May 31, 1847.

18. *Ibid.*, August 1, 1850.

19. Liberty, about thirty-five miles southwest of Lynchburg, is now Bedford.

20. Lanty's Diary.

21. Lanty to his grandmother, February 23, 1853. R F B Collection.

22. Her readings from Shakespeare must have been delightful: they left a lasting impression on her hearers. But when Lanty saw "Launcelot Gobbo" in the *Merchant*, he inserted a "u" into his name and demanded his family observe it. It must be admitted that Mrs. Blackford was careful to expurgate what she read: Launcelot first read *Othello* in the spring of 1855 (after he had left home) and concluded "Shakespeare was a dirty fellow."

23. Mrs. Blackford to Mary Isabella, October 1, 1851. R F B Collection.

24. Lanty's Diary, December 18, 1848.

25. February 12, 1848. MS., L. Congress.

26. February 14, 1848. MS., L. Congress.

27. It would appear the family later bought a copy of Mrs. Hening's book for a copy has descended to the author.

28. MS., dated only "1852," in author's possession.

29. January 15, 1853. MS. in author's possession.

30. MS., L. Congress.

31. MS. in author's possession.

32. MS. in author's possession. Nothing further was heard from James Cephas Minor.

33. September 19, 1846. MS., U Va.

34. This quotation from W M B Diary was written December 27, 1863, following the death of Dr. Blackford. It is found in S L B *Memoir*, II, 19.

35. December 19, 1849. MS., U Va.

36. In his diary of September 9, 1865, he said: "I have about two

thousand books now. They are well selected and give me infinite pleasure."
S L B *Memoir*, II, 122.

37. He made a beautiful cabinet, the drawers of which still open. It is now in the author's possession.

38. Sixty-seven years ago Charles gave this steam engine, still in good working order and still enjoyed by his sons, "to the Smithsonian Institution, and received a grateful letter acknowledging the courtesy and commenting on the fact that such a piece of mechanism should have been constructed by an amateur at so early a date." S L B *Memoir*, II, 212.

39. Lanty's Diary, November 11, 1848.

40. February 14, 1852. This and other letters Willy wrote home are in R F B Collection.

41. Willy to his father, May 11, 1852.

42. Nicolay and Hay, *Abraham Lincoln, Complete Works* (New York, 1894) I, 174.

43. Lanty's Diary, November 3, 1852.

44. Among the many who that unsettled year forsook the conservative Whig Party to contribute to the Democratic victory was Mary's brother Lucius. In spite of a brilliant record at Yale, Lucius ever followed his own convictions — or emotions — however much the family might deplore his course. The attitude of the Virginia "quality" as to the parties of the day is illustrated in another story of Aunt Lyddy, the faithful old Edgewood servant:

Mr. Minor had lent her a small sum of money: such loans to house servants were common and scarcely ever repaid. When in the course of time Aunt Lyddy offered to repay it, her master declined to accept the money, but the old woman was insistent. Finally, not knowing of his apostasy, she gave as her final and conclusive argument the reason why she must return the loan:

"Take it, Lucius, I must pay it. I ain't no Democrat. I pays my debts!"

Aunt Lyddy was the only old Negro that Berkeley Minor (or the author) ever heard of who failed to address those she had nursed as children by a title when they grew up. Another of her idiosyncrasies was to pronounce Berkeley "Barkley."

In B M Recollections is recorded one more story that throws a sidelight on an aspect of slavery. In the division of Dr. Berkeley's estate, Aunt Lyddy was given to another heir, but she refused to leave Edgewood: "I knows that Kate and Lucius ain't goin' to make me leave home." She was right.

45. R F B Collection.

46. These murders are recounted in considerable detail in Lanty's Diary.

47. Actually this letter was written May 8, 1853. R F B Collection.

48. Charly to his parents, November 6, 1852. R F B Collection.

49. June 28, 1853. MS., U Va.

50. Lanty's Diary, April 4, 1853.

51. *Ibid.*, May 7, 1853.

52. Charles M. Blackford in S L B *Memoir*, I, 63.

Chapter V

UNCLE TOM'S CABIN

1. Lanty's Diary, January 10, 1853.

2. This remarkable letter written by Charly at nineteen emphasizes the abhorrence of the Southerner to regulation from without. The original of this (and of other letters quoted in this chapter) is in R F B Collection.

3. May 4, 1853.

4. Willy to his mother, March 5, 1853.

5. "Betsy's Story" is from M B B Notes. It has been slightly edited, but an earnest effort has been made to retain the spirit and meaning of the original.

6. Dr. Thomas S. Savage is the same physician-priest that went to Liberia in 1836 to study health conditions before the arrival of Mary's brother and the Rev. John Payne. His first wife died in Africa. He soon married another missionary and she died shortly too. His third wife was another of those fearless missionaries. Finally, in 1847, because of poor health (according to Mrs. Hening) Dr. and Mrs. Savage returned to the United States. By that time W. M. Blackford, Abraham Lincoln, and many others were losing faith in the Colonization project. Mr. Gurley never did.

7. R F B Collection.

Chapter VI

MARY'S CHILDREN GROWING UP

1. The originals of the letters cited in this chapter (except that one cited in note 24) are in R F B Collection.

2. September 25, 1853.

3. January 1, 1854.

4. The quotation is from a protest of March 3, 1837, signed by Abraham Lincoln and Dan Stone, against a resolution on slavery adopted by the Illinois legislature. See Beveridge, *Lincoln*, I, 194.

5. This quotation is from Lincoln's Peoria speech of October 16, 1854, as cited in Roy E. Basler, *Abraham Lincoln, His Speeches and Writings* (New York, 1946), 306. The comment is by N. W. Stephenson, *Encyclopaedia Britannica* (1938) XVI, 141.

6. This statement is sustained by many remarks in Mary's writings in addition to those cited, and in her children's letters to her.

7. Willy to his mother, May 7, 1852.

8. Willy to Mary Isabella, May 1, 1853.

9. May 29, 1853.

10. May 17, 1854.

11. April 3, 1854.

12. April 10, 1854.

13. March 10, 1854.

14. May 28, 1854.

15. May 29, 1854.

16. Lewis to his father, June 11, 1854.

17. July 1, 1854.

18. July 23, 1854.

19. Dueling had not yet gone out of fashion. In February 1846, Mary's old beau, James H. Pleasants, editor of the Richmond *Whig* (who had married twice since Miss Minor rejected him), challenged a man who had called him an Abolitionist — like Mary he was an ardent Colonizationist — and was killed in the duel. While none of Mary's sons ever fought a duel, her brother Lewis fought a number, according to his grandson, the late Dr. Landon White. John, on the other hand, who while at college was often reproved by his father for his quarrelsomeness (letters in B M Recollections), tried to keep his temper under control later. After John Minor's death Charly wrote of him:

"Although so gentle and lovingly sympathetic with the tender and helpless, and though he shrunk so much from public life and its notoriety, he was bold and aggressive in the defense of right and of the weak, and in matters connected with personal honor his word was regarded as law. He settled, perhaps, more personal difficulties than any one man who ever lived in the State. When two gentlemen had a misunderstanding anywhere in his part of the State, and all other means failed and a duel seemed a necessity, friends would often get both sides to consent that Mr. Minor should say what was to be done, and from his arbitrament there was no appeal. One thing was sure, the man who submitted a quarrel to his settlement knew that the world would say he did right, and also, that if he did not abide by it, he had Mr. Minor to fight, if not his original antagonist." S L B *Memoir*, I, 132–134.

20. September 23, 1854.

21. February 10, 1855.

22. February 26, 1855.

23. In a letter to Lanty, April 26, 1855.

24. Dr. Lewis W. Minor to his brother Lucius, April 29, 1855. MS., U Va.

25. C M B Memoirs. Further quotations in this section are from the same source unless otherwise noted.

26. Kathleen Bruce, *Virginia Iron Manufacture in the Slave Era* (New York, 1937), 133.

27. Lanty's Diary, August 20, 1855.

28. Mr. Blackford to Lanty, April 25, 1855.

29. January 21, 1856.

30. January 27, 1854.

31. April 10, 1856.

32. Philip Alexander Bruce, *History of the University of Virginia* (New York, 1922), I, 299. Madison was a Colonizationist.

33. *Ibid.*, 302–311.

34. *Ibid.*, 310.

35. December 3, 1857. MS., Jones Memorial Library.

36. L M B Sketch.

37. October 12, 1858.

38. Lieut. Col. Alexander S. Pendleton distinguished himself on Jackson's staff. He was frequently mentioned in Lanty's letters. He was mortally wounded at Fisher's Hill, September 22, 1864, a few days before he would have been twenty-five. Douglas Southall Freeman has much to say about him in *Lee's Lieutenants* (New York, 1942–1944); he admired him as much as he did not admire his father.

39. Randolph Harrison McKim (whom Eugene in a letter to his mother, December 4, 1859, R F B Collection, termed, "one of the handsomest and best fellows in the University") after a gallant record in the war, became a celebrated preacher, orator, and writer. He long had charge of Epiphany Episcopal Church in Washington. He remained one of Launcelot Blackford's best friends until the latter's death in 1914, and conducted his funeral. He was of course well known to the author. In 1910 he published *A Soldier's Recollections* (New York) in which he pictured his carefree youth and an enjoyment of the fighting hardly equaled by Eugene's.

40. Captain Frank Robertson served on Stuart's staff: he demanded that a letter of commendation from Jeb Stuart be buried with him, over his heart. He also maintained his intimacy with Launcelot until L.M.B.'s death, every winter spending weeks at the Episcopal High School. He was a delightful old gentleman.

41. Dick Maury will appear again in the last chapter. He and Lanty enjoyed Confederate reunions together and also remained intimate until Col. Maury's death long after the war.

42. George Washington Nelson taught under Lanty at the Episcopal High School in the early seventies, and then entered the Episcopal ministry.

43. The Reverend W. F. Gardner was the first rector of the Episcopal High School after the war. Perhaps his influence helped Launcelot to succeed him when he gave up his post to enter parochial work.

Launcelot's friendships were durable: the author has no reason to question that they endured with Nelson and Gardner, but he has no knowledge on the subject (both may have died before he was born).

44. Although a society with similar aims was organized at the University of Michigan prior to October 12, 1858, the Young Men's Christian Association at the University of Virginia was the first college organization so named. Alexander Hogg, Carter M. Louthan, Rev. J. K. Faulkner, D.D., Col. William H. Kable, David E. Russell, James C. Deming, Bishop George W. Peterkin, Dr. James M. Garnett, and Dr. Blackford returned to the University on October 12, 1908 to celebrate the fiftieth anniversary of the Association they had founded.

45. October 16, 1858.

46. January 19, 1859.

47. The day of the month was not given.

Chapter VII

SHADOWS OF THE IRRESISTIBLE CONFLICT

1. December 4, 1859. Except for those to and from John B. Minor and those otherwise specified, the letters cited in this chapter are in R F B Collection.

2. Fredericksburg *Weekly Advertiser*, June 28, 1858. Carrol H. Quenzel, Librarian, Mary Washington College of the University of Virginia, graciously brought this item to the author's attention.

3. John B. Minor, 1813–1896, brother of Lucian Minor, son of Lancelot Minor of Minor's Folly (brother of General John Minor, foster father of Mary's four brothers, Charles, Lewis, Lucius, and Lancelot) taught "the law and the reason thereof" at the University from 1845 till his death in 1895. His fame as a teacher was increased by his textbooks of law and his many graduates who gained distinction. In the South he was often referred to as "the great John B."

His letters to Mr. and Mrs. Blackford are in the author's possession. By a rare stroke of fortune, many letters they wrote him were discovered in the U Va Library. Sometimes the letters exchanged have been broken up to give the effect of conversation.

4. The Virginia Military Institute, founded in 1839, is in Lexington.

5. February 19, 1858.

6. December 14, 1859.

7. Gerrit Smith of Massachusetts was originally an ardent Colonizationist and contributed thousands of dollars to that cause. About 1835 he switched to the Abolitionists, and ever after fought the Colonization Society bitterly. Fox, *Am. Colon. Soc.* 16, 31.

8. February 26, 1860.

9. James Churchill Cooke will appear again.

10. May 11, 1860.

11. June 4, 1860. Few of Mary's letters from her husband while she was in Massachusetts have survived, but this would have been an appropriate acknowledgment of his of June 3.

12. Dick was his faithful slave-butler. He died in 1864, evidently of pulmonary tuberculosis. For a year or two earlier, because of his illness, Charly had provided him a home elsewhere. At that time of course he did not realize the danger of Dick's passing the tubercle bacilli on to his family.

13. June 10, 1860.

14. July 20, 1860.

15. August 20, 1860.

The Democratic Party had been split between Douglas and Breckenridge: Douglas straddled the question of slavery while Breckenridge advocated its extension. The Republican Party, at that time a purely sectional organization, had attracted the Abolitionists. When difficulties arose in nominating Senator Seward, the Republicans unanimously nominated Lincoln.

The new Constitutional Union Party, who nominated John Bell of

Tennessee and Edward Everett of Massachusetts, resolved simply, "It is both the part of patriotism and of duty to recognize no political principle other than the constitution of the country, the union of the states and the enforcement of the law." *Encyclopaedia Britannica* (1938) III, 372.

16. The original of this extraordinarily self-revealing, penciled letter of August 28, 1860 is in author's possession.

17. Bell and Everett polled more than half a million votes, but they carried only Virginia, Kentucky, and Tennessee.

18. Dr. James M. Minor to his brother Lucius, December 10, 1860. MS., U Va.

19. This phrenetic letter of November 27, 1860 is from B M Recollections.

20. December 3, 1860.

21. December 20, 1860.

22. January 18, 1861.

Chapter VIII

VIRGINIA MUST FIGHT

1. This paragraph is but slightly altered from one in S L B *Memoir*, I, 11.

2. As in the last chapter, the letters quoted from Minor are in author's possession; those he received in U Va.

3. MS., Jones Memorial Library.

4. This letter and all others to be quoted that Launcelot received or wrote during the war are in author's collection.

5. Reverend George Washington Bethune, 1805–1862, was a minister of the Dutch Reformed Church, a member of the American Colonization Society, and an earnest foe of slavery. He was educated at Dickinson College (as was Mr. Blackford, four years his senior). *Dictionary of American Biography* (New York, 1928–1937) II, 229.

In Mr. Johnson's "bread and butter" letter he remarked that from Washington to New York he had been accompanied by his brother-in-law, and Dr. Bethune was also grateful for the Blackfords' hospitality. Therefore the author assumed that Dr. Bethune was the brother-in-law. Mr. Blackford in his diary, however, mentions only young Mr. Johnson, so it is obvious that Dr. Bethune was not his guest in April 1861. It seems impossible to determine whether the friendship originated at Dickinson College or through the Colonization Society, and when Dr. Bethune was a guest in the Blackford home. If he had been entertained by them in Fredericksburg, it is the more striking that Mary should have appealed to him after such a lapse of years.

6. Certainly the young minister did not realize how valuable this military information might have proved to the Confederacy if she had been in a position to take advantage of it. MS., May 4, 1861, R F B Collection.

7. W M B Diary, in S L B *Memoir*, I, 20.

8. Lewis to his father, April 24, 1861. All of Lewis' letters are in R F B Collection.

9. A veteran may be allowed to paraphrase an old French proverb to, "The more war changes, the more a soldier's life remains the same."

10. May 13, 1861. He means of course that he has become a Christian.

11. S L B *Memoir*, I, 21.

12. W M B Diary, May 28, 1861, in *ibid.*, I, 22.

13. R F B Collection.

14. This clipping is in author's collection. It does not show the date or from what paper: it may be from the Richmond *Whig*, May 1, 1861.

15. R F B Collection.

16. May 26, 1861, R F B Collection.

17. Because the military careers of Willy and Charly have been presented in other books, they will be touched on but lightly in this one.

18. S L B *Memoir*, I, 28.

19. Eugene to his cousin M. L. Minor, June 30, 1861. MS., U Va.

20. *Ibid.*, July 9, 1861.

21. R F B Collection. No original letters of Eugene's except those in U Va have been consulted. Very few he wrote home seem to have been preserved.

22. S L B *Memoir*, I, 49.

23. June 5, 1861.

24. July 15, 1861.

25. August 17, 1861.

26. S L B *Memoir*, I, 71.

27. The best account of this *corps d'élite* is to be found in E. A. Moore, *The Story of a Cannoneer under Stonewall Jackson, in which is told the Part taken by the Rockbridge Artillery in the Army of Northern Virginia* (Lynchburg, 1910). The Reverend Churchill J. Gibson tells the author that this is the favorite book of General George Catlett Marshall, who began his military career in the home town of the organization.

28. W M B Diary, August 16, 1861, in S L B *Memoir*, I, 74.

29. August 21, 1861.

30. Mr. Pendleton, father of Sandy Pendleton, was rapidly promoted to brigadier general, and was appointed Chief of Artillery of the Army of Northern Virginia. Freeman has criticized him severely as a soldier (*Lee's Lieutenants*, II, 226–235, 243, 248, 662–665). After the war he returned to Lexington to resume charge of Grace Episcopal Church, where his most distinguished parishioner was General Lee.

31. Clement D. Fishburne's unpublished memoirs were placed at the disposal of the author by his granddaughter, Mrs. Staige D. Blackford. A younger brother of Junius Fishburne, while Professor of Latin and Greek at Davidson College, N.C., he was a groomsman at Jackson's second wedding.

32. As illustrated in many of his letters.

33. William H. Echols, once a student of Mr. Blackford's at the Episco-

pal High School and long Professor of Mathematics at the University, was told this story by one of Launcelot's messmates. He made use of it in his biographical sketch in the University's *Alumni Bulletin*, October 1914.

34. L M B Sketch.

35. This gun is still preserved at the Virginia Military Institute.

36. Echols, *Alumi Bulletin*.

37. October 28, 1861, in S L B *Memoir*, I, 95.

38. S L B *Memoir*, I, 98.

39. October 27, 1861. In 1894 Sue wrote: "Father always had two or three sick or wounded soldiers in his house and, as many of them were devoid of education or refinement, it was a great stretch of patriotism and philanthropy. Father was the most genuinely hospitable man I have ever known and, as is ever the case with such persons, was the victim of much imposition. Later in the war, when it was hard to get the barest necessities of life in sufficient abundance, his table and his house was always crowded." S L B *Memoir*, I, 88.

In the fall of 1861 Mr. Blackford was asked to take into his home a young soldier from a distant state, ill with typhoid, whose mother thought he would have a better chance of recovery in a private home. Three weeks later he recorded, "She wanted to pay board, but of course I would receive nothing. I think the removal of Robert saved his life. . . I may mention that she gave the cook ten cents as a reward for her extra trouble. They are in easy circumstances & have money plenty."

40. October 23, 1861.

41. October 27, 1861.

42. November 12, 1861.

43. Fishburne memoirs.

44. In S L B *Memoir*, I, 108, this letter was erroneously attributed to Lewis, who was in Norfolk at the time.

45. In the following weeks Lanty's detachment was sent up to the Potomac to assist in destroying a dam vital in the control of the water level of the important Chesapeake and Ohio Canal to Washington. The brigade then took part in the Romney Expedition, where real hardships were endured. His letters about these adventures are most detailed, voluminous, and interesting, but they do not belong here.

46. August 17, 1861. Evidently General Huger had known the elder Blackfords before the war, but the author has not been able to learn any details.

47. December 28, 1861.

48. B M Recollections.

49. Mary to her brother Lucius, May 26, 1861. R F B Collection.

50. B M Recollections. It is regretted that more space can not be devoted to Commodore Maury in this book. The interested reader will find a good account of him in John W. Wayland, *The Pathfinder of the Seas, The Life of Matthew Fontaine Maury* (Richmond, 1930).

51. Mr. Blackford wrote in his diary, March 7, 1862 (S L B *Memoir*, I, 145): "Amongst Mr. John Minor's papers I found some two or three

dozen letters written by Edmund Pendleton to General Woodford, bearing date from 1775 to 1779. We have been reading them and find them very interesting. It is curious to find him indulging in tirades against speculators and extortioners and against the supineness of the people in volunteering. With dates and names altered, so far as they refer to speculators, one might suppose them to have arrived by the last mail" ". . . *Le plus ça reste la même chose.*"

52. February 8, 1862. R F B Collection.
53. January 25, 1862. B M Recollections.

Chapter IX

BATTLES

1. January 27, 1862. R F B Collection.
2. From oration by the Reverend Randolph H. McKim, D.D., at the unveiling of a tablet in memory of L. M. Blackford in the Chapel of the Episcopal High School, February 1915.
3. S L B *Memoir*, I, 133.
4. Lanty was a wonderful correspondent during the war. As soon as possible after each engagement he wrote home or wired that he was safe. He also wrote very long letters on the installment plan, and was often days behind in his reporting. This letter was begun on March 27, 1862, and the concluding sentence is from a letter of April 3.
5. His description of his first battle is omitted with regret. These comments were written March 28, 1862.
6. "Disciple" was one of Mary's favorite words and elsewhere she spelled it in the conventional fashion. She must have been very much wrought up to have spelled it as she did on this occasion. MS. in author's possession.
7. April 18, 1862.
8. April 3, 1862.
9. June 7, 1862.
10. A few lines were sent home the night of the battle. They have been incorporated in the more detailed account written on June 7, 1862.
11. W M B Diary, May 27, 1862, in S L B *Memoir*, I, 170.
12. L M B Sketch.
13. June 14, 1862.
14. Lanty's account of the Battle of Port Republic that Sunday, written June 14, 1862, is detailed, but he never got around to writing a long description of the bloodier fight on Monday. These lines are from a short note on June 11, 1862.
15. W M B Diary, June 27, 1862, in S L B *Memoir*, I, 175.
Gildersleeve, aged thirty-two, had already been made Professor of Greek at the University. Williamson, a wealthy young man, had gone abroad at fourteen for nine years of education. He had attended the same German University as Gildersleeve, though a few years later.
16. February 25, 1862.

17. March 27, 1862.

18. April 5, 1862.

19. W M B Diary, May 26, 1862, in S L B *Memoir*, I, 168.

20. W M B Diary, May 23, 1862. *Ibid.*, 168.

21. Superb example of psychosomatic medicine! Mr. Blackford understood this type of ailment. On November 16, 1861, he wrote, "I believe the constant excitement is the cause of the disorder of my bowels. Mental perturbation always has a disturbing effect upon them."

22. Which he acknowledged in his book about the war, 64, 118.

23. From his letter of July 6, 1862.

24. August 19, 1862.

25. August 24, 1862.

26. Moore, *Story of a Cannoneer*, 121. Two days later William H. Blackford received his commission on the battlefield of Groveton.

27. September 14, 1862.

28. Ran McKim had recently been commissioned as aide to General Steuart. Lanty's letter of October 14, 1862 to Berkeley is from B M Recollections.

29. S L B *Memoir*, I, 255.

30. *Ibid.*, I, 256.

31. October 21, 1862, B M Recollections.

32. "They are the most amiable people on the earth." See Chapter II.

33. S L B *Memoir*, I, 177.

34. *Ibid.*, I, 177.

35. This Maria must not be confused with Maria West (Campbell).

36. S L B *Memoir*, I, 155.

37. W M B Diary, November 26, 1862, in S L B *Memoir*, I, 263.

38. W M B Diary, October 28, 1862, in S L B *Memoir*, I, 257.

39. S L B *Memoir*, I, 284.

40. *Ibid.*, I, 286.

41. W M B Diary, December 14, 1862, in S L B *Memoir*, I, 287.

42. Inadvertently Charly's account of the first day of the Battle of Fredericksburg (S L B *Memoir*, I, 272–273) was omitted from *Letters from Lee's Army*. The quiet second day appears on pp. 146–148.

43. Mr. Blackford turned over Eugene's account of the Battle of Fredericksburg to be published in the Lynchburg *Virginian*, December 24, 1862. This editor discarded the first part and what is given here is from Lanty's scrapbook, which is in the author's collection.

44. Lanty was saddened by the deaths of his friends and messmates of the Rockbridge Artillery, David Barton and Randolph Fairfax. Randolph Fairfax Blackford was told by his father, by Randolph McKim and Berkeley Minor, that they and Randolph Fairfax had entered into a compact early in the war that the survivors would attend the funeral of each. Minor had to bury Fairfax alone at Fredericksburg. Their ranks were not broken again for fifty-two years, when McKim conducted Blackford's funeral, with Minor in attendance. Minor and Blackford's namesake attended McKim's

livered to the Garland-Rodes Camp of Confederate Veterans in Lynchburg,
June 18, 1901 (Lynchburg, 1901), 27–28.

24. Eugene to M. L. Minor, July 1, 1864. MS., U Va.

In *The Great Skedaddle* (*The Atlantic Monthly*, CLXII, July, 1938,
86–94), excerpts from the diary of Private William B. Stark, 34th Massachusetts Volunteers, present the Yankee side of this retreat. According to
Stark, shortage of rations and of ammunition — except firebrands — caused
Hunter's army to flee so precipitately before a smaller force of Confederates.

25. S L B *Memoirs*, II, 247.

26. Charly to Sue, June 20, 1864. S L B *Memoir*, II, 247.

27. Lewis to his mother, August 15, 1864. R F B Collection.

28. Lucy Landon's son, William Blackford Davis, later studied medicine
at the University and entered the Medical Corps of the U.S. Army, rising
to the rank of Colonel. He was called back from retirement for duty in
World War I. He died in Baltimore about ten years later.

29. August 28, 1864.

30. Lanty to Mary Isabella, January 4, 1865. MS. in author's collection.

31. Lewis to his mother, February 25, 1862, already cited.

32. MS. in R F B Collection. On June 11, 1865, Charly wrote to Sue,
still at the University, on the same subject, "The Yankees are behaving
very well. While there is constant official intercourse, there is not the slightest social intermingling, of which they complain very much. There is no
one in the community who is suspected of Unionism. Mr. Kinckle prays
for the President of the U. S. because Bishop Johns tells him to, but prays
also for Mr. Davis & all our prominent men and soldiers 'in the hands of
the enemy,' — which are the words he uses." MS., Jones Memorial Library.

33. Charly to Lewis, June 11, 1865. R F B Collection.

34. June 14, 1865. R F B Collection, as are her other letters to Lewis.

35. After Appomattox many old Confederates did migrate to Central
and South America. Commodore Maury was still in England at the end of
the war and, like other Confederate representatives abroad, was proscribed.
Maximilian invited him to Mexico. That summer Eugene at the University
wrote his mother:

"The Maurys are writing instructions from Cousin Mat, who has gone
to Mexico to solicit some privileges from that Crown for emigrants from
Virginia. He then desires the whole kith and kin shall emigrate, and sends
pages to that effect, mentioning us particularly. I am studying Spanish with
no such interest, loving Virginia too well by far to leave her in her dark
hours: there are many social battles to fight yet, and for these her young
man are required, specially those of birth and breeding." (The war had
not wiped from his mind some things his mother had impressed upon him!)

Berkeley Minor wrote in his Recollections: "We got very kind replies
from Cousin Matt and Dick, promising all help and countenance they could
give us if we came, but with enough caution to make us hesitate and at
last conclude we'd better not go. Cousin Matt came back to the U. S. before
the fall of Maximilian and was one of the professors at V.M.I. till his
death."

36. R F B Collection.

37. Charly to Lewis, August 29, 1865. R F B Collection.

38. June 10, 1865. R F B Collection.

39. Charly did have two sons after the war and sent them both to be taught by Lanty at the Episcopal High School.

40. September 7, 1865. Mary, despite Charles' forebodings, never did get around to leaving the Blackfords. Thirty years later Sue wrote: "She is living with us now and we support her mother, who was also our slave, but as Lincoln's proclamation did not include us, we have never been emancipated from her." S L B *Memoirs*, II, 204.

41. November 1, 1865. R F B Collection.

42. November 5, 1865. R F B Collection.

43. November 13, 1865. MS., U Va.

44. Mr. Gurley's letter, as well as Mr. McLain's, are in R F B Collection.

45. The last letter from Mr. Gurley in the author's collection is dated August 8, 1866. He regretted that so many in the group of Lynchburg Negroes that went to Liberia had died there, but still thought it was the place for the American Negro to go.

In 1896 Sue Blackford wrote of Frances, another former slave: "After the War her husband determined to go to Liberia and, against our protest, took her with him. She was dreadfully opposed to the move, saying she 'didn't want to go to no country where there ain't nothin' but niggers.' When she bade us goodbye Mr. Blackford told her that if she did not like it and would write to him he would send her the money to come back. Her husband died soon after landing and Frances had the fever. Remembering Mr. Blackford's promise, she got some one to write to him and, though he was then almost as poor as she was, he brought her back." S L B *Memoir*, II, 29.

And so, it seems, terminated a noble experiment. But it must be recalled that, whatever the failures of the Colony, it was a most potent factor in breaking up the slave trade, and it did provide a home for slaves captured on the high seas on their way to America.

EPILOGUE

1. This bed was handed down to her daughter Mary Isabella, and in turn to her daughter Lucy Landon (Mrs. Fenton Noland of Airwell). It was destroyed in 1936 when Airwell was burned the third time in its history of two hundred years.

2. Lewis' daughter, Mary Berkeley Sawtelle, supplied the author with this.

3. The late Archibald R. Hoxton, who was born on the premises in 1876, and who succeeded Dr. Blackford as Principal, contributed this item.

4. This copy of *Uncle Tom's Cabin* was discovered among the family effects following the death of Mrs. L. M. Blackford in 1936. The inscrip-

tion was recalled by Dr. S. D. Blackford and Rev. R. F. Blackford. The book has been lost.

5. The fifth son, to whom this book is dedicated, was born two years after his grandmother's death.

6. W W B Memoirs.

7. Mam' Peggy was a most important member of the household in the author's youth: some of this account is from his own recollection, more perhaps from what he heard from his mother and other members of the family.

8. This story is from Mrs. Fenton Noland.

9. The Reverend Roger A. Walke of Towson, Maryland, was the Principal's student-secretary at the time of this incident, and he wrote it out in 1947.

10. This was a favorite story of the author's mother. On April 25, 1889, she wrote her father that both the School matron and her assistant were sick. "And I have had to struggle through the duties of both added to my own busy life." She had two babies at that time. "I think I could scarcely survive if it had not been for my colored friends of whom I can truly say — with all their faults I love them still, and, if they are not very deceitful they must love me too. First I appealed to dear old Aunt Peggy, who is a lady of great powers and great influence over her own race. She said she was not strong, but she'd 'rally round,' and so she did most helpfully. . . Whenever I'd tell her of a fresh emergency, she'd grin and say, 'Nem mind, *I'll* straddle it,' and more delightfully efficient straddling was never done I am sure."

INDEX